BEYOND BETRAYAL

Tony: Our Journey Together

BEYOND BETRAYAL

Healing My Broken Past

Carolyn A. Koons

1817

Harper & Row, Publishers, San Francisco

Cambridge, Hagerstown, New York, Philadelphia, Washington
London, Mexico City, São Paulo, Singapore, Sydney

FIRST EDITION

Koons, Carolyn A.
  Beyond betrayal.
    1. Koons, Carolyn A. 2. Christian biography—
United States. I. Title.
BR1725.K65A3 1986   280′.4 [B]   86-45018
ISBN 0-06-064766-3

86 87 88 89 90 HC 10 9 8 7 6 5 4 3 2 1

To Russell and Alva Peters
who have shared the true meaning of family with me,
and
to those of you who see yourselves on the pages of this book.
May you experience God's healing
and be set free to enjoy life's greatest adventures.

Contents

Acknowledgements

TO AZUSA PACIFIC UNIVERSITY: the administrators, my colleagues, and students—my experiences with them are wonderful memories. Throughout my twenty-five years at APU, these people have become like family to me. They've loved me, believed in me, and inspired me to be all that God wants me to be. I love them all.

TO CLIFFORD: my oldest brother, who understands what it was like to grow up in our family. Becoming friends at this stage of our lives has made him special. He encourages me to be myself.

TO LINDA TAVENNER: every writer should be blessed with an enthusiastic assistant and secretary. Everyone entering my office received the latest update of my ongoing saga as Linda eagerly pressed me for the next chapter with such flattery—how could I resist writing more?

TO REBECCA LAIRD: my friend and a gifted writer/editor at Harper & Row who helped me get this story out of my heart and onto the pages. Her insight, expertise, and encouragement kept me going to the end. Much thanks are due to Becky for her pen and people skills.

TO ROY M. CARLISLE: my editor friend at Harper & Row who took a chance on me. Through his own pain and personal discernment, he was able to guide me as I struggled to keep in touch with the past. He helped me endure the pain of reliving unbearable memories so that I could share God's healing with others.

TO ALL OF THE SIGNIFICANT PEOPLE WHO ARE A PART OF THIS STORY: you are angels. On my journey to wholeness, you were there to help me take the next, often painful, step. I continually thank God for you. I owe you my life.

Except for my friends and members of my family all names have been changed

The Phone Call

The morning surpassed my hopes for a gorgeous spring day. In high spirits I greeted my staff, evading the normal pile of telephone messages waiting in my mailbox, and quickly escaped the hubbub of students and typewriters in the outer office in order to scratch out a memo before my first class.

Over a thousand teenagers and college students are expected to participate in this year's Mexicali Outreach. In order to provide adequate staff and facilities, the Institute for Outreach Ministries has put together the enclosed—

BRRING, the telephone interrupted me in midsentence. I reached out and grabbed the receiver without laying down my pen. "Hello, this is Carolyn Koons," I answered.

"Hi, Carolyn, this is Elsie." Azusa Pacific University was still small enough for the switchboard operator to have memorized each extension and to know most of the faculty personally. "I just received a strange phone call that I thought I should tell you about," Elsie continued.

"What's that?" I asked absently, as I sketched the next sentence for the memo.

"Carolyn, is your father alive?"

My fountain pen dropped from my hand and clattered onto the wooden desktop. I paused, and a chill ran down my spine. "Yes, why Elsie?"

"Well, a man called and asked if you still worked here. I told him, 'Yes, Professor Koons teaches here.' Then I asked if he wanted me to connect him with your office."

I listened in disbelief, staring blankly at the wall in front of me. To me, my parents, especially my father, were only painful memories I tried to forget.

"He seemed really angry, Carolyn, but he didn't want me to ring your extension. He said to give you this message: *'Tell Carolyn that her dad called, and that I'm on my way, and this time it's for good.'* I asked him to repeat himself because I didn't understand what he meant. He said, *'You just tell her. She knows what I mean.'* Then he slammed down the phone. As I said, he sounded really mad. Do you understand any of this?"

Unnerved, I mustered a quick, "Yes, Elsie, thanks. Goodbye." My voice trembled.

Without shifting my gaze, I mechanically cradled the phone, and my thoughts slipped back many years and many miles from campus. Then slowly the laughter and banter of students drifting in through my office door drew me back into the present. My intercom buzzed. No doubt my secretary was checking to see if I was available.

I panicked; there was no way I could talk to anyone if my father was coming to find me. I realized, "I've got to get out of here. I have to leave." Clutching my purse, I rummaged for my car keys, and without my characteristic word of explanation, I walked through the crowded office to the door. I heard my secretary's voice behind me, "Carolyn . . ."

I didn't answer, but sped up to a brisk walk. I passed by one of the classrooms I often lectured in during my Christian education courses. Just a glimpse of the rows of chairs was enough to bring one of my recurring nightmares flooding into my mind. *My dad stalked onto our sunny suburban campus gripping his .38-caliber handgun and madly searched until he found my classroom. He stood silently in the doorway, pointed the barrel toward my head, and, without hesitating, blew my brains out right in front of my students.* The dream was so vivid that I knew what it would feel like for my body to slump limply to the floor while my students screamed in horror. My dad would turn and slip away, smiling to himself now that he'd at last taken revenge on me for the horrible injury I'd done him by being born.

The imaginary scene began to replay in my mind, and I realized I was still standing in front of the empty classroom. I looked down at my watch. Five minutes or so had passed since the phone first rang. I had forty minutes to hide before he could cross Los Angeles from Long Beach to Azusa. It took all my self-control not to break into a full run as I crossed the faculty parking lot to my car, a bronze Mercury Cougar.

My thoughts tumbled recklessly as I jammed my key into the ignition and jerked the gearshift into reverse. I gunned the accelerator as the car jolted into motion.

My dad's words reverberated in my head, *"I'm on my way there, and this time it's for good."*

With my hands clenched around the padded steering wheel, I raced around town. Turning corner after corner, I asked God, "Why? Why am I still running from my father's anger, and why is he still haunting me?" It seemed so senseless. His hatred for me had already ruined his life. Why was he so intent on ending mine? I had walked out of his life years ago. I'd let go. Why wouldn't he? Why wouldn't he just leave me alone? He'd terrorized all but the last fifteen years of my life. This time he was finally going to kill me.

I certainly did know what he meant. My father knew that just a simple call and a vague threat could trigger a barrage of painful memories in me. That gun—that horrible, cold black gun—was I going to have to run from it for the rest of my life?

A car horn blared, and I stamped on the brake pedal, seeing the red light for the first time. My car skidded to a halt with the front bumper inches into the crosswalk. A car hurtled by, barely avoiding a collision with mine. My heart was pounding.

As my car idled, I looked around. Wait a minute! I thought. I was at the corner of Foothill and Grand. By force of habit, I'd headed home. I couldn't go there! What if my father had gone there first before calling the university? What if he was already sitting on my front porch waiting?

I cranked the steering wheel all the way to the left, making a U-turn without looking in my rearview mirror. Another horn honked from behind me as cars coming from the other direction whizzed past. I pulled over to the side of the road. I had to think—I just had to think. "Don't panic, Carolyn," I told myself, and began to concentrate on taking a few long, deep breaths. I checked my watch. Thirty minutes more and he would have had plenty of time to cross town.

My worst fear was coming true. I wasn't safe anywhere— not even in my own home. I had no idea where to head for, so I eased back into the flow of traffic and just drove. At a four-way stop, I glanced up at the street sign on the corner. Instantly, I knew where to go. Straight for ten blocks I sped until Live Oak intersected Foothill. The church—Glenkirk Presbyterian, the brick and stucco sanctuary—would be my refuge. My father didn't know I worked there part-time.

I parked in the nearly empty lot and made my way into my tiny office off the main patio. I slumped into the gold-cushioned counseling chair and sat in the semidarkness, trying to force myself to think clearly.

"What am I going to do? I can't go back to the college." I could just imagine my father stomping onto the campus and yelling for me up and down the main patio area with no one having a clue as to his intent. No doubt they would be able to smell the liquor on his breath. I couldn't go home, either.

That would be too dangerous. He had probably already found out where I live. I considered going to Don and Pauline's; they were close friends. But I couldn't do that. I wouldn't dare. I couldn't subject their kids to that kind of threat.

I looked at my watch again. I now had fifteen minutes. The cabin—Big Bear—that's it! Don and Pauline would let me use it without question. I could go up there for a couple of weeks until things cooled off. It would be hard to explain to the university why I had to leave at this busy time of year, but I'd be safe. Maybe my father wouldn't be able to find me there. Maybe he is just drunk enough to be out of control for a little while. Whenever he drinks he gets violent and beats up the first person who comes to mind. Surely he'd cool down after a few days.

I envisioned driving the two hours to the mountains. I could mentally picture the cabin nestled in the sugar pines. But no, just the thought of staring through the window hour after hour, day after day, wondering when and if he would find me was more torture than facing the gun now.

Just then there was a knock on my office door. I jumped up out of the chair, startled. Sweat broke out on my forehead. I wrung my hands, noticing for the first time that they were clammy. He couldn't be here already! He doesn't know where I am. The knock sounded again.

"Carolyn, are you in there?" My heart lurched. It was Walter, the senior pastor.

"Yes, come in."

Mondays, like today, were Walter's day off, and he usually enjoyed golfing with several parishioners. He opened the door with his typical exuberant friendliness. "What are you doing here?" he chuckled. "You aren't due until tomorrow. Working overtime again, huh?" he laughed, knowing that my required fifteen hours a week usually turned into something more like full time. I loved working at Glenkirk.

"No, I was just making some plans," I answered, without looking directly at him.

He waited for a long moment. I lifted my head to meet his gaze as he studied my face. Worry lines creased his forehead. "Carolyn," he quietly urged, "what's wrong?" Obviously I wasn't hiding my distress very well.

I took a deep breath and turned to walk behind my desk. I had been careful not to tell Walter, or anyone for that matter, about my family, and especially my father. I had left him years ago in the past and believed I'd never have to deal with his anger and betrayal again. But this afternoon I had to admit that my past affected everything in the present.

"I need to talk to you," I confessed.

Noticing the serious tone of my voice, he immediately sat down. "Okay, Carolyn. What is it?"

"I received a phone call at the school. My father is on his way from Long Beach and I have reason to believe . . . Well, let's just say, he's angry and I'm afraid."

"What do you mean by afraid?" Walter probed.

"My father's a violent man, Walter. I guess I've always believed that some day he'd decide it was time to kill me."

"What?" Even after years of experienced ministry, Walter seemed surprised, "What are you talking about?"

I told Walter about the telephone call, the gun, the threats, and the fact that my mother had promised that one day he would shoot me.

Adding a few vague details to help Walter fill in some of the blanks, I checked the time. The precious minutes were rapidly ticking away. My father could be here in ten minutes if he'd left work as soon as he made the call. I knew he'd be drunk, just as he'd always been when I lived at home. He'd be red-faced and vile-mouthed. Nothing ever changed.

Walter chided me. "Why didn't you tell me this? I've known you for years." Even though he was the pastor of the church and I'd gone backpacking in the high Sierra with his family, I had never shared my painful memories with Walter. I tried to be open and vulnerable about my present struggles, but where my parents were concerned, I chose to keep silent.

"What good would it have done, Walter? Would my telling you have changed anything?" He shook his head.

"What are you going to do now?" Walter sounded deeply concerned.

"I don't know," I admitted.

He warned me, "You've got to get out of this area. Your father may find you."

"I know. But give me a few minutes." I leaned back in my desk chair and sighed audibly. After a moment, I sighed again. "Walter, why? Why do I still have to deal with this gun? I'm thirty-five years old! Why can't the past stay out of the present? I'm tired of my father's anger and hatred toward me. I've tried to forget that he may reappear at any moment and carry out his threat. Why am I still running? I'm an adult! I don't do anything to provoke any of this."

At that moment I think we were both asking the same questions. Walter and I both shrugged and lapsed into silence. The room seemed heavy with dread—an anticipation of something yet to come. I closed my eyes, trying to let the quiet of the moment bring some peace. But none came. After a few minutes I checked the time. Dad would certainly have had time to arrive. I inhaled a long breath and exhaled slowly, hoping I could calm my rising terror.

"Walter," I said, breaking into the quietness, "I just decided that I'm not going to run."

He knit his eyebrows together—evidence of his strong concern. "If your father is anything like what you've described, we have to get you to a safe place—somewhere away from here."

I assured him that everything I'd just said was true. "I can't leave. I'm tired of running. Much of my life has been spent fleeing from that man's cruelty. Walter, if he's determined to blow my brains out, he'll find me anywhere. What am I going to do? Spend the rest of my days running scared? If God really does love me, which I know he does, he is just going to have to take care of me. What kind of life can I build if my father's threats can control me?"

"So what exactly are you going to do now?" Walter worried.

"I'm going home."

"I have a better idea," Walter offered, "come over to—"

I lifted my hand to stop him midsentence. "I can't come to your house. I can't go to the university. I will not run anymore. I'm going home." I walked to the door. "Trust me, Walter, and pray. I feel this is the right answer." I reached for the doorknob.

"Okay, Carolyn, but do me a favor and call tonight. If anything goes wrong, pick up the phone. If you need our help, we'll be ready." I agreed and left.

I crossed the parking lot, leaving Walter standing by my office door, unlocked the car, and drove the short mile down through Glendora to my condominium. I paused at the driveway entrance and turned my head, scrutinizing my street in both directions to see if I recognized any of the cars. I didn't even know what model of car my dad owned. I simply searched for anything that looked suspicious. Cautiously, I wheeled into the tenants' parking lot and headed toward number 164. At the last minute I turned left and looped around the back, just to check and see if anyone was parked alongside the driveway at the back street entrance. Pulling around the back, I punched the button on the garage-door opener and squinted to see into all the shadowy corners to make sure no one was in my garage. "He'd be crazy to go inside," I reasoned. But he'd do it. He would do anything to terrorize me.

I inched the car into the garage and quickly shut the door behind me. Walking outside and down the sidewalk, I hurried to test the doorknob. The house was still secured. I unlocked the front door and left it wide open. I had confidently entered my new condominium at all hours of the day and night over the past year without a thought. But this time I tiptoed in with the eerie feeling that maybe, just maybe, someone could be hiding in my home. Terrified, I slipped from room to room, opening every door and closet. At the first creak or noise I planned to dash out the front door.

Finally satisfied that no one else was in the house, I bolted the front door. Then, with greater urgency, I hurried to each window, checked the locks, and dropped the extra safety bar across the sill, just to be sure. That done, I drew all the draperies and closed all the curtains. Time had passed quickly. My father could be anywhere by this time. Any sign that I was home would be enough to prompt him to shoot indiscriminately at a silhouette he saw from outside.

The minutes ticked into hours as I slipped from one window to another peeking carefully through the curtains. Darkness fell as I sat in the house waiting, but I was too terrified to go to bed. I was determined to meet the expected knock on the door fully alert. If he came to the front door, I planned to scurry out the back sliding-glass door, leap over the low fence, and flee the complex. If he came to the back door, I would race out the front to the neighbor's.

I sat on my patterned linen couch, a prisoner of fear in my own home. Again I got up and peered out the window into the shadow of the night. For the hundredth time I realized that my father could be hiding anywhere—behind the oak tree, in the neighbor's entryway, anywhere. This time I sat down in the bentwood rocking chair. The slight swaying motion relaxed me a bit. The wall clock chimed, and I bolted out of the chair. It was way past midnight. I paced the room to the ticking of the clock. I tried to keep moving. Nervous energy coursed through my body. I felt like a stalked animal awaiting the hunter. As long as I was moving I could keep away the memories that tugged at my conscious mind. My painful past begged to surface.

I pleaded with God as I had with Walter. "Why can't the past stay out of the present? I've had enough pain." I finally gave up and collapsed again into the rocking chair.

The dark room, the gentle rocking motion, the fear that this might be my last night alive—all joined together to take me back. I didn't want to relive the terrible years gone by. But tonight, for once, I, Carolyn Koons, had no other choice.

The Canal

"Sit there, you son of a b——, that's your seat for this trip," my dad bellowed at me, a skinny, freckled kid just a few weeks past my sixth birthday. He pointed with his beer can toward the wooden bench barely visible beneath the spinet piano that was pushed flush against the back of the front seats of the rented gray panel truck.

I froze where I was, poised to scramble over the back bumper to join Gary and Clifford, my older brothers, who were already climbing up on a huge stack of bedding and mattresses. Some metal kitchen chairs and the brown couch were piled haphazardly between the piano bench and my brothers' cushioned perch.

Even as my dad came toward me and dug his strong fingers into my arm, I knew better than to flinch or move. I closed my eyes from the pain as he jerked me from the back of the van to the front passenger door. "Get up there," he ordered, shoving me over the front seat with one hand and pulling the piano bench out a few more inches with the other. I scrambled over and cowered, seated sideways across the cold wooden bench top. I felt the keyboard ledge against one hip and the edge of the kitchen table against my other shoulder. I hugged my knees close, wedged uncomfortably into the tiny space.

My mother, a medium-sized brunette, always on the heavy side of her perfect weight, solemnly approached the van, flung a coffee jug and a bag of potato chips into the middle of the front seat, and crawled in after them. Her thin, angular nose and hazel eyes seemed harsh unless she smiled, something she rarely did. I heard my father slam the double doors at the back of the truck, and a string of profanity followed him as he sauntered toward the driver's seat shouldering an ice chest full of beer.

Looking toward the back of the van, I could see the top of Gary's tawny head as he sprawled out on the tarp covering the stack of mattresses. From where I sat, the mattress pile looked roomy and fun. Why did I have to sit squeezed on this bench?

The family move from Montana to California seemed interminable. The confinement of a snowy winter was barely past, and now sitting immovable for hours was torture. By nightfall, nearly eight hours into the trip, my dad had decided to drive straight through Utah, Nevada, and Northern California and on into Long Beach, our new home.

"Move over, you lazy kids," Dad yelled at my brothers. I awakened from a fitful sleep while Mom crawled over me. "Your mother is coming back there." Clifford reached down and pulled her up to the top of the mattress pile. They all snuggled down to sleep.

My muscles ached and my legs and arms tingled from lack of circulation. Rolling onto my side, I tried to fully extend my legs, but there wasn't enough room. I couldn't sleep on this bench. I waited, watching my father until he seemed absorbed in driving; then, gathering my courage, I quietly whispered to my mom, "Can I come up there, too?"

Before she uttered a word, my father flung his fist backward and caught me squarely in the face, sending my head crashing against the piano. "D—— it, that's your seat. I told you to stay there for the whole trip. So shut up! I don't want to hear another word out of your mouth."

Terrified, I inched out of my cardigan, rolled it into a makeshift pillow, and placed it behind my back. I turned onto my side and tried unsuccessfully to scoot down far enough to lay my head on the pillow. Finally, on my back with one leg dangling under the piano and the other knee bent facing the ceiling, I was able to stretch out my back and cushion my head. The van was cold, and I could hear the whoosh of cars passing our overloaded truck late in the night. The only sound inside the van was the crinkling of the plastic tarp as someone rolled over on top of the mattress pile.

For hours I concentrated on the cars outside, trying not to shiver, in the hope I could fall asleep. Dad pulled over once and hollered at Mom to wake up and drive. Clifford loyally followed her to the front seat to keep her awake.

The next morning everyone resumed their original seats. Gary and Clifford lay so they could see out the back window. I could see the soles of their feet and hear them laughing as they made up games out of the various sights and sounds of the passing roadside.

I'd been on the piano bench for more than twenty-four hours. My bones ached. Cautiously I got up on my knees and reached forward to tap my mom on the shoulder. "Can I sit up there with you for a while?" I asked warily. My dad looked away from the road, his arm leaving the steering wheel, and roughly pushed me back down.

"No, d—— it. I told you to stay there." He scowled angrily, his eyes bloodshot and menacing. I scooted back as far as I could against the wall of the truck—as far away from him as I could get. Why couldn't I sit up there? He never made any sense.

A few minutes passed, and thirteen-year-old Clifford asked, "Hey, can I sit up front?" "Sure," my parents said in unison and laughed. And before I realized what was happening, he crawled through the van to the front seat. The threesome began to compare their dreams of what life in Southern California would hold.

An hour or so passed as I sat forlornly hunched in my corner. I wondered where Gary had gone. His feet no longer hung off the mattresses, and he hadn't made a sound since Clifford moved to the front. A hazy cloud hung over the pile, and at first I thought it must be from the cigarettes my parents constantly smoked. But then I saw a solitary wisp rising from the back of the truck.

Carefully looking back toward my parents each time I moved, I inched my way off the bench and crawled up the side of the mattresses, finally reaching the top of the soft pile that filled most of the moving truck. "It's huge up here," I confirmed as I surveyed the empty, pillow-strewn surface. Even fully stretched out I couldn't feel the jolts or vibrations of the bumpy road. I flung my arms out wide and basked in the comfort of my private kingdom. Then it dawned on me. "Wait a minute! Gary, Clifford, Mom, and I could all fit up here at once!" Why couldn't I sleep stretched out like the rest of them?

Rolling over, I peered down between the mattresses and the back door. Eight-year-old Gary puffed hard on a cigarette and tilted his head upward trying to make a smoke ring as he exhaled. Shock registered on his face as he spied me looking down at him. He reached up and covered my mouth with the palm of his hand to keep me quiet and then motioned me out of sight. I knew he wouldn't squeal on me, because then I could tell on him. Reveling in my secret, I luxuriously rolled over, arched my back, wiggled my toes, and stretched my arms down my sides as far as I could reach.

Safe for a while, I closed my eyes. The tension in my legs and neck eased a little. My body relaxed, but I was still angry. I felt so betrayed. How could I endure that piano bench knowing there was all this room on the mattresses?

The mattress bounced a little, and I opened my eyes to see

Gary hoisting himself up next to me. He smiled threateningly and looked toward the front seat. "Dad," he singsonged, "Carolyn is up here on the mattresses."

The truck lurched to an abrupt stop, and the momentum, aided by a push from Gary, threw me from the mattress pile. I landed with my arm twisted behind my back. My knees throbbed from hitting the corner of the piano.

Clifford grabbed the steering wheel to keep us from inching off the sandy shoulder of the road as Dad spun around and pulled me to him, pummeling me with his huge fists and slamming me against the piano bench.

"I told you to stay off the mattress, you God d—— son of a b——. I told you not to move from this bench!" Tears raced down my cheeks. My mother just watched. "Don't you dare cry. You asked for it," were her only words of comfort. I tried to wipe away my tears while still keeping one arm in front of my face to shield myself from Dad's blows.

For the next day and a half, I didn't budge except to go to the restroom when we stopped. Even while two flat tires were repaired, I was sentenced to the bench. Three long days after leaving Livingston, Montana, we drove past the green freeway sign announcing we'd crossed the Long Beach city limits.

We all crowded into one cheap motel room. For several days my parents searched for a house. We finally settled into a small, nondescript white house on Eucalyptus Street at the north end of town. Dad found a six-day-a-week job at the shipyards. Within days Clifford, Gary, and I started school midsemester.

Unlike the tiny, hand-me-down schoolroom in Livingston, my first-grade classroom was large, and all the new books crackled and smelled of ink. I loved the big, sunny window and spent most of the first week daydreaming about being outside: running, playing kickball, facing each new dare with my crazy acrobatics on the rings and the monkey bars.

After a week the teachers began asking me questions. "Please tell me the time, Carolyn."

I paused for a minute, having no idea what to say. Nobody had ever taught me how to tell time. I looked at the wall clock and guessed, "It's twelve and five."

The teacher stood expressionless, staring at me. She turned to the boy to my left. "What time is it, Todd?"

"It's 12:25, Miss Reed."

"Carolyn, please count as far as you can. Begin with the number one."

"One, two, three, four . . ." I recited as far as I could into the twenties.

Miss Reed then walked to her desk and picked up a book, opened it, and placed it in front of me. "Please read aloud. Begin on the top of page ten."

There were only a few words that I recognized, *and, to, can,* and *bat.*

"This book is too hard for me," I explained. She seemed exasperated but trying hard not to show it. How was I supposed to know any of this? I blushed when I realized the rest of the class knew more than I did.

Miss Reed gave the rest of the class an assignment. While the other kids opened their desks and foraged for pencil and paper, she asked me to sit quietly until she returned.

She crossed the room to another teacher's desk. They huddled quietly, writing notes in a grade book and glancing frequently at me while they talked. I looked down and for the first time in school felt different and dumb. How did the other kids know all this stuff? In Montana, I'd tried to memorize the squiggly lines and curves the teacher had called the alphabet. But none of it made sense. I had recess to think about. Why stay inside with books when there was a big playfield outside?

The best students in the class had finished their assignments by the time the teachers motioned for me to join them. "Carolyn, you are way behind the other students in this class. Apparently California schools are ahead of the one you attended at the first of the year."

"Yes ma'am," I answered, and she admonished me to work very hard and pay attention.

And I did try for a while. Still, my classroom record remained low. During recess and physical education, however, I was always one of the first chosen whenever teams were picked. My reputation flourished on the field. Not only could I run faster and hit harder than the boys in my class, I soon found out I could make the other kids laugh.

By the end of the second grade, the teachers' concern about my reading became serious. Report cards were issued, and I flunked reading. Embarrassed, I agreed to attend summer school. Miss Joyce, my new teacher, encouraged me to concentrate. "I believe you really will learn to read." Her words motivated me to work harder than I ever had before. For six long weeks I struggled with the letters and words. I longed to be out playing football in the streets with the neighborhood kids, but Miss Joyce was nice; she spent a lot of time with me helping me to learn to read all the words on each page of a book.

On the final day I waited with bated breath for my report card. When the teacher stopped in front of me, she was beaming! "Congratulations, Carolyn. I'm proud of you." Miss Joyce handed me the envelope and moved to the next girl.

I ran to the playground, stopped near the tetherball court, and gingerly opened my grade card. A big red *A* covered the page. Jumping and whooping for joy, I ran from the grounds, and instead of leisurely counting the cracks in the sidewalk or detouring all over the neighborhood, I headed straight home.

Once at our back door I could hardly speak. I burst excitedly through the door and scattered my books across the kitchen table. "Mom, I got an *A,*" I proudly announced. "Mom!" I called again, but she was engrossed in the newspaper while enjoying a cup of coffee and a cigarette.

"Mom! I got an *A* on my report card."

She slowly turned toward me with a bored look on her face, "Sure, prove it." She resumed reading. I grabbed my reading book from the table and riffled through the pages to find the report card. To my horror it wasn't there.

"I lost the card," I moaned frantically, flipping through all my books. "Oh, it has to be here." But it wasn't.

"Oh, sure, Carolyn. Did you flunk again?" my mom scoffed, not even looking at me.

"No, honest, I got an *A,*" I yelled at her.

"Then go find it," she taunted. She took a deep drag on her cigarette as she stood up and disappeared down the hall toward her room, slamming the door behind her.

I stumbled back out the door and frantically searched every inch of the sidewalk for blocks and blocks—all the way back to school. Tugging on the locked door, I peered through the small window. The corridors were empty, the bulletin boards bare. Nobody would be back now until school started in the fall. I was devastated and didn't go home until long after dinner. Mom wouldn't care anyway. There was no question about that.

The rest of the summer was filled with street games. Mom and Dad both worked, leaving my brothers and me to fend for ourselves. Clifford, athletic and charming, made friends easily and always spent his time away from home. I tagged along with Gary and his pals. We rarely stayed on our block, often heading toward the city park where a group of kids hung out always ready for a rough game of football or basketball.

Toward the end of the summer, Gary kept sneaking away —leaving me at home alone. One day I followed him. Ducking through an empty lot, he rushed to meet up with five or six other boys his age. Lagging a few yards behind, I trailed after them to the river. Warning signs declaring No Trespassing lined the chain-link fence. The boys stopped and surveyed the barrier, deciding where to sneak over it. I walked toward them, and when I was within hearing distance, I saw one of the boys point downstream and say, ". . . and the horse and the kid riding it were sucked under by the quicksand down where the river bends."

Right then Gary noticed me and screwed up his face in annoyance. He obviously didn't want me around. I didn't care if he considered me a tagalong. I just didn't want to be left out and have to stay in the house by myself all day.

We began to walk along the fence. One of the stragglers noticed a missing support and bent the fence back enough to squirm under. I saw him emerge on the other side.

"Look!" I reported enthusiastically, "he's on the bank." Soon we'd all wormed under the fence and continued hiking alongside the dirty, rushing water. A boy in ragged jeans led the pack, looking intently for something.

"There's the pipe!" he finally declared, sounding relieved. Within seconds the boys shed their clothes down to their undershorts and dived off the unused sewer pipe into the murky water.

"Hey, Carolyn, dive from inside the pipe," one of the boys dared. "When I dive off the top you follow from inside and try to break the water in exactly the same spot as me."

Unwilling to admit I didn't want to dive into the water, I swung inside the pipe and crouched down. The image of the drowning horse and boy being sucked into the quicksand flashed across my mind. I waited in the dark and clammy pipe; the sound of the water below echoed angrily.

A banging against the side of the pipe made me jump and bump my head. The boys were all laughing, but Gary's laugh shrieked above the rest. Embarrassed, I stuck my head out to see what was happening and had to duck as a pebble whizzed past my face.

The boys bombarded the pipe with rocks. The pinging grew to a barrage as larger rocks and sticks were hurled against the concrete. The boys didn't want me around, but I couldn't escape; they would love to use me as a real target. Then something thudded against the concrete. Instinctively I knew what the sound was. I froze, knowing that I'd heard that sound before.

Back in Montana when I was four, a similar barbed-wire fence and red danger signs bordered the concrete irrigation canal at the end of our street. Though it was much smaller than the river, in the spring water surged down the narrow canal and often overflowed its muddy banks.

The canal was my brothers' favorite place to play. When they had to watch me, we'd often head to the canal to throw branches into the water then run against the twigs in a fierce footrace. We also made makeshift boats from pieces of wood and littered paper. They'd bob up and down for blocks in the white churning water until they reached the whirlpool above the steel grate that kept debris from being swept underground into the concrete tunnel.

The hunks of wood would dart furiously, faster and faster, then smash against the steel grate, repelled again and again, until they splintered or sank, able to pass under the barrier. All that would be left was the echo: the hollow thud of the log bouncing off the hard, dark sides of the tunnel. That was the horrible sound I had heard when Gary's friends bombarded the pipe. I suddenly remembered why the sound was embedded in my memory.

Once Gary had dared me and our neighborhood playmates to play a new game he called "cross the plank." Every twenty feet or so, a four-by-four plank spanned the canal. Gary was the first to crouch and haul himself out onto one of them. He stood slowly, his arms extended out and dipping dangerously, until he gained his balance. Cautiously, he stepped his way across the beam looking like a tightrope walker.

"Ha, ha! I made it! I made it! C'mon, Carolyn, try it," Gary jumped and hollered, proud and cocky. At first I refused. But Gary's taunting made me realize I had to do it. He wouldn't let me play with him again if I didn't; I'd be left at home alone. Terrified, I knelt down on my hands and knees and slipped my hands forward until my stomach touched the plank. I felt the water splash on my face and soak into my clothes while I carefully inched my way across.

On the other side, while he cajoled the other kids, I scurried up the hill on the far side of the canal searching for a branch to race to the tunnel. I found a small log, but I couldn't budge it alone. I opened my mouth to call for Gary, hoping to distract him from the scary game, but before I could call out, I heard a scream. All the other kids ran, shrieking, downstream. Sliding back down the slippery bank, I could see that a boy was already several feet down the canal being swept along by the current. Gary's game had turned into reality.

Gary raced to the next four-by-four and flopped down, extending his hands and hoping the boy could grab his fingers. The currents betrayed the plan and whisked him farther away. Some adults heard our screams. The boy was dragged, unconscious but alive, from against the steel barricade.

Even now, years after the canal incident and far from Montana, I was afraid of this California river. I would never admit it to Gary or his friends, but the fear of getting sucked into the darkness haunted me.

The boys soon tired of pelting the pipe with rocks and left me alone. By the time I crawled out they were long out of sight. I looked at the river and shivered. The rushing water spooked me. I was afraid if I got in over my head I would never get out. No one would be there to help me, or even to care. Alone, sucked under by a betraying current, was already a familiar story in my young life. But just maybe, with my strong memory and my stubborn will, I could—somehow—retrace my steps and find my way home.

The Gun

Gary and I remembered the events of the next year by our beatings. We learned to stay clear of Dad. A bottle, an empty can, or a dirty glass littering the house reminded us he'd be drunk and violent when we'd see him next. A couple of times after school I found him collapsed and delirious on the front porch just a few steps from the front door. Once, in a mad frenzy, he beat Gary so badly he missed a full week of school, too bruised and sore to get out of bed.

Birthdays usually came and went unnoticed. But the year I was in the third grade was different, Clifford got a brand-new shiny black Schwinn bicycle, which soon made him the envy of the neighborhood. According to my dad, I was never to touch it.

When Gary's birthday came along, he walked out into the backyard and discovered a beautiful blue three-speed—the latest and greatest in bicycles to date. He was ecstatic. Both Gary and Clifford jumped on their bikes and raced up and down the street as fast as they could go.

When Gary maneuvered carefully back into the driveway, he looked at me, gave me a shove, and warned, "Don't you ever touch my bike, understand?" His face sometimes looked like a cruel imitation of Dad's.

"I'm big enough. I can do it," I countered.

"You're not big enough to even touch the pedals," he scowled.

"I'm sure I can," I begged, "I'll show you." I reached out

for his bike. He grabbed my arm and wrenched it behind my back. Pain shot up to my shoulder.

"Stay away from my bike," he growled. "If you ever touch my bike, I'll kill you." He sounded just like Dad, too.

I wanted a bicycle so badly that I hinted at Christmas to my mom and dad about getting me one. The refrigerator door was covered with catalog pictures I'd cut out just so they'd know what kind and color I wanted. Every time we passed a bicycle I wished aloud I could ride one like it. But Christmas came and went uncelebrated. They must be planning to surprise me for my birthday, I reasoned.

June eighteenth finally arrived. Opening my eyes, I waited for a moment, savoring the anticipation before looking across the bedroom for the gleaming red bike they'd surely rolled into my room. When I could stand it no longer I sat bolt upright. The room was empty. My parents were yelling in the kitchen. Mom told Dad to get out, and he slammed the back door.

I lay down and pulled the covers up over my head. "Please don't let this be a bad day," I begged to the empty room. "Please, let me be happy today. My birthday only comes once a year."

I walked out into the hallway, my eyes wide with hopeful curiosity. Maybe they still would surprise me. No one said anything for a few minutes. Mom finally said, "Happy birthday," as she shoved a cereal bowl across the breakfast table. Nothing else happened. I waited, then dressed and spent several hours puttering in my room. Gary and Clifford rode off on their bikes together. Mom disappeared without a word. Alone, I wandered into the garage, found a two-by-four, and decided to build a sailboat with a string, an old white rag, and a fistful of nails.

When the finishing touches were in place, I heard the sputtering of my dad's battered red pickup in the driveway. I ran out of the garage and waited breathlessly by the back porch as he steered the truck backwards. Mom appeared at the back door and guided him with hand motions as he maneuvered around the steps. The ignition coughed and then went silent as Dad pocketed the keys and stamped from the cab to the tailgate. He crawled up on the truck bed, bent down, and picked up a bicycle.

His face twisted into a hideous grimace as he lifted the bicycle high over his head and snarled out his hateful birthday blessing. "I went to the junkyard in honor of your birthday, and here's your d—— bike." As the bike hurled through the air and hit the ground he stood to his full six foot two and pointed his finger at me from his vantage point in the truck. "Don't you ever, ever, ask me for anything as long as you live." And with that he leaped out of the truck and pushed my mom aside, banging the kitchen door after him. My mom ran inside, and I could hear obscenities filling the air.

I bent down to examine the bike. The old gray paint was chipped and the handlebars rusted until there was no silver finish left. An old chain hung limply from the sprockets. The flat tires stretched around rims that were missing most of their spokes. But it was mine.

I carefully dragged the bike into the garage, propping it upside down on its seat and handlebars. As I began to work, my parents' loud argument still poured from the house. Loosening all the bolts, I dismantled the frame. After carefully sanding every inch of metal, I brushed on a coat of light blue paint from a half-empty paint can. I sanded and rubbed the handlebars, but the corrosion defeated me. Finally I used black automobile paint to cover the rust and leave a sleek finish. I knew my friend Warren from across the street had a lot of old bicycle parts in his shed. He gladly gave them to me and helped me piece the bike back together.

For five days I did nothing but fix my bike. Then it was time for the test run. I, the proud owner of a sturdy, usable bicycle, walked it out onto the driveway. Stepping back to survey my work in the sunlight, I thought the bike looked beautiful.

I pedaled out onto the street, passing Clifford on his three-speed. The bike was heavy. It took every ounce of my strength, standing up, to push one pedal, then the other, in a full revolution. I excitedly headed toward the park to show Warren and the other kids that I had my own bike!

As twilight began to fall, I rode home and parked my bike next to the other two in our driveway. Now there were three bikes in the family! I could hear my brothers engrossed in some card game in the house. Clifford's bike caught the last rays of day so beautifully! With a furtive glance toward the house, I rolled it into the street, and my legs spontaneously spanned the frame as I stretched my toes toward the pedals. I must be dreaming. The pedals spun effortlessly and didn't grind. The bike was low, light, and fast. My bike weighed at least twice as much. As it responded to my energetic pumping, I raced toward the end of the block and back again before quietly pushing the bike back to where I found it.

"That was fantastic," I sighed. Riding Clifford's bike for a few minutes without getting caught now made Gary's too tempting. Seconds later I rounded the corner on Gary's blue three-speed. I shifted gears, mimicking the technique I'd carefully watched Gary use. Clifford's bike was fast, but this one flew. The wind whipped through my hair and made my eyes water. Amazed that anything could move with such speed, I again, reluctantly, returned the bike to exactly the spot I had taken it from. Shaking my head in disbelief, I stood there and looked at the three bikes, asking myself why. Why do I get a junkyard bike and my brothers get the best? I remembered asking the same questions when we moved to California and I had to sit on the hard piano bench. I stood there confused, staring at the three bikes until darkness set in.

For some reason my parents treated my brothers, especially Clifford, one way and me another. Why? I kept asking myself. I began to feel that none of my family cared; the bikes proved that. What happened to me or how I felt didn't matter to any of them. They weren't going to do anything for me, that was obvious! If I was going to make it, I would have to do it all alone. No one in the world had, or ever would, help me grow up. I was on my own. If I needed or wanted anything, I would have to get it myself. So from then on, I did!

For weeks I devised a plan to get the kind of bike I wanted. School began, and I hung back after recess, scouting out the bike racks when everyone else headed toward the classroom. After a quick survey, I spotted a bright red beauty. I ran to the rack and quickly wheeled it around the back of the building to another set of racks near the south exit. Carefully parking the bike near the gate, I sprinted back to class just as the teacher began the lesson. I wasn't even tardy.

When the school bell rang at the end of the afternoon, I casually walked out the back door toward the bike rack, untangled the red bike from the rest, and sped down the street.

I rode all over the north side of town. When I got home my mom asked me where I had got the bike. "Oh, it's Janice's; she said I could borrow it for a week," I answered cheerfully. She resumed her cleaning, satisfied.

"How simple," I boasted to myself. "I could keep this up all year." And I did. I exchanged one bike for another whenever I felt like it, about every week or two. Taking the bikes was simple. Soon I discovered that if I lingered before going to recess I could even steal the milk money from the teacher's desk.

The better I became at getting what I wanted, the worse things were at home. It seemed as though all Dad did was drink. And the more he consumed, the more he yelled and pushed us around. One night Dad had been drinking heavily and provoked Clifford into a fistfight. Clifford and his girlfriend tried to escape the battle by fleeing in his battered old car. My dad squealed after them in his truck. We could hear the throttled engine clear down the street. Scared, I paced across my room late into the night wondering if he would try to kill Clifford. I never knew what happened, but Clifford wasn't home in the morning. He didn't come home for days.

The next Saturday I woke late to discover that I was alone. The empty house felt eerie, so I went to a friend's home and stayed until late afternoon, when her mother insisted that I go home for dinner. When I pulled my newest stolen bike into the yard, I was startled to see my dad's truck. Saturday nights when the bars were open later than usual were the least likely times for him to be home. One glance, as he came out the door, revealed he'd already done himself in for the night. Red-faced and disheveled, he stumbled down the back stairs toward me, enraged.

He struggled out of his sturdy leather belt and grabbed my arm, yanking me from my bike. The smell of liquor on his breath sickened me. "Let me go." I knew he was out of control. As he hauled me into the house, I struggled to free myself from his iron grip, but he overpowered me. I felt as though I was being attacked by a wild animal. He threw me down on the kitchen floor and whipped me. I screamed until I could hardly gasp for air, but he just kept hitting me—the heavy belt slapped against my skin until welts rose and blood encrusted my clothes. While he struck me, he yelled, "You d—— b——. You no-good wife! Where's my dinner? I know where you go when I'm not here, you whore!"

He's going to kill me! I thought. My legs were aflame, and I rolled from side to side fighting for my life. Drunk enough not to tell the difference between me, a nine-year-old, and my thirty-five-year-old mother, he was still clearheaded enough to carefully aim and execute each strike. "I'm not Mom!" I screamed. "I'm not your wife! I'm Carolyn!" Nothing I said registered. With sweat pouring off his face, he stood up straight and leveled one last blow across my back with all his might. He left me and staggered for the door, muttering about what rotten luck he'd had in marrying.

The room was spinning. Every inch of my body hurt. I could hardly focus through my tears. I inched my way down the hall to my bedroom on my hands and knees, nudged the door shut with my foot, and collapsed on the bare floor. My legs throbbed. Unable to move, I fell asleep just inside the door. Later I was awakened by the sound of my parents fighting. In terror I silently cried out in the darkness of my room. "Somebody please help me. Don't let him come after me again. Make them stop. I can't stand it anymore!" Tears filled my swollen eyes, and I cried myself into a deep sleep— my only means of escaping the painful world I lived in.

Life continued. My reading was still poor, and I had a hard time memorizing my multiplication tables past the sixes. School was a social outlet, I couldn't care less about reading or math anyway. My mom never checked my report cards; neither would she go to conferences the teachers requested. I had nothing to worry about when teachers got angry about my schoolwork; Mom never made me stay home and study. In fact, she usually shooed me out of the house whenever I came near.

School was okay, but street football was my favorite activity. I loved sports. After the last bell rang, I sprinted home, changed into my jeans, and was the first one on the asphalt ready to warm up. The only girl allowed to touch the football, I proudly gloated over the fact that the other girls could only be sidewalk cheerleaders.

One late Friday afternoon, I peered down the empty neighborhood street, squinting. The blinding sun and heat made the air stifling. Air moving in slow motion created the illusion of heat waves rolling off the asphalt on the next block. The typical breezes were distinctly absent.

"Everyone must've gone home," I sadly concluded. All my friends had obviously escaped to the coolness of their darkened houses. Disappointed, I turned toward home.

I meandered down the cement driveway, around the shady side of the house, and through the back door. The empty kitchen led me to believe I was alone. Clifford and Gary weren't in their room. The door to my parents' bedroom was closed. I cloistered myself in my private sunny nook.

Through the single window, I could see the neighbor's tree. Not a leaf stirred. I remembered last night when the outside light from their house cast menacing shadows through the limbs onto my walls. Today in the bright light, all that seemed faraway fantasy.

My twin bed and pine dresser were pushed against the wall that faced the door. Recently, I had come home after school to find my mom's cedar chest tucked under the window. Mom claimed she could no longer keep it in the garage. Knowing she kept it locked, I absentmindedly walked over to the chest just to see if it might be open. Maybe there were some interesting old clothes to dress up in and play with during the long afternoon ahead.

My hand slipped under the smooth edge of the lid. I couldn't believe it; the lid moved! I opened it a few inches before letting the lid drop back down so I could hurriedly whisk aside the blue handkerchief and the handmade sailboat displayed atop it. The lid squeaked, and a long moment passed as I waited to listen for anyone moving in the house before I dropped to my knees and ran my hand across the blankets, towels, and old winter sweaters folded neatly across the top. The excitement was unbearable. My heart started to pound. I was afraid to mess up the tidy piles so I slipped my skinny hand between the stacks to discover what was underneath and searched slowly through the soft materials.

Under the middle pile there was something cold and hard; it felt like metal. Lifting the pile with my left hand, I gasped and pulled out a black handgun. I could feel my pulse race. I'd seen a .38-caliber like this on my dad's dresser a couple of times, but I'd never touched a gun before. As I turned it over in my hand, it was bigger and heavier than I expected. I pointed the barrel so I could look inside. Six long, shiny bullets were tucked securely in the chamber.

Why was my dad's gun in my room? He'd pushed my mom around last week when he couldn't find it. "Where'd you hide my gun?" he had slurred angrily. Why did Mom lie about where it was?

Suddenly I felt cold and afraid, even though it was horribly hot outside. Shoving the gun back beneath the piles, I bolted out the back door to Warren's house.

Running up the sidewalk, I saw him just inside the screen door. "Warren, you gotta come over to my house, right now! I found something."

Halfway across the street he caught up to me. "What's up?"

"Shhhh," I warned, "don't talk yet. I'll show you."

We tiptoed through our kitchen and through the hall to my room.

"Carolyn . . . ," he whispered, ready to question me further. I quickly put my hand over his mouth and shook my head while I closed the door behind him and motioned him toward the chest. He kneeled down beside me, and I cautiously opened the lid, reached down between the blankets, and pulled out the gun. Warren jumped back and grabbed for the door.

"Wait," I begged, "come look at it." This was important. I, no doubt, was the only kid on the block who had a loaded .38 in her bedroom.

"You want to hold it?" I coaxed, pushing the shiny gun toward him.

"Nooo, you show me," he replied, shoving his hands deep in his jeans pockets.

I took the gun and gingerly began to show him the different parts. I aimed the gun in each direction so we could inspect all angles.

"That thing is loaded!" Warren gulped as the barrel passed in front of his face.

I assured him that I knew. "The gun has been around the house before. It's okay." I was loosening up and began pointing the gun at imaginary robbers lurking in my tiny room.

Warren smiled for the first time and edged closer. "Have you ever played cops and robbers with a loaded gun?" he asked.

THUD. The door flew open and slammed against the wall. "What are you doing with that gun?" my mother screamed accusingly. The blood drained from my face, and I dropped the gun limply by my side. She lunged toward me, grabbed it by the handle, and positioned her finger expertly on the trigger with the barrel pointed straight at me. I cowered against the wall for support. She was shaking with rage, and the gun was so close to my face I could count the bullets in the chamber. She edged even closer. I could feel the coolness of the metal as she nudged me with it. Frantically, I stepped back and caught my heel on the edge of the chest. Trapped between the wall, the cedar chest, and my crazed mother, I instinctively covered my face with my arms.

"Don't shoot me, Mom, don't shoot," I begged.

Her muscles twitched; her finger tightened around the trigger. I was afraid her finger would slip and the gun would fire.

"What are you doing with this gun?" she ranted. I couldn't move. Out of the corner of my eye I saw Warren's terrified look before he darted from the room.

Rage screwed her face into a hysterical grimace. She waved the gun wildly. "Don't you know that I hid this gun from your dad? He hates your God-d—— guts. One of these days he's going to kill you."

Horrified at what she was saying, I struggled to get away, but she forced me back with the gun pressed against my face.

"Please don't shoot, Mom," I pleaded.

"He hates you. He's going to kill you. One of these days, he'll find this gun, and you'll be dead. He'll blow your brains out."

My head was spinning. My mother straightened slowly and emphasized, with the gun strategically aimed between my eyes, "I am the only thing keeping him from killing you. You'd better pray that he dies before I do, because without me, he'll kill you."

She pushed me aside and quickly shoved the gun down into the cedar chest, brusquely rearranging the blankets and sweaters. The wooden lid thudded shut, unlocked.

"Stay in this God-d—— room, you son of a b——!"

The door banged shut. I crawled into the corner between the chest and the wall afraid to move, afraid to speak, afraid to breathe.

Now the walls were spinning. "He hates your guts! He hates you. One day he's going to kill you!" The words echoed hollowly in the empty room. The spinning walls were closing in. "You had better pray . . . one of these days . . ." The blackness swept me under.

The Fire

As a fourth grader I stood in the darkened hallway one evening watching my family play cards around the kitchen table. Often when the four of them did something together, I looked on from a distance, feeling like an extra character in the family drama. It was as if my part had never been scripted in.

"Carolyn is in the hallway," Mom announced unexpectedly as she studied the cards just dealt her.

Gary turned toward me. "Why don't you come in out of the dark, rabbit-face, and let us see your buckteeth?" He laughed. The others joined in.

"Would you look at that nose?" Gary mocked when I walked toward the empty chair.

"Remember when she broke her nose? There was blood everywhere," my mom added, shaking her head as she re-created the scene for others around the table. Each family member, in turn, recounted a part of the episode. During an all-block rock fight, I ran home for safety. When I felt it was safe to venture out, I cautiously took a few steps out the door. Without warning a rock, hurled from the back alley, smashed into my face. Blood gushed from my nose, and I fainted on the overgrown lawn. When I came to again—screaming—dirt and blood had hardened around my eyes. Blindly running to the sink to flush out my eyes, I heard my mom enter the room. The trail of blood across the floor earned me a swat and a harsh reprimand. My broken nose went unnoticed.

"Ever since she broke her nose she really doesn't look like

anyone in the family," Gary taunted. "Why is that, Mom?"

My parents exchanged angry looks before Dad broke his silence with a gruff retort. "She's not part of this family. She's never looked like any of us."

Gary went on as if he wasn't listening. "My nose is like Mom's and Clifford's; Dad and I have the same color eyes, but who does Carolyn look like?"

"I said," Dad repeated loudly, "she's not a part of this family."

Mom changed the subject and told me to go to my room. Before bed that night, I examined my face in the mirror as I brushed my teeth. My eyes were light brown, and slight dimples creased in my cheeks when I smiled. The door was open, and my mom walked in.

"Who do I look like, Mom? I can't tell."

She stared at my reflection in the mirror for a long time, her expression changing as I watched. First, nothing, then a twinge of sadness, and finally the red color creeping up her face exploded into angry words. She grabbed my arm and shoved me against the sink. "You aren't a member of this family. Don't ever ask me who you look like again. Do you understand?"

I understood. I didn't belong, and I was beginning to wonder whose child I really was. My mom claimed I had no birth certificate, but she'd described the day I was born. Surely she was my mother, but *maybe* I had a different father!

From that night on, I spent even less time at home. I challenged myself on the streets; there wasn't a bike I couldn't steal or an adult I couldn't infuriate. When I wanted something I couldn't just take, I learned to steal money from my friends' houses.

Two blocks from my house, up a small hill near the corner market where I shoplifted candy, a beautiful new church with pillars was under construction. Ken, my buddy, told me one day as we walked by that the new pastor was Bobby Richards.

"The Olympic pole vaulter?"

"The same one."

The next weekend we saw workers installing uprights and a straw mat in the yard behind the new pastor's house. From behind the hill at the end of the yard, Ken and I regularly watched him run, plant the pole, lift off, hurdle over, and fall gracefully toward the mat. When he wasn't practicing, Ken and I raced our bikes up and down the steeply graded parking lot.

On Sundays cars lined the parking lot, so I didn't go there, but once I forgot and pedaled down the street. The doors swung open, freeing the sound of the organ music as I steered my way up the driveway. Nicely dressed people streamed out and up into the lot. I sat and watched. No one yelled. No one pushed or shoved. Some of the kids, even some my age, held their parents' hands as they headed toward their cars. I stood there fascinated. Small groups clustered on the front sidewalk talking and laughing. They seemed so happy that it began to make me angry. These people seemed so relaxed and kind to their families. Why did my dad hit me? Why did everyone always scream and yell in our family? I hated home. I hated the neighborhood; I hated the way we lived. Why did we have to be so different?

I heard one of the girls my age ask her friend to come over and spend the afternoon at her house. Why couldn't I ever do that? I roughly pushed the kickstand on my bike with my foot and sped toward Warren's house. I stayed for dinner and the Sunday movie that followed. Warren's father, mother, and sister all cuddled on the family room couch while he and I lay on the floor.

As soon as the production credits began to roll up the

screen, Warren's mother announced, "Time to go to bed, kids." I took it as my invitation to leave. But the carpet was so comfortable, I hesitated to get up. Warren jumped to his feet. Sleepily, I watched him cross the room and wait as his sister kissed their dad. Then, to my amazement, Warren kissed him, too! Warren kissed his dad! I couldn't believe it. Why would Warren do a thing like that? I rushed home without saying good night.

Early the next morning I banged on Warren's bedroom window. Soon, rubbing his eyes, he walked out the back door in his bathrobe. "Come on, we've got something to talk about." I dragged him to the curb where my bike was parked and pointedly asked, "Why do you kiss your dad?"

"What do you mean? We always kiss each other good night," he said, puzzled. "Why did you wake me up so early?"

"Quit kidding, Warren. Kids don't kiss their parents."

"Carolyn, you're nuts. What do you mean, kids don't kiss their parents? Of course they do."

This was all a mystery that I had to get to the bottom of. "Does your dad beat you?" I pushed.

"Oh, he spanked me when he found out we'd stolen that candy at the store, but what do you mean by 'beat' me?"

He obviously didn't understand. So it must be true, my family wasn't normal. I didn't need to ask any more questions.

Several days later, I rode my bike to the church again. The church parking lot was deserted, and no one seemed to be home at the pastor's house. Stowing my bike behind the front shrubs, I circled the building, trying each of the doors. Finding no entrance open, I picked up a fist-sized rock and walked around to the back parking lot. With one throw I broke a clean hole in a window that was partly hidden by shrubbery. I reached through the glass and unlatched the lock. With one

shove against the windowpane, I was inside a church for the
first time in my life.

I walked down a long, dark hallway into a huge, sunlit
room. Row after row of gleaming wooden benches led to a tall
wooden stand and an organ. And that window! I couldn't take
my eyes off it. Red, yellow, and purple beams of light crisscrossed the whole front of the church. I'd never seen anything
so beautiful. I slowly slid cross-legged to the floor in the
middle of the center aisle and just stared in awe.

"These church people have it so good. They come smiling
out of the front doors holding their kids' hands. They don't
care about me. I live right down the block, and they don't
know I exist or that my dad or mom have never kissed me
good night in my life." I sat there struggling with the confusion I felt. Anger welled up in me, and I started to pound my
fists rhythmically into the thick red carpet. The next Sunday,
I'd make sure they didn't have it so good. I walked in between
the pews and threw the prayer books and hymnals on the floor.
"So there," I snarled.

Heading back down the hallway, I peeked in all the side
rooms. One had individual desks and a bulletin board. The
next had a nameplate saying Pastor's Study on the door. Dark,
shiny cupboards and shelves extended from floor to ceiling.
What a gold mine! I emptied one of the wastebaskets on the
floor and began to stash blank paper and stamps in it. I found
brand-new candles in a drawer and Bibles on the counter.
When the basket was all but overflowing, I marched straight
out the back door, ignoring the gaping window.

I blinked in the strong afternoon light, blinded for a moment. Now, what was I going to do with all this loot? At the
corner of the building there was a crawl space covered by a
thin wire barrier. One swoop of my hand took care of pulling

the wire out of the way. I hastily knelt down and dragged the wastebasket in behind me.

A large space, three feet high and many feet wide, extended the length of the church. I wormed just far enough under the church to clear the wire and spread out all my valuables. After I dug little holes in the ground the candles stood tall and straight. I arrayed the paper and envelopes alongside the stamps and Bibles. I'd just build my own little church with this stuff.

"All that paper would start one terrific fire," I thought. I patted my jeans pocket. Yep, I always had a matchbook handy for the cigarettes Gary and I stole from home. I lit one candle. The flame flickered beautifully, so I lit the other six. They smelled good, too. They were so tall and white, I imagined they could burn forever. While I watched them burn I crumpled several pieces of stationery into a little pile and then reached for one of the candles. My elbow caught one of the other candles and tipped it over. The paper burst into flames as I jumped back.

I scooped up a handful of dirt, and before I could douse the flame, a man grabbed my arm and dragged me out from under the church. "What in the h—— are you doing?" A red-faced man in uniform looked down at me as another man scurried underneath the church to fling dirt on the burning paper.

I struggled against the uniformed man as he hauled me by my collar to a standing position. The second man emerged from the crawl space; it was Pastor Richards. The uniformed man kept shoving me. He was almost ready to hit me. "Go ahead and hit me," I screamed, "you're just like my dad!"

Pastor Richards moved in, shielding me from the officer. "Please, let's all calm down and go to my office for a few minutes," he said, his tanned face drawn and serious.

"I could have this lousy punk arrested and thrown in jail. She's a no-good delinquent," bellowed the man in blue. His chest heaved with the force of his anger.

Pastor Richards shook his head and waited for the man to settle down. "What's your name?" he asked as he gazed intently at me.

"Carolyn," I confessed weakly.

"Carolyn, huh?" his voice gently echoed my name. He paused then nodded toward the officer. "This man is the fire chief. He is terribly angry because what you just did was very dangerous and destructive. You could have burned the church down and perhaps even killed yourself."

He took a step forward and touched my shoulder, nudging me sideways so he could drape his whole arm lightly across my shoulders. We began walking to the church's back steps. "Where do you live, Carolyn?" Afraid to lie, I told him as I pointed two blocks down the street. He motioned for me to sit down on the cement steps and then joined me.

"You're in a lot of trouble. Do you understand that?" I nodded. With unwavering intensity he went on, "Instead of calling the police, I'm going to make a deal with you. I want you to come to the church every Saturday and work for me. Also, I'm going to call your parents, okay?"

"Yes," I murmured, not looking up.

He clapped me on the back, "See you on Saturday, then."

He seemed finished. The fire chief was already in his car. Pastor Richards stood up and smoothed the creases in his slacks. I sat and waited. When he didn't say anything more I looked up. He raised his eyebrows and motioned that I was free to leave. Amazed, I dashed for my bike. That man didn't hit me! He didn't even yell at me!

The next Saturday, bright and early, I sat on the hill behind the pastor's home. Soon he swung open the screen door wearing a red T-shirt, blue shorts, and tennis shoes. As soon as he saw me on the hill, he waved. I lifted my hand in a return gesture. He ducked under the half-opened garage door and came out with a long pole, motioning for me to come down. As I slowly descended the hill, I wondered what he would do if I got too close to him. He was smiling, so I took a chance and ventured into the yard.

"Let me explain your job, Carolyn," he smiled, holding out the pole. I stared at him without moving a muscle. "Don't be afraid, it's not such a bad job. Come on, follow me, and I'll show you what to do." I followed him to the upright standards, and he said, "It's your job to catch the pole after I make a jump. Just don't let it touch the ground. That's very important, so concentrate." He smiled and winked at me.

I couldn't believe it. For the next several Saturdays I rode my bike to the church and acted as Bob Richards's pole-vault assistant. Ken and my other buddies sat, half-hidden, on the hill watching as this Olympic champion ran again and again and effortlessly vaulted over the bar as I scurried after the pole. He asked me to come back on Sunday. But I wasn't about to go into the church again. He was nice . . . too nice. I still couldn't trust him.

After I was relieved of my mandatory pole-vault duties, I often loitered on the hill behind his house watching his every move. I figured that if I observed him enough I might discover what made him so nice, so I spent hours watching him pole vault or scurry from home to office between appointments. I never saw him cuss, drink, or fight—he surely was unlike most men I'd ever known.

Even Mr. Davis, my fifth-grade teacher, could be provoked to hurl a string of reprimands my way. Again and again he tried to convince my mom to make an appointment for a conference. Finally, at lunchtime on report card day, he came up behind me. "Carolyn, I want you to stay after school this afternoon."

"I didn't do anything!" I immediately defended myself.

"I know, I just want to talk to you."

"If you're worried that I'll forge my mom's name on my report card again, I promise I won't."

"That's not it. Just be here, okay?"

After the last bell rang, I lingered by the coat closet until my classmates left. Sure no one was around to see I had to stay after school, I slipped back into the room and sat drawing at my desk. Mr. Davis straightened the papers on his desk before joining me. Expecting a reprimand, I didn't look up as he approached. I knew I wasn't doing well in school and expected to hear the worst news. He pulled the next desk close to mine.

"I want you to see what I am giving you on your report card," he began. He pulled my grades out of the envelope and placed the card in front of me. "You have three *E*'s, or excellents, in physical education, arts and crafts, and music."

"Yeah, they're my favorites."

Mr. Davis nodded with a warm smile and pointed to the next column. "You have six *S*'s, or satisfactories." He waited long enough for me to read the list, then pointed at the last line. "These are what we need to talk about," he said, referring to a long row of *N*'s in the "needs to improve" column. "There are twenty-three, to be exact." He carefully explained each check and what behavior was appropriate and what unsuitable for improvement. Most had to do with my attitude and loud disruptions.

"Carolyn," he said in a kind and enthusiastic voice, "I have a goal for you. And I'm convinced you can do it."

"A goal, what's that?" I eyed him suspiciously.

"I would like to see you wipe out most of these 'need to improve' marks and turn them into 'satisfactories.' I have no doubt you can do it if you want to."

I couldn't believe what Mr. Davis was telling me. He thought I could do well in school. "You really think I could do better?"

"Of course I do. In fact, I am personally going to help you do it," he added. "We'll show everyone how good you really are."

I was ecstatic. For the first time a teacher was showing personal interest in me. Rather than sending me off to the principal's office or telling me how impossible I was, Mr. Davis was actually going to help me, because he thought I was special.

Starting with the next day, I could hardly wait to get to class and try to become a model student. Every once in a while I would see Mr. Davis look up and wink at me in his secret way of telling me that I was doing okay. The more encouragement I got, the harder I worked. I even found myself taking a couple of books home to study so that I'd know all the answers when Mr. Davis tutored me after school with my spelling and reading.

I was so excited as the grade cards were passed out on the last day of the school year. I carefully opened the envelope and slipped out the chart, eager to count the checks in each column. "Yahoo!" I yelled right in the middle of class.

There were only nine *N*'s, none of them for behavior or attitude. I had changed twenty-three into nine in less than three months. Mr. Davis walked up to me with a pleased smile on his face.

"You're doing very well. I'm so proud of you! I believe the sixth grade will be even better."

I daily reminded myself of Mr. Davis's words throughout

the summer. Never had the vacation stretched on so endlessly. The weeks wouldn't go fast enough. Not even spending every day from early morning until closing in the local park squelched my eager anticipation of the new school year.

September came, and I was assigned to Mr. Stokes's room. All my friends had Mrs. Craig, and I was disappointed. Mr. Stokes was okay, but he wasn't young or nice like Mr. Davis. Short and bald, Mr. Stokes operated by cracking the whip and assigning piles of homework every night. Every few weeks I'd see Mr. Davis come in and talk to Mr. Stokes. They'd always look or discreetly motion in my direction. I knew Mr. Davis was checking in to see how I was doing. As he left each time, he'd toss a quick wink my way. He made me feel special when he took the time to care like that even now that I wasn't in his class.

My new teacher didn't care about me or about any of us. As long as we remained quiet and order reigned, he ignored us. After each of Mr. Davis's visits, I'd work hard for a day, but otherwise I reverted to my old habits—I lived for recess and baseball. I loved to smash the ball into the outfield and listen to the cheers as I, the premier home run hitter, raced around the bases. When we didn't play baseball, it was kickball. I regularly cheated just to watch Mr. Stokes come unglued. The more I taunted him, the more my friends urged me on.

One day in February, a tall, slim college student walked into our class. Mr. Stokes introduced Mr. Franklin, our new student teacher for the coming three months. We all excitedly anticipated any change, and Mr. Franklin was handsome enough to even make me giggle when he smiled.

Mr. Franklin spent a lot of time going from student to student helping us with our studies. When we started acting up or not paying attention, he just moved his chair near us. We wanted to impress him, so we tried to listen to Mr. Stokes's boring lessons. In days, young Mr. Franklin completely won our hearts.

During a Friday P.E. class, I was in a wild mood—cheating by racing over the line when I kicked the ball and getting everyone laughing. I strutted around so much that the class paid more attention to me than to the kickball game. Mr. Stokes was furious, which only spurred me on. Finally, he grabbed me and physically threw me out of the game.

When he started to come after me, Mr. Franklin stepped between us. "I'll talk to Carolyn," he assured his supervisor. "I'll handle this one for you." Mr. Franklin steered me across the playground to the lunch benches, far enough from the game to talk privately. Unaccustomed to undivided attention from my favorite teacher, I tried to laugh and act tough, but he just sat calmly and watched me. Finally he reached into his jacket pocket, took out a Lifesaver, and put it in his mouth before offering one to me. Surprised at his generosity, I took a candy. He sat there a long time just looking at me before he spoke. "Carolyn, I wanted to let you know that tomorrow is my last day here at your school."

"I know," I said, disappointment evident in my voice. "Mr. Stokes told us this morning."

"Before I left, I decided I wanted to talk to you."

"Me?" I responded, startled.

"Yes. I have been thinking about you for some time now."

I looked into his kind face. I couldn't understand why he wanted to talk to me. Why just me? I'd bet every kid in the class would love to sit right here with Mr. Franklin. I felt like the most important student in the whole school.

He began, "I've been watching you for a couple of months, and I am going to be very honest with you." He looked me straight in the eye. "You and I both know that many of the teachers around here think that you're pretty bad." I just shrugged noncommittally. This was nothing new to me.

"But I've come to a conclusion. I think all your bad behavior is a cover-up. As I look deep down inside of you, I sense that there is a good person, in fact, a very good person, in there." No one had ever said anything like that to me before. I tried to act really calm.

"What do you mean?" I said a little too gruffly.

He grinned. "You really are a good person, Carolyn. I wanted to make sure that I told you that before I left. I can see your goodness and think other people need to see it too. My hope is that if we ever see each other again, you'll tell me that you've found that person inside of you. Is it a deal?"

I had never heard such powerful words in my life. "It's a deal," I whispered. I didn't know why, but I was ready to cry. Mr. Franklin stood up, gave me a gentle pat on the back, and walked back to the game. After I regained my composure I joined him.

My mind repeated Mr. Franklin's wonderful words. He thought that I was good! I must be good then. I must be! I felt as though bells were ringing in my head and in my spirit. I was elated. The person I considered my favorite in all the world had just declared that I was good. And while the kickball game went on in front of me, I actually began to believe him.

The game concluded, and the other kids filed into the school. I hung back until Mr. Franklin nodded, "Go ahead." I raced to the room feeling as if a million pounds had been lifted from my shoulders—no, from my heart. I slipped into my seat in the back row while the other kids milled around. I imagined myself rushing up to the front of the room. "I have an announcement to make." I'd make everyone sit down. Then in my fantasy, I would grab the chalk and write in huge capital letters "MR. FRANKLIN THINKS I'M GOOD." I'd twirl around in the center of the room celebrating while all the others cheered.

The kid next to me disrupted my daydream by slipping a folded note on my desk. I looked up and saw my buddy Ken anxiously waiting for me to read it.

"Oh no," I groaned. My most recent bicycle heist was in action. Our partner, Jimmy, was still outside moving the bikes we'd picked from one end of the playground to the other. We planned to steal them after school. We just couldn't do it now! Mr. Franklin had said that I was good. I couldn't steal anymore —not bikes, not money, not anything.

My desk was just a few feet from the door. Mr. Stokes hadn't called the class to order yet. I bolted out the back door and Ken followed. Jimmy was already pushing a bike down the sidewalk. Ken grabbed the bike he'd chosen and eased it out of the steel rack. I lunged in between Ken and the bike rack and clutched the handlebars, pulling in the opposite direction. "Put it back."

Ken laughed nervously. "C'mon, Carolyn, quit joking. We have to hurry."

"I mean it. Put the bikes back. We aren't going to steal anymore."

"What do you mean?" Jimmy hollered from a few feet away.

"It's over," I pleaded urgently, "put the bikes back. We have to go back inside."

"Carolyn!" Jimmy screamed, "Watch out!"

The next thing I knew, I was crying out in pain as my knees skidded across the asphalt as I fell forward. Another blow knocked me all the way to the ground. Mr. Stokes loomed over me. "So you're the one. You're the rotten bicycle thief." He yanked me to my feet and dragged me across the yard clutching my neck and arm so I couldn't break loose. We didn't stop until we stood front and center in the classroom. A complete, frightened silence blanketed the room. He shoved me against the chalkboard. I felt I was on trial for my life.

Out of control, Mr. Stokes paced and ranted back and forth in front of me. "This is the one—this is your thief. You call her your friend. You laugh at her when she cheats. You think her antics are funny. She's nobody's friend."

I blushed, horrified by Mr. Stokes's accusatory finger aimed at my face as he paced. The room began to blur, and I had trouble hearing. I tried to squeeze out the scene by closing my eyes.

He shook me to full attention. "Look at her. She's no good —absolutely no good." I looked past him to see the thirty-two stunned and horrified faces of my friends. Wasn't anyone going to help me? I was trying to stop stealing the bikes! I searched for Mr. Franklin.

A wave of nausea swept through my stomach when I spotted him. Tears streamed down his face. I wanted to tell him what had happened. He needed to know how much he'd helped me. "Believe in me, Mr. Franklin. You can still believe in me. I was trying to be good!" I pleaded silently.

He lowered his head to his arms on the desk. He, too, was helpless against Mr. Stokes and his uncontrollable anger. I had disappointed him; he wouldn't look at me. He was the best man I knew; if he wouldn't help me, who was ever going to show me how to be good?

Mr. Stokes's phrases continued to echo across the room. "You're rotten. You're no good. No one in this room should be this girl's friend." With one last angry motion, he threw me into the hallway. "Go to the principal's office. I don't want to see your face in my classroom again."

Walking down the gray-tiled hallway, I fumed, "If my crummy teacher thinks that I'm bad now, just wait. I'll show him what bad is so he'll really have something to tell the whole school!"

Mr. Stokes had humiliated me and left me without friends or a shred of dignity. How I hated him! Mr. Stokes was out of control, just like my dad. My good intentions melted in the heat of my desire to show Mr. Stokes just how bad I could really be. None of them had seen anything yet!

The Ballgame

Late in April a stack of snapshots and a map lay beside my dad's dinner plate. He hummed as he thumbed through the photos. I'd never really seen him excited before. He and Mom had just returned from a week away somewhere. They had told me it was none of my business where they went or when they left home. But tonight, with Dad's anticipatory mood and the pictures, I could tell we were going to find out.

"Well," Dad announced as he ladled mashed potatoes in a huge mound next to his peas, "we're moving."

"What? Where to?" Gary put his fork down and looked dismayed.

Mom pulled up a chair next to him as Dad opened a map of the United States and pointed to the state of Oregon.

"Is it cold there?" was the first question that came to my mind. Oregon looked pretty close to Montana. I could never get warm in the winter when we'd lived there.

"Yes, but not as cold as Montana," Mom replied.

Dad then took the pictures and passed them around one by one. There was a small motel and lots of shots of pine trees and of beautiful snow scenes. "The motel is about a mile out of town. It has eight cabins and a small house where we can live," Dad explained.

Gary and I asked questions, and our anticipation began to build. Moving sounded pretty good. Only Clifford remained sullen and silent. A high school senior with a new job as a box boy in the local supermarket, he'd just traded his bike in for a used car and monthly payments.

Two weeks later Mom, Dad, Gary, and I packed a rental truck. Clifford helped, but loaded his belongings into his own car. He was staying in California with a friend. With a promise to drive up for Christmas, he and his girlfriend, Madilyn, stood together waving as we drove off, headed due north.

The long hours in the back of the truck made me think of the last time we had moved. The horrible memories of the piano bench came bitterly back after years of lying dormant. This time the weather was beautiful, and I sat with Gary near the back window hidden from our parents' view. I kept as quiet as I could, so Dad just ignored me and sipped on a six-pack of beer.

The drive through Northern California showed off its lush hills, towering redwoods, and huge mountains. The miles passed rapidly and soon we were crossing into Oregon. Stopping to stretch at Klamath Falls, we browsed down Main Street before driving on. The timber became dense as we climbed higher due north beyond Crater Lake. Every twenty miles or so Highway 97 intersected a rural road. One gas station, a couple of bars, and a combination general store and market characteristically claimed each of the four corners. We slowly crested hill after hill as logging trucks roared past our over-loaded truck.

Mom studied the last of the three maps we'd purchased until we found one that listed "Crescent, Oregon, population 350." Late in the afternoon, she pointed to a spot on the map. "We're here!" She looked at my dad and smiled.

We rounded a final curve and climbed a small slope before finding the painted sign, hung on a metal post, near the shoulder of the road. Dad slowed and steered the truck onto the red-cinder driveway that horseshoed around the motel units. Eight white one-roomed cabins outlined the drive. A small house with one large picture window overlooked the cabins from a slight rise on the right side of the drive. Slender pines interspersed with cedars shot straight to the sky all around the shabby complex. In the center of the horseshoe was a miniature shed that housed a washer and dryer.

Gary unlatched the truck doors, and I jumped out and craned my neck to look at the overhead neon sign. BIG PINES MOTEL—VACANCY, the words blinked on and off to entice tired motorists. I surveyed the motel and the surroundings by slowly turning in a full circle. Buildings, trees, and sky—that was all there was. We were in the middle of nowhere. Walking on a few yards down the highway, I could see a low shack or chicken coop nestled in the foliage across the two lanes of asphalt.

"Load up," I heard my dad yell. "I want to show you town before we start unpacking."

"But we just got here," Gary protested, his hand on the doorknob of cabin one.

"I want to see my room," I complained.

My dad slammed the front door shut and walked over to me. "You don't have a room. The only bedroom is for your mom and me. You and Gary get the living room. So there's nothing to see and nothing more to say. Get in."

About a mile down the road we slowed as the road widened into town near some dilapidated buildings. Dad pulled over near Forest Service Headquarters. The town looked like a scene from an old-time movie. We could see three blocks of civilization. A huge stack of firewood lay neatly stacked by each tiny wooden house tucked off the main road back in the woods. A two-pump gas station claimed position as the town hub.

Long Beach, the crisscrossing freeways, the diesel buses, and the tall, crowded buildings bore no resemblance to Crescent. The only pavement was on the highway. The access roads and parking lots were cinder-covered.

"This is town?" I asked.

"You're joking," Gary laughed at Dad. We fired remarks across the backseat. "There couldn't be three hundred and fifty people here. How about thirty-five people and two hundred and fifteen skunks?"

Railroad tracks ran along the right side of the road. Behind the tracks, the Deschutes River quietly wound its way south through a meadow of tall grass. A few more houses without lawns dotted the roadside between the railroad tracks and the highway. Five logging trucks and several cars were parked in front of the Crescent Bar. Just past the tavern stood a tiny little storefront with an old board sign reading Post Office. An American flag flew overhead. "The post office is smaller than our kitchen in California," Gary pointed out to the rest of us.

Next to the post office were a few little cabins, and in the center of town was a white building displaying a Crescent Coffee Shop placard. More people were packed inside than were visible on the rest of the main street. Dad drove slowly, letting us see each building. It didn't take long. We turned onto an access road that paralleled the highway. Dad swerved around the mud puddles. Toward the end of the road, a church stood away from the road in a grove of trees.

That was it: the whole of Crescent, Oregon. No beaches, no department stores—nothing.

"This is it?" I asked, already knowing the answer.

"This is it. Bend, the nearest big town, is fifty miles on down the road. If you really want shopping centers you go a hundred miles back to Klamath Falls."

"This sure isn't like Southern California," Gary declared.

"C'mon," Dad announced, "I'll show you where I'm going to work."

We continued on, and one mile over the hill we entered

Gilchrist. On the left the Deschutes River opened up into a massive pond with thousands of logs floating on top. A dam controlled the river waters, stopping the flow from continuing downstream at more than a lazy trickle. Men jumped from log to log as they used hand-held poles to guide the logs to a ramp. The logs moved through the loading dock to the saws of Gilchrist Mill.

In front of the lake stood a beautiful, expensive-looking yard with manicured lawns and flower beds surrounded by a hand-hewn log fence. "That's Mr. Gilchrist's home," Dad said. "He's a millionaire and owns the whole town." I was impressed.

Gilchrist was different from Crescent. The cabins and houses, painted identically with Scandinavian decorative trim, lined the well-cared-for streets. They had a larger church and a row of stores, but as we passed by, I could see that only the market was occupied. The name Gilchrist was painted above each business. "I can't believe one man owns the whole town," Mom shook her head.

"He controls everything," Dad assured her. "Rumor has it that he is one of the richest men in the United States." Dad looked back at Gary and me as he drove around the mill. "I am going to work here while your mom runs the motel."

I had never seen a mill before. Hundreds of men bustled all over the gigantic structure. Logging trucks were lined up to deliver their logs down another ramp to the lake. Flagmen waved in every direction controlling traffic and machinery. Dad explained that there were crews of men up in the woods felling the trees that these logging trucks transported through the forest on a network of narrow dirt roads.

The noise in sections of the mill was deafening. Enormous blades sliced through each of the logs. A huge, funnel-shaped chimney billowed smoke. "This mill runs twenty-four hours a day," Dad declared. "They need a lot of men to keep it operating. It's not terrific pay, but at least it's something."

We drove past the flagmen onto the main highway, retracing the route to Crescent and our new home. I wondered if I was going to like this rustic place.

Dad started to work at the mill the next Monday, and Mom took over management of the motel. Dad, a new employee, ended up working the night shift. That meant Gary and I had to help rent the motel units in the evenings and clean them up and do our chores before we left for school. Fortunately the bus stop was just in front of the house.

Oro Blay, a friendly man in his sixties, drove the school bus and greeted each new rider by name. By the time the bus got to our house it had already covered thirty-five miles of the route. The bus usually was half full by the time Gary and I climbed on.

The next stop was a mere eighth of a mile down the road. As the bus ground to a stop, thirteen disheveled kids straggled on. There weren't any houses between our stop and this one. I couldn't figure out where all these kids lived. The only building around was the low chicken coop or shack back in the trees. "Gary," I whispered on the first bus ride, "where'd all these kids come from?"

Before Gary could respond, the nosey kid behind me blurted out for all to hear, "They all live over there in the chicken coop!"

"You're kidding," I said, staring out the bus window to get a better look at the long, low structure at the edge of the trees.

"Nope, you ought to see inside. They're really poor. Their mom and dad don't work so they have to live there."

"All of them are from the same family?" I questioned, never having met a family with more than four children.

"Yep, all thirteen of them, from six years old to seventeen. You ought to see their place. There are holes in the floors and the walls. You don't have to go in to see inside." Our chatty neighbor rattled on and on. "I heard that they sleep three or four to a bed."

"You're kidding," I repeated, looking at Gary. "And we think we have it bad sharing the living room."

The bus rambled along through Crescent and into Gilchrist. Oro gunned the bus to make it up the steep hill where the road veered sharply to the left beyond the church and the market. All of a sudden, as if on cue, the kids on the bus started yelling, "Hurry up, beat him, c'mon, Oro." Gary and I looked around. What was going on?

Up in front of us I saw an old yellow bus racing from the other direction toward the same parking spot we were headed for. I later learned that the other bus had spent several hours that morning picking up kids from as far away as thirty miles north of Gilchrist. There was only one parking spot reserved for incoming buses. Every morning it was a race to see which one would arrive first.

Gary and I waited while everyone else rushed off the bus. We followed up the walkway to the school. No more asphalt playgrounds; green grass, towering pines, and dirt roads surrounded us. I eyed a rousing game of baseball going on in the yard in front. This, I decided, looked like fun, as I walked up the wide stairs and into the school.

Two people, a short man who'd lost most of his hair and a woman nearly a foot taller and fifty pounds heavier, stood in front of the double wood doors that led inside. Gary and I soon discovered Mr. McGee was the principal and Mrs. McGee the vice-principal, but with one look I knew who really was the boss.

The McGees kept us aside as the other students hurried to

their classrooms. We followed the couple into the inner office and filled out forms while they summoned our teachers.

Mrs. Clements led me down to the elementary hallway. I looked over my shoulder to see Gary heading the opposite direction. The school was one long building with only heavy doors to separate the grade school from the high school. I longed to go with Gary and be with the high school kids.

Before long I sat at my assigned seat, able for the first time to get a look at my classmates. There was one kid in the class who kept raising his hand to answer all of the questions. He acted like the brainy kid, but he was cute and smiled a lot. The teacher called him Chet. He was one that I hoped would become my friend.

I learned two important things that day at recess: Mrs. McGee was a retired WAC sergeant who loved to shout orders, and there was an all-school dance scheduled for Friday. Dancing or partying occupied the number-one spot on everyone's social calendar in the logging community. I'd never heard of a dance in Long Beach.

The high schoolers sponsored regular dances in the gymnasium, but as a sixth grader, I couldn't attend. Gary, however, quickly scaled the ranks to popularity in his class, and I hit it off with Chet.

Within three weeks Chet asked me to the local Granger dance. He had cornered me near the coatracks after recess. "I don't know how to dance," I had to admit. Chet promised to teach me. Mom readily consented, and I had my first date.

Chet lived on a ranch seventeen miles north of Crescent. I had no idea how he planned to pick me up for the dance, since neither of us could drive. I dressed in my new white blouse and plaid skirt and waited near the front window.

A car horn tooted, and up drove Oro Blay and Chet.

"How fun," I thought. Everybody liked Oro. He was a great old guy. Backtracking through town, Oro turned right at the logging road leading out of town. For an hour and a half he steered around curvy dirt roads. I couldn't believe that people could cross the river and drive all these unmarked roads and actually know where to find exactly the right building in the right town. I wasn't even sure if you could call four buildings clustered together in the middle of a high-country logging road a town!

At the dance, a group of young guys, all in cowboy boots, leaned against parked cars as they downed cans of beer. Western music boomed from inside. We walked inside, and found a room reverberating with music and energy. A guitar, bass, piano, and drums surrounded the wailing vocalist. Everyone seemed to dance in the same direction as if this were a roller skating rink, but no one wore skates. The dancers swarmed on and off the wood floor in between songs.

Chet took me by the hand and led me out to the floor. He put his arm around my waist and told me to put my left hand on his shoulder. We clasped our other hands together, and he said, "Okay, take two steps forward and one step back." The rhythm of the music made it easy—one-two, one-two, back one, pause. Several people waved and hollered hello to Chet as we maneuvered through the groups of adults and teenagers. We were no doubt the youngest ones there.

The dance ended well after midnight. We had a long drive home, so Oro told us to just relax, and he would get us back to Crescent. I sleepily nestled back in the seat. Chet scooted closer to me, slipping his arm around my waist before he kissed me. I opened my eyes and leaned away, embarrassed. Oro was right beside me. Chet smiled sheepishly and threw his coat over my head like a minitent to block Oro's view. In the front seat of the bouncing truck we kissed again. Chet kept looking at his watch. Finally I whispered, "What are you doing?"

"Timing us," he said. We kissed for thirty-five minutes nonstop. That was a record for both of us. I got home at 4:00 A.M. from my very first date. No one was awake when I tiptoed to my bed.

When there wasn't a dance or a movie at the local theater, Gary and I soon learned to open up our shared room, the living room, as a dance hall for all our friends. Every Saturday a gang of kids from the high school gathered at our house. Most were ninth graders, like Gary, or older.

Chet soon was replaced by my older friends. I learned each new step quickly and so became a sought-after dance partner. After a regular group had established our house as their headquarters, we decided to form the Kool Kats Klub. The constitution and membership requirements were quickly voted on. The one problem the whole group had to figure out was what to do with me. The constitution required that all members be at least in the ninth grade, but I was three years too young. Consensus allowed for an exception to be made, and we drafted it into the constitution. "Carolyn Koons shall be the only non-ninth grader that can belong to the club forever and ever."

I soon forgot all my grade school chums. Thrust into a group of high school kids, I joined in the car races that sped recklessly over mountain logging roads. We made a ritual of stopping to circle the cars wherever we were at the stroke of midnight. The car radios, all tuned to the same frequency, blared while we danced on dirt roads in the moonlight. Beer and whiskey flowed freely. If attending a party where drinking was not allowed, we simply hid it in the cars and took lots of breaks from the hot and steamy dance halls.

When bored, we thought up all kinds of adventures. It was easy to find the most recent logging camps and siphon gas out of the trucks; that way we could run around in our cars all night. Some of the kids' fathers came home from work complaining about the vandals who had messed with the machinery the night before. Gary and I laughed over the stories together and kept our secrets to ourselves.

Any hopes about our family changing when we moved from California to Oregon soon proved futile. The rough, bawdy culture brought out the worst in my dad. His arrogant bullying became worse as he burst through the door each morning after the graveyard shift smelling like a drunk. His buddies at the mill armed him with new vulgar jokes and renewed his vigor to push us around.

Mom was supposed to run the motel, but with Dad gone every evening, her social life too soon became routine. More often than not, she would order me to stay home in the evenings and take care of the rentals while she hopped into the car and drove to the Crescent Bar, leaving me to rent out the motel units and register the guests. Standing behind the registration counter in our house, I'd try not to look at the people registering, hoping they couldn't tell I was only beginning the seventh grade.

Once a man asked me for a receipt. Not knowing what one was, I assured him, "Oh, don't worry, you don't need one. We trust you." I figured the startled look on his face meant I'd said the wrong thing. I hastily ducked out of the registration booth to keep him from asking more questions. Sometimes I'd just turn the No Vacancy sign on or call my friends to come over just so I didn't have to meet those strangers alone.

I'd now moved from the elementary school wing down the hall to the high school area. My locker was located toward the far exit. After my first English class of the year started I invited the gang to my locker. "Come see what I have in here," I beckoned. They circled the opened locker straining to see. I reached inside and pulled out a large brown bag. Checking to make sure no teachers were in view, I pulled out two full bottles. My brother popped the cork in the wine with his pocketknife. Someone else unscrewed the cap on the vodka. Everyone got a chance to gulp some down before we had to run to beat the tardy bell. From that day on, I drank my way through seventh and eighth grades.

Other than physical education class, I didn't participate much in school. Midafternoon, both junior and senior high girls joined into one gym class. On cold days we exercised inside; on the beautiful warm days, we headed outside in our blue-and-white P.E. uniforms. Up a little knoll from the school, the football field was edged by towering sugar pines. Logging trucks lumbered past a few hundred yards from the field.

Each period began with Mrs. McGee's drills. As self-appointed instructor, she lined us up in straight rows of equal numbers and marched us through calisthenics. Barking, "Reach," "Stretch," "Stop complaining, push," she rigorously oversaw jumping jacks, twists, and contortions. Her competitive, bullying attitude usually worsened as the period progressed.

Class typically concluded with a few innings of baseball. Invariably, Mrs. McGee umpired and I pitched. Bigger and stronger than any of the other girls, I struck out all but the best batters with my fast balls, and even most of them.

In the middle of one spring game, Mrs. McGee declared a new rule. "Carolyn can't pitch fast anymore. It's too hard on the batter and catcher." I proceeded under new rules, with my friends giggling at Mrs. McGee's comic authority as she paraded back and forth along the first base line.

Even using the slow pitches, I was easily striking out the other team. With the score tied three to three, I was first at bat. Straddling home base, I choked up on the bat and considered smashing the ball to left field, knowing the fielder couldn't catch. She usually let the ball roll into the woods, which allowed time for me to round the bases for a home run.

Mrs. McGee was rooting determinedly for the pitcher to strike me out. I decided to have some fun. The pitcher lobbed the ball and I bunted, dashing for first base and betting that the pitcher would be too surprised to field the ball in time.

I was right. She overthrew first base. The cheers from my peers urged me on to second. I could hear Mrs. McGee screaming from home. Once I was safe on second, the teacher ran to the pitcher's mound, hoping to help the team put me out. She laboriously ran toward the grounded ball between first and second and threw it on over the head of the second baseman as I speedily rounded the diamond on my way to third.

"Put her out, d—— it," Mrs. McGee demanded.

The second baseman threw directly to third before I reached the bag. Trapped, I danced impishly between second and third bases as the ball whished back and forth, always arriving just as I switched directions, careful to stay too far away for the basemen to tag me. Finally, the third baseman overthrew, and I rounded the last corner, gleefully darting for home.

I could hear my team cheering. The other team chorused, "Home it, home it!" By now both teams were yelling and screaming with excitement. My heart pounded. I was going to make it without a slide. As I neared home, to my dismay, Mrs. McGee stepped dead center in front of the plate, her arms raised as if to fight. I veered around her to my left, stretching my right foot to touch the side of the plate for the score.

A smashing fist threw my feet out from under me, and I tumbled to the ground. Mrs. McGee, her face twisted with anger, stood menacingly over me as warm blood spurted from my split lip and flowed down my uniform. I was stunned. Through dust and tears I looked up at the woman sergeant swaying madly over me.

Four girls jumped out from the team huddled behind the backstop to help me. My head reeled, and my mouth throbbed with pain. Within a split second, Mrs. McGee had scattered the group by flailing her arms wildly. "Leave her alone. Don't any of you touch her."

Reaching down, she strong-armed me to my feet. "Go to the showers," she demanded. Unnerved, not knowing whether to laugh in disbelief or raise my fists and retaliate, I stepped back, groping behind me for the the team bench alongside the first base line. Mrs. McGee followed me and pushed me over on my back in the dirt.

Girls from both teams quickly surrounded me to keep Mrs. McGee from touching me. I could hear her hysterical yelling even though I couldn't see her. "Go to the showers!" She shoved her way into the huddle. With her body blocking the rest of the girls from following, I hobbled to the gym, my sweaty, bloodstained clothes clinging to me. I didn't turn around, but I heard her wildly warn my friends, "Stay away from her. I don't want any of you to hang around with her anymore."

Memories of Mr. Stokes and the sixth grade rushed back. "She can't do this to me again," I thought in silent rage. "What did I do to make her so mad? I was just playing good ball! It's not fair."

I forced myself to walk steadily although I was close to exploding inside. What had I done to this stupid teacher? I wasn't even breaking any rules this time! No matter what I did, somebody blamed me. My clenched fists swung by my sides. If I could just get my hands on that woman, she'd never know what hit her.

The Motel

As I reached for the door handle to the locker room, my friend Vicky caught up with me, grabbing my elbow and guiding me inside. "You shouldn't let her get away with this," she whispered vehemently as I undressed and headed toward the tepid showers. "You might need stitches; your lip looks terrible!" Blood still flowed inside my mouth, and my head throbbed.

Vicky followed me, "You didn't do anything wrong." She waved her arms angrily, "McGee just has it in for you." Exhaustion kept me from responding. I closed my eyes and stood under the rushing water, longing to be somewhere far from school where I could just lie down and try to forget this bizarre afternoon.

Word spread rapidly throughout the small high school. By the time I appeared in the locker-lined hallway, my boyfriend, Larry, had heard the news. After one look at my puffy face and split lip, he protectively draped his arm around my shoulders and waited as I gathered up my belongings.

As we headed toward the exit and his 1948 Chevy, he told me, "Mr. McGee hustled 'the sergeant' into his private office as soon as she left the gym." A Do Not Admit sign still hung from the hook above the frosted window as we passed the office door. "You could sue her, Carolyn. You could get her kicked out of teaching." Larry was seething as we drove to his house, where his mother inspected my lip and suggested that I see a doctor. But I just wanted to go home.

Back in the Chevy we passed by the Crescent Bar. Sure

enough, our family car was parked outside. Knowing that the house would be empty when I got there intensified my pain. My family was never there when I needed anything. The split lip and bruised face were but physical signs of my deeper wounds. A nagging loneliness crept deeper and deeper inside me as we approached the motel.

Once inside I dragged myself to the couch. Larry brought me a pillow and plopped down on the floor next to me, stroking my hair. It was nice to know someone was on my side. After I quieted down, almost ready to doze off, he scurried around the house to find a washcloth and several aspirins. He bathed my forehead and held my head as I gulped down the pills. My body ached. Slowly, while Larry held my hand, I drifted off to sleep.

The next morning I abruptly awoke to a blaring horn. I opened my eyes to see Gary run to catch the school bus. I didn't move. My joints were stiff. I didn't need school or irrational teachers who hit me and told my friends not to hang around with me. I was tired of being pushed around.

I attended classes sporadically for the rest of the year, going only when I felt like it. The older kids were easily convinced to play hooky. Nightly dances, weekend movies, and racing in cars over the logging roads filled the rest of the spring and summer. Moonlight dips in the swimming hole and daylight rifle shooting contests provided free excitement. When the frosts came, bringing school back into full swing, we turned to late afternoon games of car hide-and-seek through the forest. I turned my creativity toward devising exciting diversions—anything that kept me from thinking about school or home.

One September evening, Larry led a caravan of four cars over the rutted woodland roads. As we circled back toward town, he slowed and rolled down his window, hollering to the driver behind him, "I've got an idea. Follow me."

With no further explanation, but a mischievous twinkle in his dark brown eyes, he turned off the logging road and took a path through the sugar pines. Twisting back and forth, the four crowded cars sped on until the track opened onto the football field behind the school. The high school wing emptied onto one end of the field and the faculty housing faced the school from the other.

Larry gulped down the last of his beer and threw the can out the window. "C'mon!" he waved the other drivers to follow him. He revved the motor, and the car hurtled across the dirt track onto the grassy football field. With the accelerator floored, Larry alternated between gaining speed and stamping on the brakes as he leaned to the left throwing the car into a screeching spin. Dirt clods spun up from the back tires. The other three cars followed and dug huge ruts in the field. With radios blaring, we screamed in excitement, racing in figure eights back and forth across the field trying to see how fast we could drive without crashing.

One by one the lights switched on in the faculty housing. Robed people stumbled to the doors to find out what all the noise was about. The McGees' porch light was the last to be lit up; it flooded the field with brightness. "Let's get out of here," Larry laughingly commanded, the adrenalin and beer taking full effect.

"That should drive Mrs. McGee wild for a few weeks," I thought spitefully. Larry's car had been far enough away from the houses when the lights went on. She'd never know I was involved.

The next day at school an announcement was read over the P.A. system in Mr. McGee's nasal whine: "Anyone knowing anything about the vandals who tore up the football field last night, please come to the principal's office." I exchanged knowing glances with one other guy who'd been with us. No one in my class budged. I looked out into the hall from my desk, and it was empty. I smiled. We'd promised each other not to squeal.

Each time we didn't get caught encouraged our gang to take just one more dare. Our partying continued, yet we did less and less dancing as the older among the couples retreated to parked cars or a back bedroom in one of our houses.

Late at night my mom would stumble home and sleep until early morning when Dad, bleary-eyed, would lumber loudly through the back door. Invariably they'd fight. It was the arguing and abuse that sent me out the door to school more often than anything else. When I was at home, my job was to care for the motel customers. One night a man, with his packed bags, stood at the front door when I answered a knock. After listening to hours of fighting, he was checking out, even though he was paid up for a week. He couldn't stand the yelling. I didn't even try to convince him to stay one more night. I knew nothing would change.

The next day my mom roughly woke me as I slept on the couch. Matter-of-factly, without giving me time to clear my drowsy head, she reported that Dad was taking Gary and heading for California. My parents didn't want to live together anymore. Gary balked at the plan, but he didn't have a choice. Neither of us did. Within days they were gone.

With Gary gone, the solitary late-night hours after the ritual parties at the motel seemed lonelier than ever. Some of his friends stopped visiting, and he wasn't there to drive me around. I dreaded the frequent walks home from Crescent in the pitch-black winter evenings. One night as I left a party near the edge of town, I headed down the long highway staring through the blackness to where our motel should be. Neither moonlight nor highway lights broke through the murky dark.

Placing my left foot in front of my right, I walked up the cinder shoulder of the highway, making sure that I didn't fall off the steep embankment into the trees. I inched my way toward home taking tiny, cautious steps and humming quietly to calm my nerves.

About ten minutes out of Crescent, I looked back toward town, then ahead. I was suspended in darkness. I stopped walking, realizing how terrified I was. After a moment of silence while I tried to gather my courage, I heard a clumping, running sound, increasing in volume, rushing toward me. I froze, unable to move. A hard, furry object crashed into my shoulder. I lost my footing and rolled down the cinder embankment, coming to rest against a rough tree trunk. My hands and knees stung from scraping across the cinder.

Intently listening for the creature to return, I limped up the embankment. Hearing nothing, I faced the direction of the motel, carefully checked the asphalt until I found the center dividing line, and ran down it. Twenty yards down the road I felt soft dirt under my feet and realized I had strayed to the shoulder. Groping to find my way back to the yellow line, I kept seeing wild, stampeding beasts in my mind. Was it a deer that hit me? What was it? I was never happier to see the Vacancy sign blinking in the night.

In the next weeks vacationing deer hunters from Portland and Eugene flocked to central Oregon. The cabins were reserved for a week to a month at a time as the hopeful hunters used the motel as home base for their timberland forays. Many of the men looked familiar. They'd rented from us the previous winter. After they returned from full days of trekking through the trees, my mom would always accompany one or two down to the local bar. She loved hunting season. It added excitement to her dull social life.

During the entire six-week season, the front door of our

house didn't slam shut behind Mom before 4:00 A.M. Often I was roused from my sleep by her laughter, accompanied always by a male voice outside—their forms silhouetted against the porch light. Sometimes she invited someone in, and I could hear giggling and intimate noises from the living room as I lay silently in the adjoining bedroom. Eventually Mom would tiptoe into the room, drop her clothes in a pile on the floor, and slip under the covers, thinking that I was asleep.

I woke myself for school each morning and dressed as she breathed shallowly in her hung-over sleep. Once I watched her. Her body slightly rose and fell with each breath. The disarray of the room seemed to represent her whole life. I felt sorry for her. She was lonely, miserable, and constantly searching for something or someone to make her happy. Her pain was more than I could bear to think about. I went to school depressed, wondering if I could prevent the same thing from happening to me. Was I doomed to be just like her? That thought haunted me.

That afternoon when I came home, a man, one of Mom's late-night companions, lounged in the kitchen. Each time my mom passed by him, he fondled her or made some suggestive comment. Repulsed, I changed my clothes and went back and forth between the bedroom and living room, trying to act busy until Larry came to pick me up.

Finally my mom called me. "Come here, Carolyn. You and Larry going out?"

"Yeah, he'll be here in five minutes or so," I answered from the doorway, not wanting to venture any closer to either of them.

Mom gestured toward the man, "Frank and I have a present for you." With one eye on him, she flirtatiously strode over to the refrigerator and swung the door open. Colored glass bottles of vodka, whiskey, wine, beer, and untold mixers filled the shelves. "Here, pick whatever you want. Take as much as you can carry. We want you to have a *long* evening out. Understand, Carolyn?"

The bribe made my stomach turn over. Normally, I would have ignored the offer; I didn't want any favors from my mother, but tonight I loathed the two people in front of me. The free booze would help me forget that my mother was in our house sleeping with this stranger.

I reached in the refrigerator and grabbed a bottle of vodka and another of red wine, mumbling a perfunctory thanks without looking at either of them. I rushed to the porch and was relieved to see Larry's car approaching from town.

My mom followed me and stood beside me. We both stared out unseeing across the road. Out of the corner of my eye I saw her turn to look at me. I refused to return her gaze. Sensing my anger, she defiantly declared, "I'm not sleeping in the house tonight. I'm going to sleep in unit one." I knew only too well that Frank would be there waiting. "Don't stay up for me. I won't be coming in."

My shoulders stiffened automatically, and I sucked in a lungful of air. I couldn't believe she had the gall to tell me what she was going to do. I wanted her out of my sight. I wanted to get out of the house as fast as possible.

The horn honked and I grabbed the two bottles. Larry waved, and when my mom turned abruptly back inside without waving back, his look told me he'd noticed that something was going on. Our friends Vicky and Dave shouted greetings, oblivious to my tension. I ran to the car clutching the bottles.

"What do you have there?" Vicky exclaimed delightedly.

"A treasure or two," I answered, handing the vodka bottle to her. "Tonight we're going to celebrate."

Larry and I rode in silence along the dirt road behind our

house that intersected with the logging road. We followed the tracks of the huge trucks and slowly chugged uphill. Vicky and Dave giggled and laughed, their hands all over the bottle and each other. They paid no attention to us.

At the top of the incline we pulled into the grove of trees that bordered the drop into the canyon below. The dark woods were draped in an eerie silence. Larry turned up the radio and rolled down his window. I uncorked the wine and told a crude joke I'd heard from my mother.

Everyone but Larry laughed. "What's wrong?" he asked, sensing my anger.

"I don't want to talk about it. Give me the vodka." I reached back to Dave, grabbed the bottle from him, and took a long swallow of the clear liquid. Larry took the bottle from me.

"You don't like the taste of vodka, remember? You told me that the other day. What are you thinking about?" he probed gently. He pulled me into his arms and brushed his lips briefly across mine. He was kind and full of tenderness, but I had nothing to give in return. I felt cold, like an emotional corpse. Did I really love Larry? Maybe I was just like my mom —searching and lonely, trying to fill a bottomless void.

I took a deep breath. I didn't want to explain my lousy life, but neither did I want to give in to his persistent nudges and romantic desire. The thought of getting pregnant terrified me. I knew if I did that I'd be forever stuck in this backwoods place, having babies and hustling strangers at the local bar. I could just imagine my mother back at the motel, and it sickened me. There had to be more to life than this. Where were my brothers? Were their lives any better than mine now? A million questions surged through my mind.

"Carolyn, please . . ." Larry pleaded and squeezed my hand tightly. I knew what he was asking me.

"Larry, I can't." I looked to the floor then turned my body away from him and scooted toward the passenger door.

"I can't go through with this." I opened the door and got out.

"What's wrong?" Larry called defensively as he got out of the car and walked around the front of it toward me.

"I don't understand you," he said, more subdued, when I didn't offer any answer. "You seem so angry. What did I do?" He hesitantly embraced me. Poor Larry, but how could I explain? I wanted to be free from his arms, free from my mother's choices, free from my life in Crescent. We stood staring into the dark canyon for a long time. All the muddied pieces of my life came rushing in on me.

Larry sullenly took me home.

Mom took up semipermanent residence in unit one with Frank. She crossed it off the registration book as unavailable. After a week, Frank had to return to work in Eugene. Within a couple of days some other man lived with her in unit one. How could she do this?

The second man left after a few days, too. Mom came into the house while I was there—something she hadn't done in days—to tell me, "I'm going camping. The guys are off for a hunting trip through the high country. I'm going with them as their cook, shall we say. We may stay two weeks, maybe a month. If you need anything, you know how to rent the units and clean them up for money. You can use the car if you want." She threw the keys on the sofa and walked into the bedroom to pack her clothes.

I was a thirteen-year-old, who already looked eighteen, with free access to a car and no driver's license. Gary had taught me how to drive a manual transmission pickup truck in the mountains the summer before. I could get around, but I resented my mother for dumping the responsibility for the whole crummy motel on me. This time, rather than focusing on her loneliness and searching, I felt anger and resentment burning inside me. And more than that, I was disgusted at her blatant life-style. What did she think I was? A fool?

The stock of booze in the refrigerator was all she left me. There I was, stationed in a lonely motel a mile from town with lots of bottles to drown out my anger and a flashing Vacancy sign to advertise just how alone I really was. Soon I realized it was probably a relief to have Mom gone. I could have parties night or day. But still, when everyone was gone, it was just me, the dark woods, and the silence.

Days went by and I heard nothing from her. I half-heartedly tried to convince myself that she'd never return and that I was free, but most of the time I spent rehearsing the vehement speech I'd give when she walked through that door.

Vicky, Dave, and Larry spent lots of time at the house with me. I didn't tell them what was going on, and I tried to make excuses when they asked about my mother. Her absence puzzled them. I became good at changing the subject.

By the third weekend, I asked Vicky to spend the night with me. She walked home after school to her low, Scandinavian-style house in Gilchrist to pick up some clothes while I rode the bus home to straighten the units and flip on the No Vacancy sign. My anticipation built. Someone would be in the house with me all night that night.

When her mother dropped her off, Vicky pointed to the No Vacancy sign, "You're already full for the night?"

"Are you kidding? I don't want anyone to stop and ask for a room. It scares me when men I've never seen before walk into the house wanting a room. I have to go out in the dark and show them the cabins."

"Isn't your mom going to get mad at you for discouraging business? Don't you need the money?"

"I don't know and I don't care. I just don't want to show those guys around the motel at night."

We walked up to the porch and sat on the railing. Vicky soon went inside to put her clothes in the bedroom then came back out and sat beside me.

"Carolyn, where is your mom?"

"Oh, she's off visiting some friends."

"C'mon, who do you think you're fooling?" Vicky scoffed, leaning toward me intently, "don't you know who your mom is?"

I stood up and stepped away from her. "Sure I know who my mom is. What kind of question is that?"

"I'm serious. Do you know who your mom is?"

"What do you mean, 'who'?" I demanded. "What are you trying to say?"

"I'm telling you that your mom is the town prostitute, and we all know it," Vicky said matter-of-factly.

I grabbed the porch rail and clenched my eyes shut, hoping to make her words go away. I knew what Vicky said was true. I knew better than anybody what my mom was doing, stumbling home from the bar and laughing her way into unit one with God only knows who, but I didn't know that anyone else knew. Anger and embarrassment struck to my very core. I hated the way my mother lived. Now the whole town knew.

"Your mom is the town prostitute," Vicky repeated.

What could I say? Rage welled up in me as it never had before. I wanted to tear this whole damned motel apart board by board. How could I strike back? I wanted revenge, or I wanted to die. Vicky left me alone for the rest of the night. If my mom could just wander off and do as she pleased, so could I!

On Sunday night I called Larry. "I have a plan. Let's get

Vicky and Dave and forget school tomorrow. My mom is gone for a couple more weeks."

"You're kidding! Won't you get in trouble for leaving the motel? We'll all get in trouble for skipping school."

"No, we won't." I explained my plan, and he agreed. He called Dave, who phoned Vicky. The next morning we all gathered at my house. Larry brought his dad's truck and showed me his stashed possessions: a couple of thirty-aught-six rifles and two shotguns.

"I could only convince my dad to let me bring two deer guns, I didn't tell him you girls were coming with us. Whoever isn't hunting can do target practice with the handguns."

Vicky and Dave brought the food. We packed all four of us in the cab and roared off. It was exciting to drive past the school realizing the rest of the students had to stay down there with Sergeant McGee while we went hunting.

We scanned the roadsides for miles, too lazy to get out and hike. We meandered along logging roads to the other side of the valley. By late afternoon we hadn't even seen a deer. Dave and Vicky were getting restless. Larry had been quiet too long, I knew him well enough to know he was scheming. "I know where to go," he finally assured us. He pulled the truck around in a U-turn, and we headed back down the logging road to a small driveway.

A few hundred yards past the entrance, we pulled up alongside a quaint summer cabin. The doors and windows were locked. Larry and I went to check the garage. As we checked the garage door, we heard a loud crash and ran around to the far side of the cabin. Dave had smashed the side window with a rock and unlocked it. Only his legs were visible as he crawled through.

Within seconds he flung open the front door and we all

hurried inside. Each of us took a cupboard or closet, rooting through the loot. With arms piled high we carried bundles to the truck until we were satisfied that we'd plundered all the valuables. Larry and Dave cut long branches from a pine and swept the tire tracks away as I backed the truck onto the main road. Laughing hysterically, we searched for a second cabin. By dusk we'd ransacked four. The truck was bulging. Larry even tied some spare tires on the roof.

By this time we'd crossed the valley again, and Larry headed for an open meadow on an abandoned ranch where we could build a campfire and cook some of the stolen food. We opened many more cans than we could eat and broiled the steaks we'd found in someone's freezer. We rested for a long while after eating, groaning from having stuffed ourselves.

Dave was the first to get up. "Help me put this stuff from the car in that shed over there." He pointed to a building in the shadows a few yards away. We hung the cameras and radios by nails from the ceiling beams and piled the cans in the corner, using a flashlight to guide us. Small holes in the wall allowed the moonlight to shine in. The holes made perfect targets for shooting practice. We all took turns aiming for the light.

Tiring of that, Dave aimed his gun at one of the cans in the corner. Larry followed suit, and in seconds they had blown the canned goods to pieces. Baked beans and corn oozed all over the floor.

I grabbed the gun from Larry and, laughing uncontrollably, aimed at the blaring radio. With one round I blew it to smithereens. One by one we took turns destroying all the evidence. We were far enough away from town that anyone who had heard the shots wouldn't think a thing of them. After all, it was deer season.

At least once a week we continued our cabin hunting

sprees. Evenings traditionally held a party or hanging out at the Crescent Cafe with the other members of our gang. Hamburgers and drinks were cheap, and everyone within miles stopped by.

One night after a three-cabin day, the four of us pulled up and sauntered to the counter at about 9:30 P.M. Other high school kids filled all the booths, and the jukebox played nonstop. Larry ordered cheeseburgers and orange crushes. "Have you seen the paper?" A girl in his class scooted the folded front page toward us.

"What's happening?" Dave asked before he read the headline. Larry and I didn't say anything. "WANTED—INFORMATION CONCERNING VANDALISM OF SEVERAL CABINS IN THE CRESCENT/GILCHRIST AREA." My heart pounded. It had never dawned on me that our escapades would reach the papers—or the police.

The girl who showed us the paper looked accusingly at me. "Do you know who's been doing this?"

"No," I emphasized, "I had no idea there was anything like that going on."

"Well, whoever did it is really going to be in big trouble when they get caught." She didn't say any more and left to sit with her friends near the back of the cafe.

Larry and I wordlessly wolfed down our dinners and headed nonchalantly toward the exit. I could feel the sweat on my hands as I reached to push open the swinging door.

Our fun was over, and the winter days droned on and on. The rain poured down incessantly. Mom had returned, and we left each other alone. For weeks on end we didn't exchange much more than an indifferent hello. I didn't want to talk because I knew I'd tell her just what I thought once I'd started, but I watched her. She lit up when a few of her special men friends came around, but otherwise her face remained lifeless.

Day after day she followed her routine at the Crescent Bar. I pitied her—she'd created such a boring and hopeless life.

One drizzly, depressing afternoon, Larry was busy with some school activity so I took the bus home. "I haven't seen you in a long while," Oro said when I moved to the front as the bus neared my stop. "Did you and Larry break up?"

"Oh, no, he's busy at school. I just needed another way home." Oro honked and waved as I walked down the path to the house. Smoke curled upward from the chimney. That meant Mom was home and the wood stove was already stoked. Good, I wouldn't have to go back to the wet woodpile.

There wasn't a car parked in the lot. Probably no guests would show up at this time of year. It would be a long, depressing night. My mother was sitting at the table with the telephone next to her as she read a handwritten letter. She looked as if she'd been crying, and one glance told me she was mad too. "I want to talk to you."

I hung my jacket on a chair and sat down. I felt awkward. It occurred to me that she'd never said she wanted to talk to me before. "I want to read you a letter." She turned the paper over to the front. The letter was from some woman's husband. He'd come home to find his wife in bed with my father. The letter described the man grabbing his gun and threatening my dad. Dad, naked and scared, dove through the bedroom window and ran down the street in all his glory.

Mom finished reading and said, "I've talked to the man who wrote this letter twice today. And I talked to your father. He's coming home." She then called up a girlfriend from town and began to repeat the story detail by detail. She acted appalled that Dad could cheat on her.

I sat there across the table from my mother feeling stunned. How much worse could this sick play we all lived out become? My mom's livid ranting about Dad's behavior was incredible. Who was she to rage about the injustice of my dad's unfaithfulness? Who had the right to be mad at whom? The ugliness of the world was suddenly unbearable. Between listening to my mother's phone calls to her friends as she played the role of wronged wife, I called Larry. "Get me out of here!"

Within minutes he drove up. "I'm leaving. I don't know when I'll be back," I told my mother as I left the house. She was too absorbed in retelling the story for the umteenth time to respond.

Larry leaned across the car to open my door. "Are you okay?" he asked.

"I don't want to talk about it."

"Whatever you say." He knew when to be quiet and when to pry. I knew I was fortunate to have a sensitive friend who would stick with me through thick and thin.

Larry drove for a long time. Slouched down, I rested my head against the seatback and stared, unseeing, out the passenger window. A heavy pressure weighed down my chest. The bleak clouds outside only mirrored, in part, the darkness in my heart. I didn't have the energy to respond to Larry's occasional questions. I felt tears rising, but none came. I couldn't remember the last time I'd cried. Maybe I didn't know how anymore.

Larry gently took my hand and squeezed it. We'd driven the seventeen miles to La Pine, turned around, and retraced our route. A few miles north of Gilchrist, we turned off the main highway and headed toward the cinder pit, a natural quarry mined for use in highway construction.

Our headlights bobbed up and down the road as we lugged up the hill. Trees lined the sides of the road. We drove slowly; Larry was aware of how easy it was for a car to slide off the road into the pit. At the top, Larry steered the car in a complete circle, flashing the headlights into all the parking spots to make sure we were alone. I felt the breeze as he rolled down his window. The stars were beautiful in a moonless sky. Inside the car the red lights on the radio glowed.

"What's wrong?" Larry insisted. His brown eyes clouded with concern.

"My dad is coming home."

"Oh, no," he groaned. "Does that mean your parents are getting back together?"

"I don't know. I don't know anything anymore. I can't stand it, Larry. I want to get out of here."

"Carolyn, you can't leave!" His voice sounded shocked. Just my putting into words my desire to start over set him off. He droned on and on trying to convince me that I had to stay. I leaned my head out the window to stare into the blackness. I remembered the night the furry animal had knocked me into the blind darkness of the forest. "You could live with us for a year or two, then we could get married. I'm sure there's a way to work it out," Larry continued.

The darkness began to close in. I felt lost. "Larry, get me out of here."

"Carolyn, I'm trying to talk to you." He shook me to get my attention.

The blackness moved in closer and closer, I panicked and reached for the ignition, turning the key. Larry's foot wasn't on the clutch, and when we bolted forward, my head smashed against the front window. "What are you trying to do? Kill us?" He screamed and stamped on the brakes, looking at me in amazement. "What are you doing?"

"I just want to get out of here. The darkness scares me." Hysterical fantasies about unseen animals roared through my mind. I reached again for the ignition.

"Carolyn, no!" Larry flipped on the headlights. The car sat angled at the very edge of the cinder pit. If he hadn't hit the brakes so quickly, we would have plunged downward in the night.

My heart sank. "Oh get me home, please get me home," I whimpered, and slumped down in the seat.

The trip home was wordless. I opened my door and looked into his confused, stormy eyes. His chin was set—whether in anger or concern I couldn't tell. "I'm sorry. We'll talk about all those things another time. Larry, believe me, I do love you."

"Sure. Good night."

I sensed his disappointment. I stood and watched him drive away past the Vacancy sign. The darkness moved toward me. I turned and ran wildly up the stairs and threw open the front door, glad for the bare light bulb glaring from the ceiling.

Two days later, Gary and Dad arrived. Tension grew, and no one would answer my questions. Gary only admitted he hated living with Dad because he was drunk all the time. At the end of the week Mom announced we were selling the motel and moving back to California. Dad had a new job on a railroad construction crew.

Just like that, three years of my life ended. Larry encouraged me to stay with him, but that meant staying in Crescent. I had to escape the life my mother led, I would not live like my parents. I didn't know what railroad life or Salinas, California, would offer. I just knew that maybe out there where I had never been something better waited.

We packed up our bags and boxes in yet another rented truck and left the way we came.

The Farm

Dad purchased a nondescript forty-two-foot-by-eight-foot aluminum trailer in Salinas. Cheaply made bunk beds, with thin, lumpy mattresses, were installed in the sole bedroom for Gary and me. Mom and Dad chose the dark green foldout couch in the living room.

Both Mom and Dad predicted we wouldn't stay in Salinas long, and for once their words proved trustworthy. In less than a month, not even enough time to enroll in school, we hitched the trailer to our pickup truck and headed south to Long Beach.

Within days, more than two and a half years after I'd left Mr. Stokes's sixth-grade class, I stood in the halls of Wilson Junior High School. Many of the faces were familiar. Most of the kids were taller; like me, they'd filled out. We were no longer gangly kids but teenagers. Yet for me the memories remained. Eerie reminders of Mr. Stokes's judgment and Mr. Franklin's disappointment descended on me from the very first day. It made me feel as if I'd stolen the bicycles last week instead of years ago.

Ken and Warren, my old friends, tentative and wary, perhaps because our age made friendships between two boys and a girl awkward, asked questions and sometimes invited me out with their new friends. But things had changed. I didn't fit anymore. Again, it didn't matter much since we moved once more six weeks after arriving.

A long trip across country, ending amid open miles of farmland dotted with an occasional tractor or combine, brought us to Topeka, Kansas. The Midwest would be a fascinating adventure.

Each weekday a battered bus drove up to the trailer park by the freeway that skirted the edge of town to take Gary and me to school. The kids from the tidy farmhouses stared curiously out the windows. Brought up to be polite, they never said anything, except one girl who admitted she'd never met anybody from a big city, especially Southern California. Gary and I were not like them.

As the bus slowed to let us off in the afternoon, the kids gawked at my dad and the other railroad workers, just home from work, sitting on the tiny trailer porches, day after day, drinking beer or playing cards and telling dirty jokes.

Neither Gary nor I ever invited any of the kids from school to our trailer; we didn't want them to see anything more of how we lived. The whole park was full of crude-mouthed railroad workers, always partying. Some even traveled in their own trailers. Like a band of gypsies, the motley railroad families migrated from one construction site to the next. One family in particular, the Fribergs, became my parents' best drinking buddies and card partners. They soon tired of cheap trailer parks full of transient laborers, however, and left the railroad to buy a small farm in Minnesota. How I began to wish we could settle somewhere and get out of this nomadic life.

Embarrassed to ask kids home, Gary and I stuck to socializing at parties and dances. Dancing was big here in Kansas, too. With our varied repertoire, learned all over Oregon and California, Gary and I never lacked friends as long as there were dances Friday and Saturday nights.

Within a couple of months, just as we began to settle in to midwestern life, we were uprooted from Kansas and were on our way to Crown Point, Indiana. Even as we traveled I dis-

covered humidity like none I'd ever experienced. I could feel
the sticky air get heavier and heavier, and when we stopped
to rest and I ran lightly trying to stretch out my stiff legs, I
noticed that my lungs had to work harder to breathe.

This time the trailer park wasn't desolate. The spring rains
had left the grass and trees verdant and welcoming. I was soon
back in school, though my teachers were dismayed that over
the year I'd missed a full month in Salinas and six weeks while
in transit. I had no proof of which grade I was supposed to be
in. Even after many phone calls they couldn't locate any test
scores to verify my academic skills. The counselors finally
assigned me to the grade I assured them I was in, with hopes
that my scattered school records would catch up with me
before the next time we moved.

The Crown Point High School Dance Contest was scheduled for the week after we arrived. In a gym decorated with
crepe paper, Gary and I paired up to test our expanding talents
against this new crowd. We were near the end of the scheduled pairs. They all danced just alike. When it was our turn,
we felt the curious eyes of teachers and students alike intently
turned on us. They didn't know us, and this was our first
chance to make an impression. The music started and with the
first note I forgot that there was an audience until I heard the
clapping. I looked around and the whole crowd was applauding. I knew there weren't many things that I did well, but
could I dance! We won hands down.

By this time my parents had acquired a flatbed slat-sided
truck somewhere along our route across the country. I often
piled in the back with my friends as Gary, urged on by his
friends in the front, raced all over the windy hills of northwest-
ern Indiana. Those of us in the back clung to the stakes on the
side of the truck in terrified delight. In the evening we'd head
toward the drive-in movies.

At school my friends kept talking about a new movie star, Pat Boone. I knew he sang on the radio because he sang one of my favorite dance tunes. I heard that he was in a new movie, *Bernardine.* This guy's handsome, all-American picture first stared out at me from a movie magazine, when I stopped in the local drugstore after school.

One day, a few weeks before the movie was to open, a girlfriend asked me, "Did you know that Pat Boone is a Christian?"

"What does that mean? Is he good or something?"

She assured me, "It means he sure isn't like us!"

I was fascinated. People all over town said Pat Boone was good. Somebody actually was good. Everybody said it. I collected every magazine I could find. They all confirmed it; not only was he good-looking and talented, this guy was different.

The movie title, *Bernardine,* finally appeared on the theater marquee. Close to the front of the line for the first showing, I pushed and shoved until I found a seat on the aisle right in the middle with a perfect view. I hoped that I wouldn't be disappointed.

From start to finish, Pat Boone smiled and laughed on screen. Portrayed as kind and helpful, he seemed different from the characters in the usual adventures or westerns I saw. After I'd seen the movie, it seemed that no matter where I went someone would start talking about Pat Boone. Reports from the magazines promised that this guy was just as popular and good in real life. I wondered if being a Christian meant being like him. Seeing a happy and exciting life, even on a movie screen, made me curious. Maybe everyone else's life wasn't as miserable as mine. I don't know what came over me, but I couldn't shake it. I saw the movie eight times while it was in Crown Point. I hoped that if I watched enough just maybe I'd figure out what made life happy.

A month later, I passed the eighth grade, before my transcripts arrived. It was Mom who, again, broke the bad news. We were on the road once more.

Heading northwest through Illinois, Wisconsin, Minnesota, and North Dakota, we backtracked to Havre, Montana, a barren cowboy town thirty miles south of the Canadian border. I hadn't been to Montana since the third grade, and I'd never been this far north before. The railroad company made space for all the welders and their families in a trailer park outside town near the city dump. Undoubtedly this was the worst place yet. Compared to Havre, even Crescent was a booming metropolis. This place was desolate. For the first time I prayed that we would move. I barely left the trailer during the month and a half before we hitched it up to the truck and headed back toward Indiana.

Saint Paul, Minnesota, marked a little more than halfway on our journey. Mom and Dad had stayed in contact with the Fribergs, so we headed there to see their farm. When we reached the outskirts of the Twin Cities we left the main road and traveled an hour before branching off onto a dirt road. Mile after mile of rolling green hills and patches of tilled soil stretched before us.

We stopped at a farm every mile or so asking for directions. We finally found their narrow, old two-story farmhouse at the end of a rutted lane. A peeling red barn stood to the left of the house. From a far corner of the corral a horse watched us.

Before Dad allowed us to get out, he backed the trailer under a big, leafy oak tree in the front yard. I couldn't wait to stretch my legs and look around. What a place! The cornstalks in the closest fields looked twice as tall as I was. The Fribergs, Bob and Phyllis and their two sons, rushed out to greet us. Everyone soon disappeared into the house while I headed to the barn to explore.

Several holes in the walls revealed two horse stalls with hay-strewn floors. A few chickens scurried between my feet, and I thought about how different these people's life was from mine. I walked out behind the barn and leaned up against the fence post watching a beautiful brown-and-white Moroccan quarter horse graze.

"Come here, boy," I coaxed, tempting him with a handful of alfalfa. His ears perked up, and his long, lean legs began to carry him toward me. He came within ten feet and stopped short. "Come here, boy," I said gently. His ears flattened against his head while he nervously pawed the ground with his hooves. I waved the alfalfa in front of him. I could tell he wanted it. He stamped hard and snorted, refusing to budge. I talked to him soothingly. Nothing. Finally, I threw the wad of grass several feet inside the fence, halfway between him and me.

Cautiously he approached, grabbed the alfalfa, and backed away, never turning his gaze from me. When he was a safe distance away, he galloped to the far end of the field.

I headed to the house and heard loud chatter. Inside, the house was a disaster. Bob, now retired from the railroad, tiled floors and roofs. He must've decided to do his own house in his spare time. Phyllis saw me in the doorway. "Come on in, Carolyn. Bob's just getting the drinks."

She told me of her new job as a cocktail waitress in Saint Paul while Bob popped the tops on the beer. Soon tongues wagged long and loud as stories flew across the room about everyone who'd ever worked with them on the railroad. My father boasted about beating up some guy in Havre, which somehow got my mother to arguing with him about money.

I sank down in my chair, only half-listening to the stories I'd heard a million times before. With each beer can added to the pile of empties, the tension increased.

Bob got tired of hearing my parents argue. "Let's go outside, I wanna show you my new horse." I jumped up, eager to get back to the corral, but my dad lagged behind. "Give me another beer," he said, without budging. Mom threw him a disgusted look, shifted her attention to Bob, and followed him out the front door. As we walked behind them toward the horse, it became obvious from his wobbly gait that Bob was drunk.

He opened the corral gate, grabbed a short whip that hung from a nearby hook, and headed toward the horse. The animal backed away. Bob, swearing every step of the way, pursued the horse into a corner of the corral. When the horse had no room to move, Bob grabbed its mane and swung up onto its back. The first sharp kick Bob aimed at the horse's haunches sent them both off in a frenzied gallop.

The horse flung its head up and down in protest. It ran wildly, making quick turns and abrupt stops trying to rid itself of the crazed rider. Bob responded with savage strikes of the whip. With a whinny, the horse reared up on its back legs. Somehow Bob hung on. When the horse landed, Bob jumped off and raised his arm high to level blow after blow on the horse's neck with the rawhide whip.

"Stop it. Quit hitting him. He's afraid of you!" I pleaded aloud, grabbing at Bob's arm.

"Shut up!" my mother ordered, lunging toward me to push me out of the way.

"Throw me a harness," Bob yelled to his oldest son. The boy obeyed. Then Bob roughly forced the bit into the horse's mouth, flinging the reins over its head. He attached the lead rope and pulled the horse toward the lone tree in the corral.

He looped the rope over the lowest limb and tied a knot leaving only a little slack for the horse to toss its head. It couldn't reach the grass to graze.

"D—— beast is wild. Must've been beaten by the guy who sold it to me. I'm gonna break that horse if I have to kill it— or it kills me." Bob spewed out the words as he walked back to the group by the gate.

I remained after the others left. The horse hobbled to the tree watching Bob's every move as he staggered away. I couldn't understand how he could beat that horse. The poor thing was trapped inside the corral. It had such a confined and hopeless life. How I knew how that felt! I wanted to run over, untie him, and set him free, but Bob yelled at me to come to the house. Helplessly, I followed.

As if nothing had happened, we went back inside. Bob headed toward the refrigerator and reached for another beer while Phyllis touched his arm in an effort to stop him from drinking any more. With his free arm he slapped her soundly across the face. She fell back against the sink. She tried to laugh it off, but the red spot on her face showed how hard he'd hit her.

Bob headed toward the living room with two beers in his hand. Phyllis followed. I sat down at the kitchen table near the window, staring out at the farmyard. I could see a corner of the barn and the chicken coop, surrounded by lush grass and trees and covered by the wide, open sky. I longed to live on a farm, in a house, anywhere but the trailer. I hated the trailer. Somebody knew everything I did. I couldn't get dressed without someone bursting into the room to get something. I hated the way we lived. People should live in houses. They shouldn't be living in trailers, moving all over the country.

Mom walked into the kitchen to resupply the beer in the other room. I stood up and leaned against the sink next to her.

"Isn't this a neat place?" I said haltingly—unsure about how to initiate a real conversation with her.

"It's okay," she shrugged and began to walk out of the room.

"Hey, Mom, I want to talk to you about something."

She turned around with a defiant look on her face. Rarely did I talk to her about anything, so the moment was unnatural and strained. "Why don't we buy a place like this? Why don't we get off of the railroad and live in a house? I don't like living in a trailer or moving all the time. Can't we have a house like everybody else?"

She just stared at me, her eyes fixed and cold. The moment seemed endless. When she spoke her voice shot through me. "Carolyn, why don't you just leave? Why don't you just get out?" I backed toward the table, not knowing what she meant. "Carolyn, I want to be really honest with you. Since the day you were born, you have been *the* problem in our marriage. Your dad hates your guts, and he will never change. Every fight we have ever had has been about you. You need to understand that he hates you, and one of these days, he's going to kill you. So why don't you just leave?"

I felt the way I had that summer day years before in Long Beach when she stood over me with my father's loaded .38. Nothing was different. Nothing! Not even her message: "He hates you. One of these days he's going to kill you." I stood there, still, stunned, as those painful words sunk deeper, dredging up other horrible threats and memories.

"I think it would be best, Carolyn, if you just leave." She paused, watching for my reaction, but I had none. "I have to make a choice. You just turned fourteen, and you have your whole life ahead of you. I don't have anything left. The choice is between you and your dad. I choose him. You need to leave."

There was nothing for me to say. I was overwhelmed with disbelief. She continued, "The only way that any of us are ever going to be happy is for you to leave." She turned, without another word or look back, and left me standing alone.

I watched her grab Phyllis and guide her out onto the porch, as Dad and Bob told stories that were vulgar at best. I walked to the back porch and stood looking across the fields that had just seemed so peaceful. "What is she talking about? How have I been the cause of every fight they've ever had? That's not true. God knows I've heard every word of enough arguments to know she's not being fair."

My parents fought about everything and anything. The angrier they got, the more they drank. Why did they blame me for everything? No one had to come right out and say it; we all knew that I was a constant reminder of her infidelity. My dad is not my real father. Why else would he hate me so much? But why is all of this *my* fault? Living with them was as awful for me as it must be for them. I wanted something more, but I didn't know what. How could I just leave? Where would I go? Not back to Oregon; I'd just end up pregnant or in trouble with the law. Oregon meant a prison all its own.

While I considered all the places I'd lived, Phyllis joined me on the porch. As if she was just making conversation about the weather, she said, "I hear that you want to leave home." My mother had already told her. I couldn't answer. Besides, she wouldn't believe that it was Mom who had told me to leave; I hadn't said a word! Phyllis seemed almost to be talking to herself. She didn't even look at me. "You can stay here for a while, if you want. We have a spare room off the attic."

Before she got any further Gary burst through the screen door. "I can't believe you're going to stay here by yourself!" In a matter of minutes, my whole life had changed without my consent. I wasn't going to have a choice in the matter.

I heard Mom's voice from the kitchen. "Phyllis says you can stay here. Let's get your clothes." I didn't move. She repeated her order. Still trying to get my bearings, I trailed after her. She pointed me toward the little room in the back of the trailer when we both were inside and threw an empty cardboard box to me. I carried the box to the closet and packed my few clothes. I took the box out of the trailer and laid it down halfway up the path to the house.

My dad walked past me without a glance and opened the passenger side of the truck for my mom to get in. Gary scooted in beside her. Dad walked around to his door and stepped up into the cab, and I heard the motor turn over.

Not an hour had passed since I'd asked my mom why we didn't buy a house and settle down. A few minutes ago I was on my way to Indiana, now I lived in Minnesota. What had I done? Would I ever see them again? Did I want to?

I remember asking myself as they drove up the rutted driveway with a cloud of dust behind them, "Is life always going to be unfair?" I turned around and looked at the Fribergs' house. They had already gone inside. I stood there alone. A loneliness like none I had ever known washed over me. I felt small. I was very afraid.

The Attic

I stood straining my eyes to see, far in the distance, where the road that carried my family away blurred into the expanse of Minnesota farmland. As the dust settled, I began to notice the toll of a long, scorching summer deceptively hidden beneath the greening harvest. The cracked, hard dirt spoke of little water. Here, too, life was harsh.

I glanced over my shoulder toward the farmhouse, then looked back to the road. Nothing stirred. My chest constricted slowly as the minutes slipped past. The memory of my mother's last words to me acted as the final turn of the emotional vise squeezing my heart. I was the problem, she'd said —not her, but me. She was wrong, yet it was I who felt like stone.

My feet felt as though they were embedded against their will in the Minnesota soil as I shuffled toward the barn. The farmhouse to my right seemed a comfortless place that I couldn't yet bear to enter. The whole scene, as far as I could see, told me that this was a lonely land for a nobody like me.

The worn boards allowed little light to filter into the stale, cobwebbed barn. It was farmers from the past, no doubt, who had carefully crafted the old, decaying halters and bridles that hung here and there on rusty nails. A few randomly stacked hay bales leaned against the two horse stalls. One stall was empty; the other, obviously used but rarely cleaned. The odor stifled the air. I walked to the heavy double doors and pushed until a stream of light flooded in.

After a cursory look into the loft, I meandered past the

barn and up the dirt path to the barbed-wire fence that marked the boundary of their land. The farm was in disrepair. I stopped to lean against a fence post near the corral. Duke, the Moroccan quarter horse, was no longer tied up and seemed to have forgotten his cares; he walked around the paddock, munching aimlessly. I envied him. Duke looked up from his grazing as if he knew I was watching him. I wondered if horses had feelings. Did horses have parents that left them alone in the middle of nowhere? Did they have to plan their future or decide what to do tomorrow or the next day? Sometimes I wished I could change places with Duke—exchange his life for mine—even though I knew he was mistreated too.

A frugal ration of hay was strewn near the barrel of stagnant drinking water. I figured Duke would love some of the abundant alfalfa that grew beyond where he could crane his neck. The barbed wire next to my arm hung loosely from the fence post. I easily lifted it up and stepped through heavy alfalfa into the dusty corral. I carefully reached back through the fence and yanked a handful out of the ground.

"Here boy, here's something good for you to eat," I coaxed, stepping cautiously toward the wary animal. Only a few steps in his direction made each muscle in Duke's body ripple tensely. He trotted skittishly to the far corner of the enclosure.

I wasn't in the mood to chase him and tossed the alfalfa on the ground, turning back toward the fence. A few feet ahead of me I noticed a gopher hole about the same diameter as Duke's hoof. I feared he might step in it and break his leg. Nudging the parched dirt with my shoe, I tried futilely to fill in the hole. Spotting a stick near the fence, I grabbed it and intently poked the sides of the hole until they crumbled.

Suddenly I heard galloping hooves behind me. Duke's shadow fell over me as I heard the first violent snort. "Get back," I yelled, spinning around, stick in hand. Duke lunged, then reared, his front hooves barely missing my face. I jumped back, stumbling into the gopher hole.

I fell and rolled to miss Duke's second attack. He reared again, and I rolled just inches past his landing point. My eyes and mouth were filled with dirt; my heart pounded wildly. At last I rolled under the fence and lay still as the horse continued to whinny and stamp.

The screen door of the farmhouse clanged open as the four Fribergs ran, yelling, toward the corral. The boys scooped up rocks and fired them at Duke, who ran to the far fence. Bob dashed for the whip and for the second time that day chased the horse to the corner, leveling savage blows all the way.

"It's my fault," I frantically hollered at Bob. "Don't hit him!"

Duke's nostrils flared, his eyes frenzied. Bob, gloating in his cruelty, ignored me. When he had the horse cowering against the fence, Bob walked back toward the house without a glance in my direction.

"Come into the house," Phyllis said coolly as she passed by, "dinner's ready."

Danny and David, still hanging over the fence, continued to bombard the corral with rocks even though they couldn't begin to throw far enough to hit Duke.

"Stop throwing rocks, you guys," I told them.

"It's not your horse," Danny scoffed, throwing the next rock at me.

"We can do whatever we want. If we want to hit him we can," David added.

Duke pranced nervously in the corner. The boys' taunting continued, but they were afraid to go near him.

"You're just like me, Duke," I thought sadly. "Nobody cares enough to get near you except to hurt you. I'll try to help you. I know you're just afraid, because . . . so am I."

Once on the porch, I turned for a final look at Duke. His eyes seemed to have followed me. Maybe he felt as alone and despised as I did. In the dusky evening I wondered if today really was happening. It felt like some insane, pain-filled fantasy that I hoped would soon be over.

After dinner I moved into my room—an alcove in the attic. The Fribergs moved a dresser with three narrow drawers in from another room. When it was placed alongside the single bed, it left barely enough room to stand. There was a doorless closet with no hanging rod, but I was able to hang my two pairs of jeans and a few blouses on metal hooks and fold the rest of my belongings atop the old boxes stored in the closet.

Sitting on the bed, I peered out the tiny window. If I sat just right, I could see Duke in the corral. I dropped back on the pillow. The whole day still seemed like a bad dream. I wondered where my folks were. Did they feel anything when they left me? Will my mom really be happier now without me? I doubted it. My parents didn't know what happiness meant, and for that matter, neither did I.

The night came quickly, extinguishing all light, and the fading of the last few rays of sun seemed to isolate me from everything I had ever known. A few twinkling stars seen from my window shone as very small beacons of hope. I could neither sleep nor banish the pain while the day replayed moment by excruciating moment. My chest tightened even a notch more with loneliness until I wanted to cry, but couldn't. "I don't even know how to cry," I moaned.

In the dark night hours I withdrew from the intensifying pain into my fantasy world—the only place I knew where there was any hope of escape. I imagined myself alone in a prison cell with five beds. The dark gray walls and barred windows held me captive. Someone heard about my plight, and soon the uniformed guards escorted a man I'd never seen into my cell.

"Carolyn," he said tenderly, "my family wants you to come and live with us. We want to help make the rest of your life happy."

I envisioned sitting despairingly on a cold steel bunk shaking my head sadly. "I want to come with you, but I can't. I don't know how to be happy."

The man replied, "Don't worry, we'll show you."

The hours passed as I lived in this make-believe peace until even it began to blur and fade away. I fell into a dream-filled sleep. Again and again good people like Pat Boone or Mr. Franklin, my sixth-grade student teacher, rescued me from my prison of isolation. And in each dream my rescuers gave me the most wonderful thing I could hope for: they hugged me and assured me that my life would be okay . . . someday.

I awoke to the clamoring farmyard dawn feeling almost hopeful, and the first couple of days at the Fribergs weren't too bad. Phyllis immediately assigned my chores. My job was to help with dinner and do all the dishes after each meal. David and Danny adamantly refused to help; they claimed they'd done enough in the past couple of years.

Each morning after sunrise, I gathered eggs from the chicken coop and tended to Duke by pitching hay across the barn, cleaning his stall, and filling his water barrel. Before long my duties included moving the mountainous haystack from outside the barn to the loft using an old-fashioned rope pulley, repairing the rickety fences along the property line, and cutting and stacking the winter firewood.

The Friberg boys continually managed to find ingenious ways to get out of helping. Bob and Phyllis yelled at them, but as they were skilled at making excuses, I soon was saddled with their chores as well as my own; I was a real convenience for the whole family.

The ponderous chores and lack of love sent me willingly to my secluded room in the attic each night after dinner. From early evening until the wee hours of the morning, I relived my fantasy of being rescued. I pleaded to my imaginary friends for help. Won't someone, anyone, please help me?

Thursdays each week meant payday for Bob. The first week, I sensed a tight-lipped tension all day. Phyllis outdid herself and had heaping bowls and platters steaming in the kitchen at mealtime. Danny, David, and I migrated hungrily to the table. We fiddled restlessly, hoping Bob would hurry home.

Phyllis paced for a while then angrily yelled at the boys. An hour and a half past dinnertime, she swore as she bustled by me and shoved me against the wall. "Get out of my way!" Not knowing what I'd done, I withdrew to my room until she hollered at me to come and eat. Bob's chair remained empty while we wordlessly gulped down the cold food.

Darkness had fallen by the time the sound of Bob's truck could be heard outside. We sat for a long time anticipating his face at the door. I tired and began to gather the dishes.

Suddenly the front door flew open, and Bob stumbled into the kitchen attempting a drunken smile. His glazed eyes stared into the distance beyond all of us. Phyllis turned toward the counter and whirled around, a paring knife in hand. "Where's your paycheck? What did you do with the money?" Phyllis raged, jabbing the knife in the air just inches from Bob's startled face.

She kept yelling, her voice rising a pitch with each sentence. Bob wrestled the knife from her grip and pointed it back at her. "I drank it, and I'll drink it every time. You and your fancy, no-good job can pay the bills. Don't your boy-friends pay you enough for your company at the bar?" He forced her toward the counter.

Danny darted past his father into the living room, and I followed. David came last, slamming the kitchen door behind him. Phyllis screamed; I heard the all-too-familiar sound of a plate smashing. Bob was going after her.

"What's happening in there?" I cringed, staring at the boys.

"This happens every payday. He gets drunk." David shrugged nonchalantly, calmly turned on the radio, and turned up the volume. Danny grabbed some army men and a truck and started playing as if the commotion in the kitchen weren't happening. I was shocked. The screaming coming through the door couldn't be ignored. It sounded as if they would kill each other.

Horrible memories of my mom and dad arguing and throwing things raced to mind as I paced in the dimness of the shabby living room. The sound of broken glass and china crashed from behind the kitchen door. Bob and Phyllis were no different from my parents; I'd just moved out of one hell into another. This prison had different people, but it was a prison all the same. I was trapped again.

It seemed as though hours went by before I heard the back door slam, followed by the car door. Phyllis demanded, "Don't you ever come back." Bob's truck swerved across the dirt road and careened over the front lawn as he gunned the motor.

Two days later he drove back as if nothing had ever happened. I got the feeling this scene had been played out before a number of times.

Summer waned, and school registration began. I had to take the school bus fifteen miles, which translated into a forty-five-minute stop-and-go ride to the nearest high school. Since I had no parental permission forms or transcripts, the principal threatened to hold me back a year—but didn't.

Each day after finishing my long list of chores, I spent any free time with Duke, talking with him for hours trying to win his trust. One crisp October day I came home to rake the fallen leaves in the yard. When I was done, I ran to the barn and found Duke with his head cinched so tightly against the wooden gate that he couldn't eat or drink. He rolled his eyes in fear, his nostrils flared, as I came near. He wrenched his whole body back and forth trying to break the rope as I struggled to untie him and release the pressure on his neck.

I discovered him tied up again a few days later. This time as I reached up to untie him he flinched, afraid that I would hit him. I began to wonder if I'd ever be able to ride him, the many beatings had made him so skittish. As I filled his water barrel, Bob and the two boys stormed into the barn. "Why did you untie him?"

"He couldn't reach his food or water. The poor horse couldn't move!"

Bob grabbed the halter out of my hands and shoved Duke's head roughly against two overhanging boards before retying him. "I am going to break this horse if it kills me."

Danny laughed and picked up the whip. Duke couldn't move except to kick up his hind legs. I quickly grabbed Danny's hand to keep him from hitting the horse, but Bob shoved me against the wall so hard that I dropped roughly into the hay. I smelled liquor on his breath. Bob took the whip himself and began to lash Duke with it. I surged forward and locked my hands around his arm, pulling with all my weight. He easily shook me loose and sent me sprawling. He raised the whip high over my head. I threw my arms up to protect my face as the whip cracked on the floor just inches in front of me.

Danny had found a two-by-four and, leaning over the side wall, proceeded to smack Duke's hind legs and rump. Finally, as the screaming and yelling intensified, Bob, who was drunk enough to have trouble walking, grabbed the boys and walked out the door, throwing the whip at my feet. "If you like him so much," he sneered, "you can just sleep out here tonight with this good-for-nothing piece of horse meat."

When they were gone I crawled toward Duke, listening to his heavy breathing. "Duke, Duke, it's okay," I whispered, reaching through the gate to untie him. "They're gone. It's just me now." He wildly tried to bolt away. "Whoa, easy, boy, I'm not going to hurt you," I soothed, patting his mane gently until he stood still. "We're just alike, Duke. You can trust me." I reached my arm around his neck and nestled my face against his strong neck. "Trust me, boy. I won't hurt you." That night, Duke and I, two outcasts, slept in the cold barn.

Fall turned into a snowy Minnesota winter. Where once the Friberg farm was shaded by leaves from huge elm trees, the same trees now stood silhouetted barren against gray skies. The temperature, with the wind chill factor, plunged to a record twenty-nine degrees below zero, blanketing the entire valley in an angry chill.

My tiny alcove, the room farthest from the heater, was unbearably cold. I could tell by the temperature in my room whether or not Duke's water would be frozen solid. Each morning, dressed in all my clothes, I would chip away a hole hoping he'd get enough to drink before it froze over again. The long, cold walk to the end of the property was brutal as the winds whipped snow from the high drifts across the road. The bus stop was buried and often hard to find. Each day fewer and fewer kids boarded the bus. An Asian flu epidemic spread across the country. Within weeks less than a third of the school population attended.

One day riding home on the bus, my bones began to ache. By the time the forty-five-minute ride was over, I could hardly drag myself up the long road to the house. For two agonizing weeks I lay in bed. For the first time the boys had to take over my chores. At least once a day, I'd muster the strength to sit up and look out the window hoping to see Duke. I couldn't. I imagined myself able to walk down the stairs and across the yard to greet my four-legged friend, but my bones ached so much that I worried that I'd never be able to walk again.

During my first bedridden weekend, the Fribergs decided to drive to Saint Paul since the snow had temporarily stopped. Alone at the farm, I determined to see Duke. Carefully I edged myself out of bed and bundled into my clothes. I cautiously descended the staircase, leaning heavily on the banister, and made my way slowly across the driveway to the barn.

I opened the small door and was horrified. A heavy rope had again been wound awkwardly around Duke's neck then cinched tight against the wall. Huge welts were raised on his haunches. There wasn't a piece of hay or a drop of water for him. He only whimpered as I approached.

"Duke, how could Danny do this to you?" I loosened his rope before carrying a pail to the pump. Tears streamed down my face as I held the water out for him. I stroked his neck and mane. Seeing this helpless animal was more than I could bear. I couldn't cry for myself or for my family, but watching this horse be abused over and over again loosed my tears. I found a sack of oats in the tack room and pitched a pile of hay for him before leaving. Neither Duke nor I looked like we were going to make it here.

Spring was nowhere in sight. The long hours spent inside added to the Fribergs' family problems. Bob and Phyllis repeated their Thursday routine two or three other nights a week. To compound the pressure Danny and David learned to team up and blame me for messing up their rooms, not doing their chores, or stealing what they stole. I couldn't stand it!

One March morning I stepped on Phyllis's scales. In the six months I'd been in Minnesota, I'd lost twenty-five pounds. I sensed anew that my strength was slowly waning—as was my spirit. I wanted more than anything to survive. I had to find some happiness, if any dwelt in the world. I kept hearing people sing or talk about happiness, but what was it? I knew it wasn't here.

Each day began to erode my spirit more as the hostility increased. I knew I had to get out of Minnesota. But where could I go? I searched my mind for a point of reference, any person who might be able to offer some hope. All my friends were in Crescent. As I imagined myself going back there, overpowering despair filled my heart. Crescent would trap me too. I couldn't go back there. My kind grandparents might welcome me, but not for long—my mother would never let me live with them. I had nowhere to go, but I still had to leave.

By offering to do odd jobs for neighbors, I eventually earned enough money for a train ticket to Chicago. As the money accumulated in my tin can bank, I tried to figure out how to tell Bob and Phyllis. I feared the vindictiveness I'd discovered in her. Finally I found Bob alone as he worked on retiling the kitchen floor. I grabbed the next piece of tile and dropped to my knees to help him. I worked side by side with him for a couple of hours deliberating how to tell him about my plans. But as each tile was neatly cemented in place and then grouted, I sensed Bob's approval and enthusiasm at having a good partner who took an interest in his work. Finally, I blurted it out.

"I'm leaving on Saturday, Bob. I bought a train ticket to Chicago." I didn't look up until all the words were out of my mouth.

He put down his tools and studied my face. I was surprised when he smiled sadly. "I understand, Carolyn. For your sake, get out of this hellhole. I'll take you to the station in Saint Paul if you'd like. Let me know."

He went back to work. The day I was to depart Bob told Phyllis over breakfast I was leaving. The icy weather couldn't begin to match the cold hate and anger her silence conveyed. If she was stuck in Minnesota, why should I have another chance? I fixed a piece of toast and gulped down some milk before nodding at Bob. He lifted my small suitcase and led me out the door.

I turned around as we drove off and looked at the dilapidated two-story house. I felt that an invisible dark cloud of doom hovered over it. My only sadness was at leaving Duke. That poor beast would never survive another year of being brutalized. Bob and I sat silent all the way to the city. When we arrived at the train station, Bob accompanied me to pick up my ticket and wait for the train. When the conductor announced it was ready to board, he looked at me with yearning, pathetic eyes. I sensed that his own world of alcoholism and loneliness was something he too wished to escape, but he knew there was no train awaiting him.

He leaned over—the same man who fought violently with his wife and drank himself crazy each week—and gave me an awkward hug. "Good luck, Carolyn. I hope you find a better life." Tears came to his eyes, and he ducked away, headed toward the car.

I found a window seat on my train. Only two others boarded my car. The train squealed forward out of the station. I sat mesmerized as the miles disappeared behind me. That same engulfing loneliness filled me. I was drifting around the country, and absolutely no one cared. I was riding along moment by moment into a stark, wintery place I'd never been before.

The Knock

I spent the day on the train, lulled by the rocking motion and my thoughts. I felt tremendously small in an enormous world. I could disappear, and no one would know. Carolyn Koons could start all over, change her name, choose a whole new story of the past . . . No one would ever find me. As I watched people get off at stops along the way to be greeted by family and loved ones, reality dispelled my fantasy. It wouldn't matter if I tried to become another person, nobody cared who I was now.

But I wanted to survive. Maybe, just maybe, there was some peace or happiness—perhaps even some love—in this ugly world. Even if I had to find it all alone, I was determined not to give up.

The train began to slow near dusk. Hundreds of black metal tracks crisscrossed as we entered the train yard alongside dozens of other trains. Chicago Central Train Station, a looming, sooty brick structure, was filled with hundreds of passengers, all seeming to have someplace to go in a hurry.

As my train pulled to its berth and I disembarked to identify my luggage, I searched the faces of the people waiting. None of them was familiar. I'd called my mother before leaving Saint Paul and asked if she'd drive over the Indiana border to get me. She'd been noncommittal on the phone. She must have decided not to come. I had no idea where to go.

Rows of upright wooden benches filled the main terminal. I saw an empty bench near the front doors and sat down, not knowing what else to do. A half hour passed. More trains came and went and with them dozens of the milling people. Another half hour passed. Finally, suitcase in hand, I headed toward the door.

"Carolyn," a woman called from my right. I turned toward the voice. My mother and another woman were walking from a side door. "Sorry we're late. Your dad and I had a big argument. He didn't want me to come." Her false gaiety barely masked the mockery and her underlying annoyance at having to see me again.

"Meet my friend Diane," Mom continued. "Her husband works on the railroad. They live just a couple of trailers from us." I mumbled a hello and sensed her awkwardness as my mother and I stood a few feet apart, not knowing how we should greet each other after many months of no contact. We never really had known how to react to each other. Even when I was a child we didn't hug or kiss. I recognized this woman as my mother, but we were more like strangers.

Mom looked at Diane then back at me, a strained smile on her face, "You know your dad, he's the same animal." The two women laughed and nudged each other. They started to giggle over some private joke and headed toward the door. I picked up my luggage and followed.

Mom and Diane chatted like good buddies during the several hours' ride back to Crown Point, Indiana. Only a handful of remarks were tossed my way as I watched out the back window.

The trailer was in a tiny trailer park on the outskirts of town. Less than twenty other trailers filled the lot. Gary was waiting inside with a couple of his friends; he brightened and welcomed me with a friendly, playful punch. "Do you want to go to the dance tonight? We can show 'em how to really move." It sounded fun to me after all the months of being alone.

Later that afternoon, Dad walked in. "I see that you're here," he said, without really looking at me.

"Yeah," I answered hopefully, gesturing awkwardly.

"You can't seem to make it anywhere, can you?" he chided. That was the end of the conversation.

After three days I realized that nothing had changed at the Koons home. Dad, very obviously, didn't want me there. Mother was preoccupied with her newfound friends, and when she offhandedly suggested, "Why don't you go out to California and stay with Clifford or some of your old friends for a while?" I decided to take her advice.

Seventy-two hours after my arrival, Mom agreed to drive me to Southern California to live with Clifford. She said she wanted to see Clifford and Madilyn's new baby. None of us had made it to their wedding a couple of years before. Mom and I drove for days in silence. I'd lost count of how many times that year I had left the past behind.

The weather in Long Beach was great, but Clifford and Madilyn's house was already cramped with a new baby. He was kind but nagged me often about my decision to leave home before I was eighteen. Evidently, the account of the past year my mother had given him was far from the truth.

Even with my record of only sporadic school attendance over the past three years, I was able to register as an eleventh grader at Artesia High School. Most of the students came from the dairy farms or small communities surrounding Long Beach. Without really trying I found a group of friends; they were tough and rowdy, just like me.

Hiding vodka in our lockers was as easy as it had been in Oregon. Nothing much varied from school to school. Partying, dancing, gangs of rebels were common to all. One thing this school had was new to me, however—a vocal group of Christian kids. This weird bunch walked around the open-air campus toting Bibles, and at lunch they sat in a circle reading and discussing things. I couldn't understand why they would sit silently with heads bowed and listen to one person pray. It was something about the way they talked to each other, though, that got to me most. They listened when someone in the group—no matter who—said anything. And too, they all spent lots of time together, never raised havoc, yet still seemed to have a good time.

My friends and I considered them easy prey for a laugh. We called them names and did everything we could think of to distract them. Often one of the guys and I stood very close to the group and talked as loudly as we could so they couldn't hear each other. These Christian kids put up with our taunting no matter how unmerciful we were. They never tried to fight; they had guts even when it was obvious they were scared to death. I couldn't figure them out. They were a pretty popular group of kids, all things considered. That made me curious about what it was they were committed to. It took a lot for them to sit in the middle of campus. They could've picked an out-of-the-way corner, and we'd never have bothered them. But they didn't.

Eventually my parents straggled back to California, battered trailer in tow. They parked on an old, run-down, barren lot near Artesia. Once in a while I stayed there, but I preferred Clifford's, or better yet, a friend's house, as did Gary. No matter where I stayed, we all avoided each other as best we could.

Gary returned to California more rebellious and angry with my parents than I'd ever seen him. The years had taken a toll on him too. One day, just weeks after the move, he unexpectedly announced that he'd joined the army. Within days he packed his belongings and at seventeen was gone for good.

My mom's parents, Grandma and Grandpa Goodson, lived in an apartment near the beach. I loved my short, plump grandmother, who fit the role just right, and my suntanned grandfather, whose physique outranked most thirty-year-olds for taut muscles and fluid grace. He lawn bowled and swam nearly every day while Grandma worked to keep the cookie jar stocked. They always welcomed me to their home, but they always seemed to maintain a certain distance. They believed that I was just a disobedient, drunken "juvenile delinquent." One day I overheard an over-the-fence conversation while I was visiting.

"Yes, my daughter Marjorie is back in California with her no-good husband and wild kids. Actually that's her daughter, Carolyn, who's staying with us today. She's already drinking and can swear like a seaman. Her brother Gary just joined the army. I don't know if either of the kids are going to make much of themselves with all the partying they do."

Grandma went on to say she thought I was hard to love or get to know. How I longed to reach out to her and Grandpa. They were two of the kindest people I knew, and I wasn't all the things they thought I was. I wanted to be good, but hanging out with friends was the only life I knew. From what I heard, I began to sense my mother had fed them lies too.

November in Southern California was lovely. The cool winter mornings and sunny afternoons were perfect. I went to school but wasn't very active. Attending so many schools in the last few years had left me floundering in every subject. It was easier to be uninterested.

One Tuesday in the early evening, the phone rang at the trailer. I was alone because my parents were away working a temporary job for a couple of weeks in central California. "Hello, is Carolyn Koons home?"

"This is Carolyn," I answered absently.

"Hi, my name is Jean Fonner. I was talking to a friend of your grandmother's the other day. She was telling me about you."

My mind quickly clicked into gear. I could imagine what this lady had heard about me, but why would she be calling?

"Carolyn, I wanted to let you know that I am a member of Bethany Baptist Church in Long Beach; it's about four miles from your house. Your grandmother's friend said that you weren't involved in any particular church. We have a wonderful youth group. In fact, I think some of the kids go to your high school." Mrs. Fonner listed a few names. I recognized one of them as part of the lunchtime circle at school. "I just want you to know that we would love to have you come and visit our church this Sunday morning. We have a Sunday school class at nine-thirty and an evening group meeting every Sunday night at six."

She just kept talking. Who was she? Who did she think she was calling me up out of the clear blue sky to ask me to go to church?

"Well, no thanks," I answered, trying to end the conversation. "I'm not interested."

"You'd really love it. I'll bet you know some of the kids already. They have a lot of fun."

"No, I'm not really interested. Thank you." My abrupt answers didn't seem to affect her persistence.

She quickly changed subjects. "How do you like Artesia High School?"

"Not much."

"What's your favorite class?"

"I don't have one." I answered each question noncommittally, determined not to prolong the conversation.

"Carolyn, we certainly would love you to come to the

youth group. In fact, I'd be glad to meet you there on Sunday."

Stronger than ever, I repeated, "I'm not interested. Church isn't my thing."

"Well, Carolyn, I want you to know that I'm praying for you. Good-bye."

I hung up the phone and sat in the stillness of the trailer unsettled by her last statement. This woman I didn't even know was praying for me. She didn't know what I was like. I'd made it to eleventh grade through fifteen tough years by myself. I could just keep making it. What made her think I needed church? Where had all these Christians been when I'd really needed them, anyway?

The fantasy I'd had of Pat Boone as a "good man" came back into my head. I hadn't thought about him for a while. He went to church, but not me. It was too late to start all that now. I drank more than usual the next few days.

Thursday afternoon the phone rang again. "Hi, Carolyn. Just wanted to check up and see how you were doing. This is Jean Fonner."

I couldn't believe it. This lady had nerve.

"How are you doing?" she repeated in a cheery voice.

"Oh fine." I matched her tone in my most polite and restrained voice, although it had little to do with my mood. I had lots on my mind, but nothing that I wanted to discuss with her, although I was a little afraid that if she'd been praying for me she might be able to read my mind.

"I want you to know the invitation to church will always be open. I'd be glad to pick you up on Sunday morning. You'd like the kids in the youth group."

I was shocked at this woman's persistence. She gently encouraged me to give church a try. As soon as I could get a word in, I declined.

"But, Carolyn, if you gave it just one chance, I think you'd be interested . . ."

I stopped listening as she began describing the upcoming teen events before repeating her invitation. I made my parting comment, "No, absolutely not. I told you I'm not interested."

"Carolyn, I do want you to know that I'm praying for you."

She hung up. I couldn't stand it. Her words cut through to my heart. Why would anyone pray for me? What good would it do? I was who I was, and I wasn't going to make changes.

The next day at school I didn't go over and give the Christians a hard time, but I closely watched the kids in the circle. They seemed to be having a good time. They laughed and joked. They smiled. I didn't remember the last time I'd smiled. My life was so empty. Jean Fonner's voice echoed in my mind, but I couldn't give in and join them. I was going to make it on my own.

My parents both worked Saturdays. I spread my stuff all over the trailer and decided to go through some old boxes of paper I'd kept. Someone knocked on the door. I figured it was one of my friends from the neighborhood gang. I opened the door and saw a lady neatly dressed in blue, with her curly brown hair tucked underneath a silk scarf. She smiled as if she knew me. "Hi Carolyn," she said, surveying my slender frame.

"Hello," I replied, wondering what she was selling. Wait a minute—she knew my name!

"Hi, I'm Jean Fonner. I just happened to be in the area driving around visiting some people and thought that I'd stop by and introduce myself in person."

I awkwardly stood in the door staring at her. I couldn't believe that she had the nerve to come all the way out here.

"Do you mind if I come in? I have something for you."

I wanted to say no, but couldn't. I opened the door just wide enough for her to come in. She walked over to the couch and waited for me to sit opposite her. I felt strained and uncomfortable, but Mrs. Fonner didn't seem to notice. She asked me about school, and we chatted about how I was doing.

"Carolyn, I have a pamphlet I'd like to leave with you." She went through it and repeated the invitation to come to church. I didn't listen much. I was trying to figure out how to get this woman out of here and out of my life.

"Well, okay. Maybe. We'll see," I responded to her remarks, hoping she'd be satisfied and go away.

"That's great!" She smiled broadly. "Do you mind if I pray with you right now?"

I blushed. "Okay," I said, trying to cover my embarrassment.

"Lord, thank you for Carolyn. I pray, Lord, that you will become an important person in her life. In Jesus' name, Amen."

She went then, leaving me to feel uneasy all afternoon. It made me nervous that someone had actually taken the time to seek me out. But that night wasn't the time to think about it. Dad came home from work drunk, and the tension that had been building since they returned exploded. He screamed at me to get out. That night I went to stay at Clifford's, where the baby kept me awake all through the night with her crying. In the morning Madilyn and Clifford, tired and edgy from lack of sleep, didn't have any energy to talk about what was going on inside me, so I decided to give them some room. I dressed and left for a walk.

The streets were bare. An occasional car, filled with nicely dressed people, pulled out of a driveway. I figured they'd be on their way to church somewhere.

I walked aimlessly for hours, covering block after block without paying attention. I didn't have a destination in mind. Without a real home, I just wandered. Midmorning, cars filled up a parking lot on one street and began to line the adjacent curbs. I looked up to check where I'd walked to. I stood across the street from a church. A steeple sat atop a white-pillared building with a tall section that looked like a chapel. A smaller building could be seen behind it. A whole bunch of teenagers stood in front of the church. All of them, except one great-looking blonde guy with the build of a quarterback, walked inside. He stood outside, looking like a football player who spent a lot of time on the beach.

I walked over to take a good look at him, pretending to head toward another part of the church. As I approached the door I heard laughter and loud talking. I looked up, and the cute blonde guy caught my eye and smiled.

"Hi," he said, coming closer, "my name's Skip."

His charm and good looks took me aback. "Oh, hi, Skip. I'm Carolyn."

"Carolyn," he repeated excitedly, "Carolyn what?"

"Carolyn Koons." His smile blazed unexpectedly. What did I do?

"I'm Skip Fonner! My mom was at your house yesterday."

I groaned inside. This couldn't be happening. I had inadvertently stumbled to Bethany Baptist Church. What kind of crazy coincidence was this?

"Come on in," he encouraged, grabbing my elbow and guiding me in.

Every seat in the room was filled, and kids were lined up against the walls. Skip led me to the second row and turned to address the group chatting among themselves.

"Hey, you guys, this is Carolyn. She goes to Artesia."

"Sue goes to Artesia too!" one red-haired girl said in

greeting, pointing to a friend of hers that I recognized from the lunchtime prayer group. Before I knew it they'd scooted together and found another chair for me while they told me their names. They bombarded me with questions about where I lived, what I liked to do, who brought me. I had the strangest feeling that they had known I was coming.

An energetic, compactly built man with reddish hair and an easy smile strode to the front of the room and waved his arm to get the kids' attention.

"Who is he?" I asked Anne, the red-haired girl.

"He's Wes Harty, our Sunday school teacher. He works at the church. Ella Marie, his wife, is back there," she whispered, pointing to a tall, smiling brunette with glasses who was standing near the door.

The room was quickly silenced. The rapt respect the kids gave to Wes was something I'd never encountered before. They followed him, loudly and happily, singing songs. I listened, soaking in every moment.

After the songs, another energetic man, this one with jet black hair and Indian features, stood up and made announcements about a meeting that night, a trip to a mission somewhere, a beach party the following Saturday, and the deadline for deposits for some camp the kids buzzed excitedly about as he talked. Skip leaned over and explained quietly, "That's Louie Files, our youth sponsor. He's really great. He has great ideas for things for us to do."

When Louie was finished, a group of five kids swarmed to the front, hats and props in hand. They did two skits that left us all laughing.

Wes then walked forward with a big Bible in his hands. Opening it with familiarity, he spoke with a friendly earnestness. I looked around the room when he referred to a Bible verse because I heard paper rustling. I realized that almost everyone in the room had a Bible and was following along. The stories he read out of the book were good. When he began to read about "The Prodigal Son," this kid that ran away but was later welcomed back, I was enthralled—and also a bit surprised. I couldn't believe he was getting all this stuff out of that book.

The longer he talked, the more uneasy I began to feel. I looked down and for the first time noticed that I wasn't dressed nearly as well as most of the kids. The other kids understood this kind of life, but I didn't. They listened to great talks like this all the time. These Bible stories told the kids how to live. That wasn't my style. Me, I was tough. No matter how nice the kids were to me, my friends and I didn't need any book to tell us what to do.

I tuned in and out of Wes's stories. The sixty or seventy kids in the room were all soaking in what he said. That made me nervous. I turned around toward the door, but by now there wasn't even a path, just a mass of kids standing up and sitting all along the counters. I was trapped; I would have to stick out this hour.

Wes was almost finished. He closed his Bible and asked us all to bow our heads for prayer. The kids all dropped their heads forward, some with their faces in their hands. Wes, out loud, talked to God as the kids listened, some nodding their heads, other murmuring affirmation. I didn't understand this. All I wanted to do was get out of here.

The prayer was the closing. The kids began to mill around then slowly leave the room. Skip and his friends kept talking in their seats. He finally stood and reached out his hand to help me up. "Come to church with us, Carolyn. It starts in a few minutes and only lasts a little over an hour."

"I can't."

"C'mon, Carolyn. I'm sure my mom will give you a ride home if you want."

Louie immediately elbowed his way over, approaching me with his hand extended. "I'm Louie, it's good to meet you. I understand you're Carolyn. I don't live too far from you. If you need a ride to or from church, I'm available."

I protested as we walked out in the middle of a group of kids. They headed directly toward the sanctuary. I was confused. The friendliness and acceptance was wonderful, but this church life I wasn't so sure about. How could I be friends with these kids from good families? They'd never understand me. Before I could make a decision, I was whisked, in the midst of the group, to the third row.

Within a few minutes a bunch of people in long, beautiful blue robes filed into special pews on the platform, and the pastor took his place behind the pulpit. Organ and piano music began playing softly. The pastor introduced himself to any visitors in the congregation as Dr. Bob Hubbard. As he sat down, Wes Harty took his place. The next thing I knew, I was trying to read the words to a song out of a hymnbook. Before long Dr. Hubbard stood up again and began to talk about Jesus and his love and miracles. I forgot about the kids around me and just listened. For the first time I was hearing about Jesus, a name people I knew just mentioned in passing or in bad jokes.

When he closed his Bible, I took it as a sign that he was almost finished. But he went on. "Jesus wants us to give him our heart so that he can take all the past hurt and replace it with love and forgiveness. We must recognize that our lives belong to God and place them in his care."

His words pierced me. I couldn't do that. Never. I had to survive on my own. No one had ever helped me. I couldn't trust anyone, especially someone I couldn't even see, to ever care enough to help me be happy. I wanted that, but it was just a dream.

My heart pounded as Pastor Hubbard lifted his hands, signaling for the congregation to stand. Wes led us in a quiet song. The room seemed to close in. I felt trapped in the middle of a pew, surrounded by people singing or praying silently. Then some of the people moved. A man and then a young woman walked down toward the pastor and talked briefly to him before kneeling down at a wooden benchlike thing at the front. I grabbed the pew in front of me for support, afraid that my legs would take over and walk up in front of all of these people just as they had carried me to this church this morning. I would die of embarrassment if these people thought I would turn my life over—whatever that meant—to God or Jesus or anybody. I glanced at Skip to my right, checking whether he could see my flushed face and hear my heart beating. He just smiled a bit and went on singing, seemingly unaware of my panic.

Finally I heard the quiet sound of hymnbooks closing and being deposited in the racks. I was never more relieved. After yet another prayer, I was able to slip past the kids and make a beeline down the aisle for the door. Sue raced to catch up with me. "Are you coming back tonight to the youth group?"

"I can't," I answered coldly, trying to discourage any more invitations.

Skip had caught up to me. "I'll pick you up and take you home afterward."

"No, I'm not interested, and I already have plans, a party to go to tonight." I whirled around and ran outside before he could respond. Several blocks away I slowed down and walked the rest of the way home. All day long I kept thinking about the church, the kids, and how different it all was from my life.

Everyone I'd met just accepted me. I was accustomed to proving myself and fighting for respect. Why did they act this way? The idea of turning my life over to some Jesus person bothered me, even though something inside warned me that those people might be right. I just didn't understand. I was learning how to survive—just barely. I had a terrifying feeling that if I let go and gave my life to this Jesus I might die. I wouldn't be me anymore. No, I had to survive. I wished I had never gone inside that confusing church. But why had I walked there? And why were those kids so nice to me?

A few minutes after five, I heard a knock. I got up from my bunk and answered the door. A man whose smile was wide in his tanned, Indian-looking face reached out his hand. "Hi, remember me, Louie Files, from the church? I didn't get a chance to talk to you much this morning. I had to drop some stuff off a few blocks away. I'm on my way back to the church; why don't you come to youth group tonight? You'll love it. Several kids come from Artesia. I'll bring you back later, and we can get acquainted on the way." His warm enthusiasm persuaded me, although I wasn't sure why.

About the same number of kids as this morning were reassembled in the youth room. The skits were crazier than the ones earlier in the day. Wes was right in the middle of everything—his antics the zaniest. After the skit, he became a little more serious and told us about some of the things Jesus had done so that our lives could be different. We ate after he talked and played some games. It was great. Then we went to church again—that made me nervous.

These people went to church in the morning and again at night! I wanted to sit in the back, but the others wouldn't hear of it. It went by more quickly this time, and the pastor didn't ask anybody to come to the front to pray.

When Louie drove up to the trailer that night I climbed out

of the car before it had come to a complete stop. Puzzled, he called to me, "Where are you going in such a hurry?"

"To a party," I called over my shoulder, even though I wasn't going anywhere.

"I'll phone you this week sometime," I heard him promise before I slammed the door to the trailer. I didn't want Louie to talk to me. I didn't want to go back to church. This whole day had been too confusing. I went right to bed, but I couldn't sleep. For hours I lay there thinking. I tried to erase the day from my memory, believing I'd be better off if it'd never happened.

The Tunnel

Three weeks went by, and each Saturday Louie, Jean, or Skip telephoned. I planned to stay with friends on weekends, hoping they couldn't track me down. They always did, and someone would drive by and pick me up both morning and evening. I soon found myself in church twice a week, then they excitedly asked me to come every night during a "Spiritual Emphasis Week." A special "evangelist"—whatever that was—was coming. Adamantly I assured them all that I certainly wasn't going to sit in church for seven straight evenings in a row, but I would come on Sunday.

Sunday morning I sat with the other teens near the front, but Sunday night I chose a pew only a few feet from the back door. This evangelistic preacher was powerful. Just that morning a large group had gone forward to pray. Lost in a crowd that numbered over a thousand, I listened hesitantly at first, then slid to the edge of my seat as he intensely explained the love of Jesus.

"Jesus offers to you, this very night, a new life." This bald preacher in a gray wool suit minced no words. Steadily, with compassion and undeniable conviction, he promised, "A life in Christ is the most exciting, fulfilling way to live. He offers you peace inside no matter what you've done or what kind of family you come from. Jesus is in the business of forgiving and healing the past."

I searched the faces in the crowd around me. What he said obviously made sense to them, but I couldn't believe that anybody could make my life any better. Not me, I couldn't give my life—what little of it there was—to anyone. My heart began to pound.

Wes led us in singing before they asked people to come to the front of the church and pray. People streamed down the aisles during the first verse, not even waiting to be asked. I was just watching, and then suddenly I was walking with them. I found myself doing what I'd sworn I would never do. Something drew me forward. Alongside a couple of dozen others, I stood in front of the congregation.

A woman, one of Jean Fonner's friends, approached me and led me to a side room. Not knowing what to expect, I just waited, feeling that I needed that something in my life the evangelist had been preaching about. The lady and I sat in metal chairs and clasped hands as I asked Jesus, the man these people had been telling me about for weeks, to come be a part of my life. The woman read verses of Scripture to me explaining the meaning of salvation. I felt a warm, friendly feeling inside.

I raised my hands to my face; tears spilled freely from my eyes and down my cheeks. Disbelieving, I stared at my hands wet with tears. I had not cried freely for myself in years—not in Minnesota or Oregon or any place in between. Abandonment by my parents had not loosed my tears, nor the rebellion or anger at my mother in Crescent. In the side room of a church, a simple prayer at the side of a stranger melted my heart.

A hope I'd never known flooded through me; just maybe there was life in me. There was a person inside to be discovered—a good person. The lady embraced me, only to release me into Louie's arms. His energetic hug of affirmation was but the first. Within moments several of the kids surrounded me. "So glad for you, Carolyn. You've made the best decision of your life!" Together, we headed toward the sanctuary. Wes rushed over and pulled me in close to him. I felt so loved! It was as if these people considered me to be a part of them.

"How do you feel, Carolyn?" Bill, one of the teens, asked.

I didn't hesitate, "I feel as though I've been lifted in the air and turned around one hundred and eighty degrees." This was what good people had. I had no idea what was ahead, but I had a hunch that maybe my dreams of learning what good meant were coming true.

For what seemed a long time people waited their turn to share a special insight or word of encouragement and a promise to pray for me. Louie gave me my first Bible, a leather-bound red-letter edition.

Bill tapped me on the shoulder. Thinking it was one more person celebrating with me, I spun around expectantly. "Carolyn, your mom and dad are outside."

"What?" My shoulders sagged. How did they know where I was?

"Yeah, they're outside in a car. They said something about just getting back into town."

I paled, my thoughts wild. How had they found me? What did they want?

Louie shooed the kids away. "What's wrong?" he asked, studying my face.

"Nothing. I've got to go."

"Tell them I'll take you home."

"No, I have to go."

I turned and left the church. I could see the shape of my parents' car in the dark driveway. Two forms, apparently my mom and dad, motioned to me. I opened the door and climbed into the backseat.

"What in the h—— are you doing here with these d—— religious people?" my dad bellowed and grabbed my arm, shaking me. I didn't answer. Clifford had told them where I would be when they came back from their two-week job search around the state. "I want you to stay away from this place." Dad pushed me back and ground the gears as he stamped on the gas pedal.

I turned slightly, enough to see Louie standing underneath the outside lights of the church. "God," I prayed, "for just a few minutes everything seemed okay. I was so happy."

My parents filled the car with criticism of religion and stories about the hypocrisy of every Christian they'd ever known as we drove to their trailer. They profaned every pastor or church they knew or could remember. I left the car without a word and walked into the tiny back bedroom. I hid my new Bible under my windbreaker long enough to rummage through the closet for an old flashlight.

Under the covers, in the dark stillness of the dreary room, I opened the big Bible. As I read, God was real to me. I could read about him in my Bible and feel him. Even with my parents in the same small space, I was happier than I'd ever been. Maybe life *would* be different.

The next morning I remembered the evangelist had encouraged us to share what happened in our lives with others. Not sure how I was to do that, I thought of the kids that met at lunchtime on campus and placed my big, new Bible on top of my schoolbooks. I was thrilled to be a Christian—whatever it meant.

"Hi, Carolyn. Are you up for a party tonight? Glen's house, after nine," one of my school friends greeted me as I walked onto campus. He didn't notice the Bible.

"What are you doing with that?" Julie, another member of the gang I hung out with, noticed.

"I'm reading it," I retorted. "What do you think you do with a Bible?"

At lunch I headed toward the snack bar to buy a sandwich

before walking toward the group of Christian kids on the center lawn. Six or seven girls sat interspersed between as many boys as they flipped through their Bibles, obviously looking for an answer to something.

"What are you doing?" I asked shyly, my Bible on top of my books.

"We're having our Bible study," one guy answered after a long moment, his incredulity showing.

"May I join you?" I requested. The few kids that recognized me from church seemed delighted. The others looked at me suspiciously, a bit shocked, no doubt recalling the many times I had stood only a few feet way disturbing them with my crude comments.

"Do you go to church?" Mary, a pastor's daughter, asked.

"Yeah, I've been going for three weeks. I became a Christian last night."

"What happened?"

"Well, there was this special speaker, an, uh, what do you call them?" hoping someone could prompt me.

"An evangelist?" the girl prompted, seeming a little surprised for some reason.

"That's it. He talked about Jesus offering a brand-new life, and I wanted what he talked about so bad that I went forward," I continued with all the fervor I felt.

That evening and every other that week I went to Bethany Baptist Church. I wanted everything they could offer me. The first in the sanctuary every night, right up front with my Bible, I felt happy for the first time.

During the next month some of the youth group went with Louie to the San Pedro Skid Row Mission on a special outing. I had no idea what we would get ourselves into. We pulled up and parked about half a block away on Main Street.

Inside the brick storefront two hundred men jammed the

hall to hear us. The disheveled look, the bleary eyes, the smell of liquor stopped me short. I didn't need to go inside that building, I knew the kind of life these men lived all too well.

"Carolyn," Louie motioned for me to come to the front, "I want you to share your testimony tonight."

"I can't," I thought, reluctantly scrutinizing the group. Behind each face I saw my dad. The odor in the room became unbearable as the men filed in to rows of metal chairs. The deadness in their eyes mirrored everything I wanted to leave behind. Already my new life seemed so different. I was still trying to just understand what had happened to me. People like my father didn't want to have anything to do with religion. What were we doing here?

Louie started the service with a prayer and a simple chorus before he beckoned me to the front. I surveyed the group and fought an urge to flee out the back door. Instead I stood up tall and shoved my hands deep into my skirt pockets, feeling very self-conscious in front of a whole roomful of men with the same problems as my father; hesitantly, with downcast eyes, I began to tell what had happened to me in the last few weeks. The nods I caught from the corner of my eye forced me to look up as I described—sketchily—the deep pain of my life. Why were these men agreeing? Could they really fathom how much I had hurt and how much God's love had freed me? Maybe these men did know what being at the bottom of life's pile felt like!

Amazed as I was, I was careful not to expose many details of my past. It wasn't so much that I cared what the men thought, but the opinions of Louie and the kids meant everything. If they knew that I really didn't live anywhere or that my parents were violent alcoholics, they might reject me.

Still, with each minute that ticked by as I spoke, I realized anew how much my new faith meant. "Jesus took the rejection and picked me up, turning my life around. Now, for the first time, I have a purpose. I feel I'm on the first rung of a ladder and God is going to take me on an exciting journey up for the rest of my life."

The excitement of my newfound faith carried me through the testimony. There was quiet in the room when I had finished. Louie smiled at me, and the rest of the kids went forward to sing while the chaplain invited the men to pray. Several stood, and my heart lurched in wonder as they walked forward to accept Jesus. I felt wonderful. These men weren't just like my dad, they were more like me—filled with pain and loneliness.

Afterward, when the men filed into the dining room to eat, Louie and the chaplain took me aside. Louie put his arm around my shoulder, "Carolyn, God is going to use you to touch people that the rest of us can't touch." The chaplain thanked me, telling me he'd never seen so many respond before. Most of the men came only to eat.

Driving home, my heart sang. For the first time in my life I had done something good. I had actually helped other people. Maybe I had even been instrumental in turning a sad life around. If this was being a Christian, I couldn't get enough of it.

Wes and Louie had all the youth group involved. Before I knew it I was helping put together conferences, youth rallies, evening youth programs, and our youth retreat. I lived for the church, and for time to read the Scriptures.

One night as Louie and I sat making lists for the winter retreat, he put his pencil away in his shirt pocket. He looked at me with an inquisitive grin as he nestled back in his desk chair. "May I ask you a question?"

"Sure," I answered, eager to help him with the plans in any way I could.

"Carolyn, tell me about yourself. What's your family like?"

I felt my eyes widen with surprise before the immediate onrush of fear began inside me. "The retreat, Louie. We're planning the weekend, remember?" I tried to joke my way out of answering.

"C'mon, Carolyn, you don't have to hide your past," he encouraged. Louie had a persistent way about him—he could chip away at your resistance and get inside your heart. This wasn't the first time he'd tried to persuade me to talk.

"I'm a new person now. That's what Wes says, so let's forget the past." I started to reiterate the retreat plans we'd discussed thus far.

Louie shrugged, willing to give up this time. "Carolyn, all of us are still affected by the past to some degree. Christ wants to redeem all of your life, even the parts you don't want to think about."

"Louie, please." I wasn't ready to let him—or anyone—in on my painful memories.

"Okay, Carolyn, you win." Louie smiled warmly, but his eyes, filled with compassion, seemed to bore through me. He wasn't meddling; I could tell that, but there was no way I'd give him the chance to reject me because of where I came from.

I soon developed a close group of friends in the youth group: Bill, the good-looking, curly-headed president, a straight-*A* student, the kind of kid I didn't know existed before; Bob, the budding preacher who looked much like a wavy-haired, laughing version of his father, our senior pastor; Sam, the tall, silent intellectual, bright but also wise beyond his years; Marv, the short, blonde comic, both loyal and questing; and Jane, my opposite, a calm, sensitive, quiet brunette with long, straight hair. We were inseparable as eleventh grade ended and we headed toward our senior year of high school.

Louie kept us active. If we weren't at the mission, we were on the other side of Long Beach helping a small church start a Sunday school or planning a youth rally. No matter how many times I said things I shouldn't or acted impulsively, everyone, especially Louie, kept loving me. My life revolved around the church.

The newness of being a Christian didn't fade, just deepened, getting better all the time. Reading the Bible and praying were wonderful ways to fill my free time. For the first time I was enjoying people and life.

I wanted to just be a Christian, the other parts of my life just shouldn't exist anymore. No one, even me, needed to think about any of that. I knew God forgave me for all I'd done, and the kids would probably, too. But I wanted to erase the rest: my father and his drunken, filthy life, my mother and her many men, and all the other betraying relationships in my life. Why did my new friends need to know any of this? I was trying to start over.

Louie persisted. I'd catch him watching me. "Why did you do that, Carolyn? When Bill surprised you from behind, you almost slugged him. What makes you so ready to fight?"

He continued to push me, however gently, to talk about myself. I didn't want to think or talk about any of it. The other kids might conclude I was trash if they knew. I craved love and approval. For the first time, maybe, I'd found lasting friends and personal respect. When asked about my family I kept my answers vague, never revealing much. I'd just say that I'd had rough times and left home very early.

One Sunday following Bible study I made some flippant remarks about the men at the mission as a bunch of us hung around not wanting to go home.

Louie stood up, "C'mere, Carolyn. There's something I want to talk to you about." He motioned toward the adjoining room, where we sat down at a small wooden table. We joked for a couple of minutes, amiably catching each other up on the past few days. Louie was watching me curiously. I began to squirm a little.

"Okay, Louie Files, why did you call me to this powwow?" I tested, hoping to bring him around to the point.

He didn't hesitate. "Sometimes when I hear you make some crazy offhand remark I realize it is a subtle clue to the past that you don't talk about. I want you to tell me about your past."

I clutched at the edge of the table, and my mood swung instantly from easy bantering to anger. "I'm not going to tell you a thing. Who do you think you are?"

My ire startled him. "Carolyn, what's the problem? Why are you afraid to tell me about yourself? You know you can trust me."

I didn't answer. With a simple question Louie had set off the raging battle that was always buried inside just a bit below the surface. I wanted to let go and tell someone my pain, and if I could be vulnerable with anyone he'd certainly be the one —but I couldn't.

He persisted, unable to believe that my reticence was absolute. "Tell me about your folks. What's your dad like? What about your mom?"

Rage that I no longer knew could take such full control of me welled up and burst out as I slammed my fist down savagely on the tabletop and jumped to my feet. "D—— it, Louie, stop it," I shouted.

He calmly put his hand on my shoulder, trying to ease me back into the chair. Instinct took over; I wheeled around and threw him back, pushing his chair to the floor. I bolted toward the door and flew down the stairs two at a time.

By the time Louie scrambled up and around the table and down the stairs, I was already in Clifford's Ford with the motor roaring. I sped out of the driveway, my tires squealing, past some of the kids who were lingering by their cars.

"Get out of my life, Louie," I demanded aloud. "Leave me alone, just let me be." I gripped the steering wheel, my foot pressing ever more heavily on the accelerator. "For the first time in my life I've found something good. I don't want the past. I don't want to have anything to do with all the ugliness of my family. Let me go. Let me go!" Alone and sobbing, I screamed to Louie as if he were there, "Let me go!" The memories of pain and betrayal blurred in a dull roar in my ears. I thought that when I became a Christian I left it all behind. Why now? I wondered. Why did Louie have to unleash all the layers of painful emotion when I was just beginning to get used to being happy?

I was racing down a lonely access road in back of the airport making the tires squeal each time I spun around a sharp curve; the headlights barely kept enough road in front of me. The speedometer inched past sixty-five to seventy-five, then eighty-five, peaking just over ninety as the car entered the tunnel that burrowed under the runway.

Closed in by the cement tube, I fantasized about guiding the wheels just inches to the left. At this speed, just a slight movement and the car would smash into the wall. I could envision the impact and feel the car demolish around me. Then it would be over. I wanted out. I couldn't stand any more agony.

I decided to do it. Just one swing of the steering wheel, and it all would be over. I floored the throttle and took a last deep breath. I concentrated on the movements of my hands. I swerved.

I swerved back, righting my course. I couldn't do it. Slumping back into the seat, I took my foot off the gas pedal and began to pray. "God, I can't stand this pain. How long am I going to have to live with my past? I'm a Christian now, why do I have to think about this?"

I exited the tunnel and managed to slow and pull off to the side of the road while the tears blurred my vision. "God," I begged, "will I ever be set free? Will anyone ever love me for who I am if I tell them?" I sat there a long time.

When I finally drove back up the driveway to the church, it was late. Church was long over, the only cars left were for those who were straightening up and preparing for the next day.

I carefully pulled between the white lines of a parking slot. Before I took the key from the ignition, my door was pulled open. Louie reached in and pulled me out of the car throwing his arms around me.

"I was afraid I'd never see you again," he cried quietly.

I knew I didn't need to say anything. He already knew I'd come a long way that night. There was something I'd discovered for the first time: I really wanted to live.

The Rally

It was a crisp October night, and Bill, Marv, Sam, Bob, Jane, and I lay sprawled across the gold carpet in Louie's office finishing last-minute plans for the evening session of the annual Pastors Conference we were hosting. Housing arrangements for the lastcomers were in a snarl.

"The guy staying at our house is from somewhere in Nevada; Lovelock, I think," Mary said, pointing to the name she guessed belonged to him.

Louie added, leaning over the master lists on his desk, "I met a pastor last night from somewhere up north who stutters a lot. He's staying with the Eatons. I think the guy has courage to stay in a job where he has to preach every Sunday."

"I used to live in Crescent, Oregon, and there was a pastor who stuttered at the community church up there." I made the remark offhandedly as I penciled in the names of drivers who had agreed to transport some of the pastors across town that afternoon.

Louie looked up, moving from behind his desk. "What town did you say?"

"Crescent."

"You'll never believe this," Louie continued in an astonished tone, "but that's where that pastor is from. It's the same one."

The pastor I remembered from Oregon probably wasn't even in the state anymore. Louie was getting excited over nothing, yet before I could temper his enthusiasm, he rushed out the door, only to appear about ten minutes later with a man in tow.

"C-carolyn K-koons," the short, gray-haired man said incredulously, "of all the p-p-people in the world, I never d-dreamed I'd ever s-see you in a ch-ch-church."

"Hi, Pastor Everett," I beamed, surprised that he'd remember me, a girl who'd never darkened the doors of his church. "Of all of the people in the world, I was the last to guess I'd ever be in a church either!" Before the words were fully uttered everyone in the room burst out laughing, leaving me to blush in embarrassment at the unexpected attention.

The pastor turned to Louie, "D-do you know how notorious th-this g-g-girl is? They st-still t-talk about her all over the c-c-county."

"Hey, that's not fair," I protested good-naturedly. "I've been gone for more than three years now."

"You'd b-be amazed at the impact you had. I c-c-can hardly wait to t-tell everybody that I ran into you." Pastor Everett shyly smiled at me.

The kids, spurred on by the pastor's innuendos, began to fire questions at me. "What were you like when you lived in Oregon?" "What did you do to become so famous?" Without answering I sat down a little sheepishly.

"I'd g-give anything for you to c-c-come and g-g-give your t-testimony. Louie t-told me just a little of what has happened to you s-since you've b-become a C-Christian. What a miracle. People b-back in C-Crescent and G-Gilchrist will b-be s-so excited when they hear the news!"

Louie looked at me and grinned broadly, the wheels of his imagination obviously spinning. Then he turned and pointed at Reverend Everett. "I want to talk to you." He prodded him gently with his elbow, and together they went out into the hall.

About twenty minutes later, after I'd dodged most of the kids' questions, Louie came back in. "We've got a plan. I was just talking to Pastor Everett, and he's serious about you going back, Carolyn. He can't quite get over your being a Christian, let alone one of the most involved people in the church. We talked about taking a small group to Crescent during our spring break. He says we could hold services at the church or the new Crescent community clubhouse and even hold assemblies at your old high school. He thinks he could get us on some radio stations out of Klamath Falls and Bend, too!"

I couldn't focus on the idea. Go back to Crescent and my high school? What would Larry and the gang think? What if Mrs. McGee was still there? She'd never let me talk in front of the students. Visions of the dark nights at the motel spun my mind into a terrifying maelstrom of pain. The past came crashing back in on me. My heart began to pound, and my hands felt clammy. I was half-excited and half-apprehensive initially, but my fears overtook me as I listened to the kids reinforce Louie's dream. The drinking, the vandalism, and the lonely nights at the motel—did I want the kids and Louie to see that?

Bill suggested that we pray about the trip. The group, caught up in the unexpected enthusiasm, prayed fervently in a circle around the room. We decided to plan for the next few months and see if God would help us work out the many details for a trip like this.

A few weeks before Easter, as plans snowballed, Louie received a phone call from a family in the church. They wanted us to use their station wagon to drive to Crescent. It actually looked as though our trip was going to happen. We intensified our practicing. Sam would preach; Bob could lead singing; Bill could emcee; and the new additions to the team, Marsha and Ron, would play the piano and the trumpet. As for me, I would give my testimony.

The Sunday before we were to leave, Bethany Baptist held an emotional send-off service. They commissioned our trip and prayed for a welcome reception in Crescent. Monday morning, before dawn, we piled in the tan station wagon and headed north.

We drove straight through California, stopping only for gas and to grab a quick meal. The hundred miles between Klamath Falls and Crescent whizzed by at dusk. Logging trucks rumbled past through the pines that towered over the narrow, two-lane strip of asphalt. I recognized many of the side roads that Larry, Vicky, Dave, and I had raced around on. Once, we had even used the long, two-lane highway itself for our racetrack. Larry had set his all-time record of 120 miles per hour just beyond the motel. Seeing the familiar sights confused my sense of time and place. I had an uneasy feeling that I was being physically transported into the past, the years I'd so carefully refused to disclose. Now, here it was, unchanged, as if I'd never left.

"Slow down, Louie," I asked, unusually subdued, as we crested the knoll near the motel. We parked in front of the Big Pines Motel sign. The long nights and embarrassment at letting the renters in; all the parties; all my parents' fights—it was eerie to sit there staring at the eight small white cabins. Three years of history hadn't changed a thing.

"Okay, let's go," I sighed, smiling guardedly at the kids, who cautiously watched my face for any reaction. Louie drove us the last mile into Crescent, and I prayed all the way. If I'd been having a nightmare, seeing the town again couldn't have been more unsettling. Any minute I expected to wake up in Long Beach, assured that this wasn't really happening, but as we drove into Crescent, it was just as I remembered it, terrifyingly so. Only God would be able to help people see the change in my life. Being thrust back into this made me feel as if I'd never left.

I pointed out the one-room post office. The Crescent Cafe

was filled as usual with loggers, teenagers, and an occasional traveler. On into Gilchrist we passed the neatly lined-up Scandinavian-style houses and the high school, which was in session that week. Time stood still. We headed back to Crescent to find Pastor Everett.

We found him stoking the fire in a quaint little neatly painted white church nestled among trees on a back street. From the first evening service on, the church was packed. The curious ones who'd known me only by sight came, and the McGees couldn't believe that I, Carolyn Koons, was really standing there in a church talking about God. They kept telling stories of our tearing up the football field, stashing vodka in our lockers, and everything else they could remember. After the first service they decided to cancel classes twice that week for all-school rallies.

The first rally was scheduled for Wednesday. I awoke, tense and unsettled, long before the others in the little room the pastor had provided above the post office. I realized that Vicky, Dave, and Larry still attended the high school. In such a small town it amazed me that I hadn't already bumped into them, which perhaps was a relief at first. Today I knew I'd see them; there was no way to delay. My desire to catch up on our friendship and tell them about my new life overruled my nervous questions about whether or not they would still accept me. In the long morning moments, while the others slept soundly, I prayed they'd listen.

We planned the rallies around two science films designed to get teenagers to think about the marvelous wonders of the world and the Creator. Once the kids were stimulated to consider the mysterious handiwork of God, each team member was to give a personal testimony, mine culminating the rally.

As Bill effortlessly emceed, I sat behind him surveying the

crowd of kids in the facing bleachers. Most faces seemed familiar, and I must have looked the same myself, for I sensed many pairs of eyes focused on me. My heart pounded, feelings of inadequacy rising with each of Bill's words as I searched the rows for Larry and Vicky. God had changed my life—this I knew—and he could change their lives too. I reminded myself of this over and over again until my confidence returned.

Row by row I searched the faces. My buddies weren't there. Bob was singing; I was next. Then I remembered where we used to congregate during assemblies. I looked to the left, and sure enough, Vicky and Dave stood next to Larry leaning against the brick wall near the exit. Larry looked away when I spotted them. We had been so close; now he acted like an uncomfortable stranger. Vicky just crossed her arms and stared at me defiantly. Only Dave smiled in encouragement.

Praying all the while for God to help me be brave, I stood when introduced and strode determinedly to the microphone. This could be the only chance these kids, my peers, would have to hear about the wonderful Jesus who gave purpose to my life. Motionless, the audience listened, seeming to cling to every word. The searching, hungry looks across the crowd reflected back what I once felt. How I wanted them to understand how completely I was changed.

A simple prayer closed the rally, and I immediately saw two of my former teachers heading right toward me, eager to talk, no doubt. Pretending not to see them, I hurried over to Vicky, Larry, and Dave.

"Hi, you guys," I said cheerfully, trying to hide my nervousness as I grabbed them all in an awkward half-hug.

"Good to see you, Carolyn," Dave was the first to respond. "You look great. You really said some great stuff!"

Larry forwent the compliments, "So you came back. But you brought religion and your new boyfriend with you," he scoffed, tossing his head in Bill's direction so that I knew who he meant.

Vicky pushed Larry's shoulder. "Shut up," she ordered and turned to confront me. "We weren't sure where you'd ended up after Indiana."

"I know. You guys remember me; I've never been much of a writer. We moved seven times in less than a year. Then my parents drove off and left me in Minnesota, but I finally made it back to California."

"How's Gary? Still causing trouble?" Dave asked. We all grinned, knowing exactly what he meant.

"Probably as much as you can in the army. He joined over a year ago."

"I guess people will do anything they have to if it means getting out of Crescent." Larry obviously hadn't forgiven me for going away with my family. The class bell rang. "Gotta go, Carolyn. See you around." He walked away with Dave, leaving Vicky and me alone.

After an awkward silence, I summoned the courage to speak. "Why don't you come to church tonight. I'll introduce you to my friends. Maybe we can all get a Coke afterward."

"I don't think so, Carolyn. Church isn't my favorite place to be, you know." Her insolent reply reminded me of the way I first answered Jean Fonner's invitation to church.

Not wanting to give up, I persisted, "That's how I felt at first, too, but I know you'll like it." She looked down at her books and began to make a feeble excuse about homework. Dubious at best, I declared, "I think that I still know you better than that, Vicky. You aren't going to study tonight."

"We'll see, Carolyn. I don't have plans for the night yet."

Rather than push forward, I changed the subject. "Are you and Dave still going together?" I asked, wondering why he hadn't stayed to walk her to her next class.

"Yes, but only on and off."

I could see Bill walking toward me. Vicky anxiously shifted her feet, obviously wanting to leave.

"Try to come, okay? It would mean a lot to me." She smiled slightly and rushed off.

"Is that a friend of yours?" Bill asked, offering me his arm and guiding me back to the rest of the group, who were busy tearing down the stage while they compared impressions of their encounters with the students.

"Vicky was my best friend," I corrected. Desolation poured through my heart as I felt the distance that now lay between me and my old friends.

"Is she coming tonight?"

"I hope so, but I don't know." Bill threw his arm around me comfortingly, and we walked back toward Louie.

Some teachers had invited us, in small groups, to talk to their classes throughout the day. The pointed intensity of the kids' questions revealed their search for something more in life. The descriptions and stories told me many of them felt trapped, just as I had.

It was a busy day. We ate hurriedly after setting up overflow chairs in the church aisles and practicing our songs and skits. Promptly at seven Bob led the overflow crowd in the opening hymn. Word had spread quickly that we were in town. For the second time that day I scanned the faces of people sitting in the pews and standing around the back aisles hoping to see Vicky. My heart sank; she wasn't there. But just as disappointment threatened to overtake me, in walked Vicky, followed by seven other kids from school. She didn't look at all comfortable.

When it was my turn to occupy the space behind the pulpit, I waited a minute, taking in each individual face in the crowd before narrating the days since I'd left Crescent.

The pain and agony were very real as I described, in more detail than ever before, the yelling, the drinking, the rejection —the fragile pieces of my life before, as if drawn to it, I found my way to that Baptist church in Long Beach. For the first time in my life I had something wonderful to live for.

The room was silent, and my words flowed easily. It was one of the times God graciously gave me the words to speak clearly of what he'd done for me. In some crazy way, even as I spoke, I could imagine myself sitting in the audience just listening to my testimony and thanking God for literally re-shaping my life.

At the end of the service, several came forward. As the other team members moved to pray with those who had come, I wound my way through the dispersing crowd toward Vicky, catching her in the aisle only a few paces from the back door. "Wait," I eagerly hollered and felt relieved when she turned and offered a cautious smile.

"Thanks for coming. I'm glad you were here to hear my testimony, even though you knew a lot of the Crescent stuff already. What do you think?" I asked, curious to hear her reaction to the service.

"Well," she paused, then looked me directly in the eyes. "You'll have to prove it to me, Carolyn. You'll just have to prove that something is different." She challenged me, her eyes hardened and defensive. She was direct and straight to the point, just as she was the day she told me that my mother was the town prostitute.

"Vicky, I can't prove anything. I can only tell you that my life is completely changed."

"We'll see, Carolyn. Just be sure that I'm going to watch every move you make this week."

And she did. For the next several days, whether at the church, the high school, or sipping an orange crush at the

Crescent Cafe, every time I turned around Vicky lurked in the background studying my actions and listening to my words. She reminded me so much of myself—wanting to give in, yet afraid to let go and believe.

The pressure I felt not to slip and say the wrong thing or do anything that might turn Vicky off increased the pressure I was already feeling just from being back in Crescent. Louie, with his all-too-perceptive eyes, noticed that I was closing up a little, trying to hide some things that being back brought to mind.

By the end of the week, feeling distanced from the team, I dreaded having to be the key speaker, the one who had to tell the horrors of my life. Reverend Everett couldn't quit raving about the impact we were having. People were driving in from the other side of Bend and up the hundred miles from Klamath Falls just to come to church after they heard the radio interviews aired all over the county. I didn't want to disappoint him, so I kept on testifying, hoping God would keep working overtime on me. Yet the expectations I felt people had of me, especially Vicky, bore down like lead on my soul.

By Friday we'd moved into the community clubhouse, a larger hall set in an idyllic spot on the banks of the Deschutes River. The place was full to capacity. "They've come to hear you!" Pastor Everett whispered as he headed to the front of the church. I tried to be excited, but I felt just anxiety and intense inner pain. No matter how much God had done for me, I still knew about all the areas inside me that needed work and healing. Years of learning were ahead. Even in my present victory I struggled with feeling like a hypocrite. Who was I to stand up in front of this eager crowd?

More people, professing Christians I'd known in Oregon, raved about my helping them by sharing my story. Looking out over the audience, I couldn't help but ask myself why none of them had ever told me about Jesus or reached out to love me three years ago. Yes, I was the wild, destructive kid in town. Each time I was introduced, a few titterings in the crowd told me that many probably whispered, "Can you believe this is the same Carolyn? Why she was one of the wildest kids in the entire high school!" But why hadn't anybody seen how much I hurt? What were they doing for all the other empty people scattered in the surrounding towns?

By Friday afternoon, I was being sucked under, back into my old, sad life in Crescent. Long Beach seemed light years away. Pastor Everett proudly predicted a record attendance for the final service everywhere we went in town. As the scheduled hour drew closer, all my restraint fled. I wanted out.

One precious hour of free time was scheduled before dinner. The team and Louie gathered in the lounge of the rented guest rooms. They all chattered excitedly about that night's service. Not me. I didn't want to think about it. Walking outside and around to the back of the house, I began to pace in front of a row of sugar pines that lined the acre lot. With each step my mind dredged up yet another hurtful time, which intensified my rising panic. My pace quickened.

"What's on your mind, Carolyn?" Louie's voice startled me from behind.

"Nothing," I retorted, my voice revealing the growing anxiety I had tried to hide all afternoon.

In his usual joshing manner he countered, "I don't believe you. It's being back here, isn't it?"

"Leave me alone, Louie," I snarled, refusing to turn and face him.

"When are you ever going to realize that you're not as tough as you think you are? We all love you, Carolyn. Don't you think we can tell when you're upset? Let me in on what you're feeling."

With a flash of wild anger I clenched my fist, flinging my arm with all my might as I spun around and slugged him between the eyes. Only as he fell, blood dripping from the bridge of his nose, did I realize what I'd done.

"Oh my, what have I done?" The most influential and important person in my life, the breath knocked out of him, lay stunned on top of a thick pile of pine needles. His eyes glazed, and for a moment he stared unseeing at me. With a shake of his head to clear his vision, he drew up as if to strike back, his black eyes steely.

As if in the same instant, his eyes widened and his expression crumbled as he shrank back, catching himself ready to retaliate.

"Hit me, Louie," I screamed uncontrollably. "C'mon, hit me back. My dad always did. Why don't you!"

With his eyes closed, he bowed and shook his head.

I looked down at my prized possession, the bloody high school class ring on my right hand. Impacting his nose at just the right angle, my ring had ripped through the tender skin. What had I done? Never again would I wear that ring! I pulled it off my finger, ran straight into the woods, and hurled the gold band as far as I could into the trees.

Louie left me, remorseful and embarrassed, until the hour for the final service, when he reappeared with a bandage across his nose and wordlessly ushered me to the auditorium, guiding me supportively by the elbow. His confident squeeze just before I headed toward my chair told me everything was okay between Louie and me. He was my vital friend and encourager. Never had I needed his assurance more. Tonight was going to be one of the most difficult nights of my life.

Every chair and table ledge was taken. Lining the entrance and aisles near the windows were more people eager to hear us sing and share our faith. The stuffy room surged with emotion and anticipation. The service began much like the others, but when Louie introduced me, I hesitated, terrified of the crowd and my tender feelings. He beckoned me again. Unable to hide my pain, I grasped the lectern sides for support and let the words pour passionately from me. The presence of God moved through the raptly attentive crowd.

"Night after night I sat huddled by the window in the Big Pines Motel hoping the car headlights would pass on by and not flash into the office and force me to meet another stranger. Nearly everyone in my life seemed like a stranger, existing in the same world but never wanting to know me. My heart was empty, like a hollow, echoing tunnel, made for some purpose but never filled. I doubted anything could ease my longing to be loved . . ."

Tears traced down a few cheeks by the time Bill invited any who wished to, to come forward and meet us for prayer. Dozens of teens, adults, and young kids slipped from their chairs. A deep sense of gratitude mingled with repentance filled me as I watched one after the other step out to pray. The past had engulfed me, threatening to overtake me, but instead God had brought perspective and used me in spite of my pain. "Thank you, Lord," I quietly whispered as I watched the scene unfold in front of me. "Thank you for changing me. And thank you for tonight."

Vicky stood at the back. As others knelt and wept, she folded her arms protectively. I tried to catch her eye, hoping she'd understand the depth of friendship I felt for her. She seemed to look at me across the room momentarily, then turned and walked stiffly out the door. Unable to leave the platform, I frantically pleaded, "God, don't let her leave." But as I went down to pray with those who were seeking, my heart heavy, I knew Vicky had turned away.

Many lingered long after the service. When all had drifted

out and just the team was left, a man from the weather service returned to tell Louie that a major spring snowstorm was brewing. By midnight we were packed and on the road. The night was cold and menacing. Only a short distance from Crescent, the heater quit, while snow fell heavier and quieter. In the chilled car, we huddled together, unable to sleep at first, praising God for what he had done. During the long night as we headed through Northern California, one by one the members of the team drifted off to a cramped and fitful sleep.

My feelings fluctuated between happiness at the changes we'd seen in people's lives and tremendous sorrow at what I'd seen on Vicky's face. In so many ways she was just like me; and I wanted so much to prove my faith to her, but I couldn't. The rebel she'd known in Crescent had taught her how to trust no one. I was beginning to see that I, in my own angry way, had been fighting the pain of my family in all my relationships. I acted out, every day, the fear I had of my dad and his gun. His drinking, his violence and cruelty, all spurred me on. How I wanted to let Vicky see that God now forgave me and really loved me; he was my heavenly father who cared.

Louie heard me searching around for a tissue as I wiped away silent tears while the others slept.

"Carolyn?" he whispered.

I leaned over the front seat and smiled. He spoke a little louder. "I want you to know that this has been one of the most powerful weeks of my life, and I've been a Christian for a long while and seen God do many wonderful things." He paused as his voice cracked slightly. "Carolyn, I want to tell you something." I leaned over closer to him, listening carefully. "God is going to use you in a unique way. Everyone in this car is chosen by God, but he has a special journey for you. Your life is going to be different—something very special."

"It's scary, Louie," I picked up. "Something, but I don't

know what, is happening to me. I feel as though I've already lived a thousand lifetimes, but my one desire is for God to use me."

"He will," Louie assured, "more than you will ever dream. You are very important to him."

He lifted one hand from the wheel and reinforced his prophetic words with a gentle squeeze of my hand. As he reached back to the wheel, I glimpsed through the reflection of the moonlight the dark scab that had formed across the bridge of his nose.

"Hey, Louie," I said, embarrassed, "I'm really sorry that I hit you."

He threw back his head and tried to muffle his laughter so as not to wake the others. "Don't worry about it; I can always claim that I'm the only person that Carolyn Koons ever knocked out."

We didn't talk any more. I rejoiced that God had allowed me to walk into a part of my past and take a good look back. It was the first freeing step toward moving on, but I had a feeling there were memories scourged upon my heart that would take years yet to be healed.

The Beach

I wasn't the only one, I soon discovered, who had come home changed from Crescent. Every time the youth group met, kids, surfacing from everywhere, joined us, excited about helping other people. Projects or ministries sprang up, one right after the other. Watching lives change and seeing other kids' faces as they discovered hope and purpose because someone cared sent tremors of resolve through my soul: being a Christian in ministry to others was what I wanted to do with my life.

Sometimes, when a rare respite allowed me time to reflect, I thought about the long, lonely evenings in Minnesota when I lay in my attic room, imprisoned in my pain, dreaming that someone, anyone, would reach out and help me. I'd wondered if anything good would ever come to me. The warmth of my new faith assured me that now it had. My life was worth living. I was going someplace, and I wasn't alone.

In June, against all the predictions of my past, I walked proudly across the platform of Wilson High School stadium in my black robe and mortarboard, my head held high in response to all the teachers who'd thought I couldn't do it. One of hundreds of graduates, I felt elated until, diploma in hand, I faced the cheering crowd as cameras clicked all around. There was no family out there celebrating for me; they hadn't changed one bit. This major accomplishment went unnoticed. I still had to make it on my own, but God, loving and very present, was applauding my growth inside. I knew I'd make it.

That evening as I wobbled a bit on my first pair of high heels, Bill escorted me to the church graduation party. What a wonderful guy! Attentive and sensitive, and validictorian of his class, he was headed for Wheaton College in the fall. That was still three months away, and we had a full summer scheduled starting the very next day.

After a short night's sleep, Louie drove some of the youth group to the Choctaw Indian Reservation just outside of Oklahoma City where he'd grown up. Louie's mom, standing inches under five feet tall, welcomed us to a spotless, but makeshift board house. His father, a tall, gangly man who looked fully at home in his well-worn denim coveralls and khaki work shirt, spent much of his time outdoors, repairing things and coaxing what little life he could from the soil. One of our tasks for the two-week stay was to build them a new outhouse in the spare hours between morning Bible clubs for children and nightly services all over the reservation.

The reservation church had a circuit-riding preacher who made monthly visits. Our enthusiastic entourage delighted everyone with music and crazy, fun children's activities. We used small lean-tos and shacks for our church services when we couldn't meet outdoors. The subsistence life the Choctaws maintained with so few resources of any kind made me think of pioneer America.

As we went from tribe to tribe sharing our faith and telling stories of what God had done in each of our lives, we found wine and beer distilleries hidden back in the woods and bushes. It was just like the old movies depicting the hidden caches and bootlegging during Prohibition.

The Friday before we were to leave, an old Indian, his face bronzed and deeply lined beneath plaited black hair, described the "nigger picnic" scheduled for that night. Shocked at the name, I balked until Louie assured me that everyone called it that. When night came we headed the station wagon fifteen miles down a twisted, narrow dirt road that seemed to stretch straight to nowhere. Over a final butte, we came upon dozens of people, bronze and black, congregated in a clearing. Strategically placed torches cast playful shadows on the dark prairie. A black man with his fiddle was joined by two others who played the saw and the bass. The other blacks in the crowd danced up a low cloud of dust. To the right of the picnic area, a skewered pig, head and all, rotated over a huge flaming pit.

"Haven't you ever been to a real ethnic event before?" Louie teased, as I stood wide-eyed watching the locals drain the still, whoop and dance, and down huge slabs of steaming pork. I refused the first five offers until I was persuaded that the meat was well-done, then I tested a tiny, delicious bite.

The next morning, I awoke writhing with excruciating abdominal pains, sure I was about to die. Louie, worried but puzzled, assured me that no one else on the team or at the picnic who'd eaten the pork felt a thing.

Before setting out for the marathon drive to California, we visited a doctor, who prescribed medicine sure to make me well. It didn't help, and I spent the entire trip prostrate in the back of the station wagon, envisioning burning coals smoldering in my stomach.

Within thirty minutes of pulling into Long Beach, I lay atop another cold, steel examining table. After a complete physical exam, I was sent out and Louie was called in. I flipped through the magazines in the waiting room, too much in pain to concentrate, until the doctor stuck his head out the door of his office. "Carolyn, you may join us now." He motioned for me to sit in the black vinyl chair. "I want to tell you something." In doctorly fashion, he rattled off some unknown terms and the anatomical location of my pain.

I looked at Louie. His face was pinched with concern. "Carolyn, he's saying that you have three ulcers."

The doctor continued, pulling out a chart that showed exactly where the ulcers were, "I don't know anything about you. I have asked Mr. Files a few questions, but the only thing I can say is that ulcers are known to be emotionally caused. I don't know what's bothering you, but you're too young to have ulcers of this severity. Louie can probably help you in ways that I can't. If you don't start dealing with whatever haunts you, you may have to have surgery. If that happens, you are no doubt in for much more physical and emotional pain in the years to come."

He then handed me a diet sheet and ordered me to eat only mashed potatoes, bananas, Cream of Wheat, and Jello, drink plenty of milk, and take my medicine regularly for the next six weeks.

Shaken by what the doctor had said and growing weaker from days of unending pain, I had to have help getting to the car. The worry lines etched in Louie's forehead told me of his concern. I had to get used to having people who actually cared if I lived or died, even though at that moment I would have bet that dying was more likely.

Louie got into the driver's seat and pulled the door shut with more strength than he needed. "You've got to quit holding back, Carolyn. You've just got to begin dealing with whatever is going on inside you. Don't you understand that we love you? What you've done in the past or where you come from doesn't matter." He paused and started the motor. "The doctor was too gentle with you. He talked quite intently with me. I don't want anything to happen to you."

I sat silently, staring straight ahead at the road as he drove me, this time, toward my parents' apartment. How could I tell Louie, my friend, my youth pastor? How could I tell anyone the details of what I'd been through? Maybe, despite what he said, they'd judge me on the basis of what I was doing then rather than now. Which spoke the truth—Louie or my fear?

Day and night for the rest of the summer I was sicker than I'd ever been in my life. I nightly dragged my pillow and blanket from the bedroom to the bathroom, whether I was staying at my parents', a friend's, or even on the couch in the youth office at church. The diarrhea and vomiting continued with even the softest diet. My expectations for a summer of ministry were met flat on my back, too sick to even walk.

The beach was three blocks from the two-bedroom apartment my parents leased. Since they were both gone during the day and worked in the evenings, leaving the place empty, I headed there in the mornings. Every other weekend or so we might cross paths.

The first morning after it sank in that I'd be spending the summer alone and inactive, I laboriously struggled to the beach and sprawled inert on the sand, without enough strength to venture close to the water. The hours dragged endlessly on. The next day I took my Bible, and my boredom turned to peaceful excitement. Slowly and tediously, squinting against the glare of the sun, I'd read a few verses then lie back and meditate until I was rested enough to pore over one of the many Bible studies that I'd collected for when I had some spare time. The Bible I had proudly carried to and from my high school classes became more than a symbol of my faith: it was now my companion.

After a few days, one morning I looked up to see a lone figure approaching slowly across the sand. I could tell by the loping gait that it was Louie.

"Hey, look who I found!" Louie teased. "Great-looking tan you're getting."

He brought me a packet of materials based on a system of

memorization. Bill, Sam, Bob, and Jane had already started. I couldn't remember having memorized anything before. Just simply reading was a struggle.

Daily, I rested and learned while my body became beautifully bronzed. The dire need for physical healing had forced me to work on my inner pain. I noticed that I was spending more and more time thinking about the future. This was new to me. I'd always concentrated on mere immediate survival. I felt rejuvenated; my strength was coming back.

The warm days mirrored the light I felt flooding into my heart.

But in the early evenings, around dusk, when I'd shuffle slowly through the sand back to the apartment, depression would replace my joy whenever Dad's car was parked outside. My reading my Bible and going to church only made him more hostile and abusive. I'd done yet one more intolerable thing by becoming a Christian.

Whenever Mom and Dad were home, liquor and beer bottles cluttered the coffee tables and counter. No friends ever came to visit. Once in a while the relatives, Grandma and Grandpa Goodson or my mom's three brothers, stopped by, but none ever stayed for long.

One Saturday in August my uncles sat around the kitchen table conferring about Grandpa's money. During the Depression he'd invested wisely and eventually accumulated a considerable estate. Each of the children knew they would someday inherit a substantial amount.

"How can we get the old man to fork over the money now?" Uncle Babe, the oldest, asked, as he dealt the cards around the table.

"I just got six thousand more out of him last week. I told him I was going to lose my house. And believe me, I'm not going to pay one red cent back," Gilbert joked; the rest joined the laughter.

Babe had his story to tell too. He'd managed to borrow several thousand for his Belmont Shore delicatessen. He'd never paid back a dime either.

It sickened me to hear the greedy four plot how to cheat their parents. Grandma and Grandpa, the only kind and generous pair in the whole lot, had no idea. When I walked into the kitchen for a glass of water, they all dropped to hushed tones.

"How's the Christian fanatic?" Babe tossed, his mustached face staring at me with a sarcastic sneer. "Have you told that youth group of yours how you used to chug more beer than all your friends combined?"

I ignored him, walking to the sink, but he wouldn't stop. As I left the room the stories of all the things Carolyn once did were flying around to uproarious laughter. Unable to stand it, and feeling too weak to find another place to stay for the night, I crawled into bed, my head under the covers, hoping I could drown out the sound of their voices. My family didn't know how to care about anyone or anything. They wanted me to suffer just because they lived rotten lives. Dreams, fitful and vivid, kept me tossing all night until my mother roughly shook me. Through a foggy head, I saw her tousled hair and rumpled clothes. "Huh?" I mumbled after she said something.

"I said you're going to have to leave." I thought I was still dreaming and half-rolled over before her arm pushed me flat on my back.

Pain. The fire in my stomach made me hug my knees tight against my chest. Leave? What had I cost her? A few boxes of Jello? A bag or two of potatoes? She didn't pay for my clothes. My anger only intensified the spasms. I made all my own spending money! I didn't take up any of her time or space. She only laid eyes on me a couple of times a month!

"Your dad and I have separated. He left me, this time for good, and I don't have any money. You've got to go. I want you out of here today." She lit a cigarette, threw the burnt match in the corner, and left.

How many times had I heard that line before? "Your dad left and is never coming back." Those two had never been happy together. Fighting and screaming at each other was their way of life. One more round had begun.

By afternoon, my packed vinyl suitcase sat in the spare bedroom at Jane's; her parents offered the bed, not believing that my mother really meant it. Unpacking in the neatly wallpapered room and sorting my clothes into the nicely lined drawers, I thought a lot about the summer day in Minnesota when my family had left me once before, but this time the desperate loneliness didn't quite overtake me. I had friends and, in a way, a new family.

Once my things were in order, I mounted my bike and headed toward my grandparents'. I hadn't seen them for a couple of weeks, and they always wanted to know where to find me. Their towering apartment building overlooked Ocean Boulevard to the east and the beach to the west. The weather invigorated Grandpa; he never missed his morning swim. Grandma was content, too. There were always cookies and milk waiting after she hugged me in her flowered housedress. I couldn't love them enough. How often I thanked God for my dear old grandmother complaining to her neighbor about her unruly granddaughter! Without her, I might not be a Christian, or have the loving family at church that helped me in times like these.

They both greeted me at the door, and I could tell by the

open book by each of their favorite chairs that they'd been reading quietly.

"How's my granddaughter?" Grandpa boomed in his exuberant voice.

"I'm fine, Grandpa, I just needed to let you know where you can get hold of me if you want to. I'm staying at my friend Jane's."

"Why are you staying there?" Grandma asked, a strained look crossing her face.

"Mom asked me to leave," I answered quietly, staring at the rag rug near the front door.

Grandpa motioned for me to sit down on the couch. His brow was furrowed and angry. "Why did she ask you to leave?"

"There's no problem, really, Grandpa. I'm better off at my friend's."

He repeated his question, leaning forward in his chair, "Tell me why she asked you to leave, Carolyn."

I looked at the floor and didn't answer.

"Tell me why. I need to know the truth."

I looked at him. His blue eyes were blazing, but he reached out his hand and patted my knee and smiled kindly.

"Grandpa, she said she couldn't afford to keep me around now that Dad has left, and there's only one income. But that doesn't make much sense. I hardly ever stay there and barely cost her a cent!"

Grandpa jumped up and thrust his hands deep into his pockets as he began to pace. He looked at Grandma, and she shook her head in disbelief.

"What's she talking about?" Grandpa muttered. He faced me. "I just wrote her a check for ten thousand dollars three days ago, because she said she needed money. I thought that would tide her over for some time. She knows if she honestly needs more she can get it. She has more than enough money to take care of the both of you—but I'm glad you're getting out of there. You deserve better."

I didn't need to answer. He was upset at her, not me. While he went to get his jacket for a long walk on the beach, Grandma bustled me into the kitchen for cookies and small talk. It was nearly dusk when I left.

I had to ride past Mom's apartment on the way to Jane's. I'd left my record albums, but now I thought it wise to get everything out of there for good. No more staying there for me, anymore—even once in a while! The wire basket on my bike was big enough to hold everything I still wanted.

Mom hadn't asked for my key, and the front room was dark when I let myself in, yet a dim light came from the back bedroom. Mom must've forgotten it when she left for work. I walked down the hall without turning on any lights and began to rummage through my closet for the records until I heard muffled voices, then giggling, through the wall.

I felt my way to the door and turned on my bedroom light before heading down the hall toward the other bedroom, whose door was slightly ajar. I knocked timidly.

"Who the h—— is there?" my dad's voice slurred. My mom giggled.

"It's me, Carolyn."

"What are you doing here?" he demanded.

"Getting the rest of my things. I'm on my way out."

"Hold it, wait!" my mother yelled, rolling out of bed, half-trying to tie her robe around her. She pushed me toward the kitchen.

"What is he doing here?" I asked, my anger rising. "I thought you said that he left you."

"Nope."

"You told me he did. Grandpa gave you money because you said he'd gone."

"So, big deal," she was searching around the counter for a cigarette. "If he isn't going to give me any money until he dies, then I have to figure out a way to get it now, right?"

"You mean you made the whole thing up to trick Grandpa? Dad never left at all?"

"You win first prize for that answer, Carolyn." She smiled smugly and strutted back to the bedroom, the smoke from her cigarette iridescent in the darkness.

Grabbing my records, I ran for the door and slammed it viciously. My mother had lied to her own father so she could rip him off for ten thousand dollars! How I hated her! I hated my dad just as much for playing along with her stupid plot. Their deceit made me so angry, my feet pumped wildly at the pedals. I was at Jane's in no time.

The Microphone

With flushed cheeks and moist hands, I fumbled through the pages stapled together on the small student desk while the thousands around me in the Long Beach State University auditorium bent intently over their college entrance exams.

I read the first set of directions. What was I doing here? Why did I think I could even pass these tests? College didn't have anything to do with working with Louie and Wes in the church. Day-to-day survival sure was easier than trying to plan the future. Now that I had something worth living for, everyone encouraged me to think ahead, first one year, then two. But now, as I painstakingly read each question, trying to come up with some logical answer, I felt like an alien in this academic world.

Most of the students trickled out of the auditorium long before I did. When the final buzzer rang, I handed in my unfinished test, identified myself to the clerk, "Koons, Carolyn A.," and left, feeling humiliated. I couldn't imagine knowing all the things they expected me to even *after* completing college.

The last two weeks of summer sped by before a long, white envelope appeared in Wednesday's mail. The California State University at Long Beach address alerted me to the contents. I threw it on my desk, unopened, not in any state to deal with more rejection.

I left for Bible study right after dinner. Louie enthusiastically led us through a passage of Scripture the way he always did, but I wasn't really hearing him; that letter was on my mind.

After Bill took me out for a Coke and dropped me off, I made up my mind; it was now or never. I picked up the envelope and tore it open before I could change my mind.

This is to inform you that Carolyn A. Koons has been accepted as a provisional student at Cal State, Long Beach. The following pages indicate the classes that will be necessary for Carolyn to take in order to continue as a student at Cal State after the fall semester.

I turned the page, and a sinking feeling came over me as I scanned the test results. How embarrassing. I had an eighth-grade reading level. I could just hear the kids at church stifle laughter when I listed my college class schedule. "I'm taking dumbbell English, dumbbell reading, psychology, literature, science, and P.E." Everyone would now label me even if they never said it out loud; my poor background was showing.

The letter gave me three days to decide. I'd either have to figure out something else to do with my life or swallow my pride and take remedial college classes.

The first day I wasn't going to accept, then I was, and soon I stood, not knowing my major, in interminable, twisting registration lines. Choosing a profession had never occurred to me before, but now I was a college student.

Studies and church took up all my time. I was back to my fast-paced lifestyle. As long as I regulated my diet my ulcers didn't bother me much. I'd bike from the library to the youth center nearly every day. As midterms approached, Louie and Wes called me in for a talk. They began describing the junior high school group. The high school and college groups were burgeoning, but less than ten junior high schoolers came to church regularly. I was flattered that they were making me privy to their discussion but couldn't figure out why. When I asked, Louie came straight to the point. "Carolyn, how would you like to take over the junior high group?"

"Me? You're kidding. I just finished high school. You wouldn't really consider me, would you?"

Wes smiled broadly. "Of course. We both have been watching you. You can do it. I'll help you with the programming, and Louie will give you all the support you need."

Louie didn't give me a second before he asked, "So, do you want to work with the junior highers?"

"I'd love it!"

The three of us worked every free afternoon for the next few weeks planning and then recruiting all the volunteers we needed. In November, on a Sunday evening, I stood before thirteen eager faces that spurred me on as I began to share the dreams I had for them. Before we closed for the evening, we all hugged each other, nearly delirious with expectation. I was in love with each one of them.

It took the first month to get all thirteen actively involved in a special task, but all of us could feel the enthusiasm building. The second month flew by with holiday activities, and when January ended my thirteen had become sixty-five. By now, I was eating, sleeping, and breathing the junior high group. We met before school for Bible studies. An all-girls small group grew to nearly forty before spring.

The kids affirmed me constantly. Focusing on their excitement and boundless energy helped me to forget the reality of college. As long as I was with them, I didn't think about my "dumbbell" classes or my past. The same Carolyn who had spent her early teen years nearly destroying her life was helping these kids do fun, constructive things. I was doing "good."

Louie and Wes gathered all the youth and college groups together one Sunday night after church. Another youth pastor, Al Johnson from Downey First Baptist, wanted three or four churches to join together and travel down the western gulf coast of Mexico to Guaymas and Empalme over Easter break. The missionaries' plea for help aroused the whole group. When it came time to vote on the project, we all chorused a unanimous yes. So from that Saturday on, we learned Spanish songs and Bible stories and crafts the Mexican kids could relate to. We even had to translate our testimonies and a simple sermon.

Friday night, after my final exams, I joined seventy-five others crowded onto three church buses. For two days we rumbled from California into Arizona before crossing the border and heading down along the Gulf of California.

We didn't expect such an immediate change of scenery between the United States and Mexico. The pervasive poverty contrasted sharply with the disarming hospitality we sensed. Person after person smiled broadly and waved us into their village. As we headed toward the beach towns, each quiet village seemed to be the most beautiful place we had ever seen —until we pulled in to the next.

Red and blue fishing boats in various sizes and states of repair lined the beach as we entered Guaymas. Small brown-eyed boys and young teens worked alongside the fishermen toting the day's catch. Everyday life seemed exotic in its simplicity.

We soon were busy unloading and setting up our base camp in an abandoned house patched together with planks and cardboard. Holes were dug and blankets hung to serve as our outhouses. Louie assembled teams to carry water from the local well to the house for cooking and washing while others of us swept out the spiders and scorpions that had occupied the empty building. After the main camp was functional, the group split into four ministry teams that would focus on a particular neighborhood in either of the villages for the next seven days.

The first morning, my team anxiously prepared for Bible school, scavenging for rocks to pound in the support stakes for our portable tent. We allocated enough supplies for each child and rehearsed our Spanish for the final time as the children began to appear. First timidly, then eagerly, as the first few helped newcomers feel at home, dozens of little brown faces surrounded us. Our hesitant and faltering Spanish had to be bolstered by lots of gesturing and hugs. The joy mirrored back from the wiggling, squirming kids inspired us. We soon sang loudly with all our hearts, hoping the words we mispronounced would be understood out of our sheer desire to communicate.

Afternoons found us working with the missionaries in the center of Guaymas where hundreds of *braceros* (Mexican farmers) camped awaiting visas from the government office that would enable them to enter the United States to work the fields.

Evangelistic churches in the two towns opened up their sanctuaries to us each night. It was a struggle for us to share our testimonies and preach, but the people responded. As we sang, they joined us. As we cried, many would show how moved they were by bursting into happy tears along with us.

By the end of the week, the graciousness and appreciation the villagers showered upon us made it seem impossible to leave. We had grown to love these people and had been changed by the experience. I'd expected that the people we preached to would benefit, but what had happened to me and the other kids amazed all of us. We slept on the ground, bathed only partially, and wore the same clothes until we'd forgotten about all we'd left at home, but never had we been so happy or fulfilled. This week was just like the time in Crescent. God had brought me to be a part of his work to transform lives. I felt wonderful!

When it came time to reload and head toward home, we lingered over sad farewells, yet most of us were sound asleep from exhaustion before we were thirty miles from town. Too wound up to sleep, I found a front seat near Al Johnson, who drove our bus. George Rivera, the missionary evangelist who had come with us as a translator, sat next to me. The three of us, all sure we'd return someday, began to dream aloud about the potential for other ministry trips we'd thought about all week.

"How about Thanksgiving next year?" Al suggested, his lanky, slouching frame straightening a bit in the driver's seat.

"If we started planning now, we could bring more kids!" I added, my mind racing.

Already we'd begun. Al made lists in his mind of youth pastors to enlist from all around the Los Angeles area while George described towns he'd scout out closer to the border in the Mexicali valley.

The sun set with golden tones fading quickly over the ocean as we wound along the narrow roads. George and Al traded places during a stop where the leaders of all three busloads determined to drive straight through the night so that we could be in our respective churches for Easter on Sunday morning. With George now in the driver's seat, we kept on imagining what might lie ahead. By the wee hours of the morning we had decided to call our ministry plans YUGO —Youth Unlimited Gospel Outreach. We felt we could do anything.

Easter morning at Bethany Baptist was electric. The testimonies and stories the kids told about Mexico brought the church soundly behind us in our plan to go again. Soon Al asked me to handle the administration for him. He considered himself a visionary, who needed someone to plan the training programs and logistics.

Al's offer was unbelievable. Me, help *him?* The idea that this man whom I deeply admired needed me was hard to accept. For so many years no one had believed in me at all. I still struggled to trust the confidence others had in me. But I got busy, and soon I was developing a training manual. Somewhere deep inside I believed that Mexico and this kind of ministry would always be an important part of my life.

College, the junior high group, and YUGO filled my life to overflowing. In the summer I substituted odd house painting jobs for classes to earn a few dollars, but soon my sophomore year at Long Beach State began.

In November, YUGO transported over four hundred teens and young adults to the Mexicali valley, where we camped en masse in the First Baptist Church of El Centro. Each morning after a combined chapel service, we separated into twenty ministry groups. Each night we reassembled as representatives from each team shared the miracles that seemed unending.

Al, Wes, Louie, and I worked endlessly. Struggling up out of my sleeping bag when the gray sky was just brightening enough to be called morning, I simply dashed through the day, handling more questions and ministry detail than the incredibly packed day before. I thrived on this new life.

The trip was soon over, and I found it increasingly difficult to go back to school; classes and boring lectures couldn't measure up. I just bided my time, often daydreaming about Mexico, until Easter vacation and our next trip. It was another phenomenal experience. Long hours of planning showed tangible results, something no amount of slaving over books could give me.

As my second year of college wound down, George Rivera approached a few of the college group, offering to take a small number down to Mexico for the whole summer. Two and a half months would allow us to hold crusades throughout mainland Mexico down to Monterrey.

Tired of college and the constant beating it gave my self-confidence, I decided that maybe God was calling me to be a missionary. Bob Hubbard, Jr., and six other veterans of Mexico trips prayed about the summer ministry for a few weeks before accepting the challenge, as I did. I'd learned to play the guitar and the accordian, and Bob and I already had a two-song duet repertoire in Spanish!

The energy of the summer we shared was electric—from visits to orphanages that housed dozens of rambunctious kids in dwellings no larger than a small apartment to citywide crusades in local parks and plazas all along the way. When roads were impassable or nonexistent, we rented burros, piled our gear and instruments on top, and trudged for hours to reach the remote villages George had periodically preached in during his years in Mexico. Some of the mountain people had never seen *"gringos"* before. We slept in tiny cabins, or outside, or wherever was offered. I ate goat meat for the first time, and three long days between villages without food of any kind taught me to not worry what I was eating. Hunger made me less discriminating about food.

On the way south from Monterrey to Saltillo, we found large numbers of *braceros* in what looked like huge refugee camps. Thousands of men just lounged around haphazard shelters waiting for news of their applications to go north to the United States for the harvest.

Local missionaries working the largest camp, with nearly five thousand inhabitants, asked for our assistance in their gospel crusade. They rigged a film projector and screen atop their van for the men in the huge courtyard to see a film that shared the gospel message, and we built a portable platform the height of the van so our team could sing and speak.

As we drove through the camp, a sea of faces pressed close to the window. When we stopped in the center of the compound and began to set up, the men began to move in, closer and closer. By the time Bob and I scrambled up the platform to sing the opening song, we were locked in on all sides by the crowd. As I stood next to Bob and sang my alto part, it dawned on me that, besides the missionary's wife, who was in her fifties, I was the only woman in the entire mass of men. I had an overwhelming sensation of being a Daniel thrown before this lonely lion's den of men who were far away from friends and companionship.

The program called for me to follow our duet with a number of Spanish songs. I accompanied myself on the guitar, and just a few bars into the song, I found it hard to keep my balance. The men began to press in on the van and rock it back and forth. The missionary panicked and tried to crawl up and grab me. Before he could reach me, I instinctively stopped my song and took hold of the portable microphone. "Get back," I ordered in Spanish. "If you want me to sing, get back. Move away from the van!"

There was a brief hesitation, and I could sense that the missionary stood just behind me. While I demonstrated by waving the men back, my heart clutched in fear, praying that they would obey. For a long few minutes, the missionaries and I weren't sure if any of us were going to get out alive. Finally the men began to move, and I softly resumed my song, forcing the men to be quiet to hear. From my vantage point, I watched a wave of movement go through the crowd as each man took a step or two backward. I continued singing, as confidence welled up within me. After the first song they applauded, and a hush fell over the crowd; they were waiting for more.

I sang every song that I knew in Spanish. The missionaries shrugged and motioned for me to continue. I laid my guitar down on the platform—I felt compelled to share my story. I told them how, at one time, my life was no different from theirs—empty and waiting for something—but one day I heard about a man named Jesus who loved me no matter what. He gave me a reason to live.

"Once I would have given my life away or changed it for someone else's at any opportunity. The emptiness of my life seemed more than I could ever escape," I emphasized, looking closely at the sea of faces in front of me—some angry, others betraying their loneliness. "But now, I look forward to each day. God has shown me in amazing ways how much he forgives me and wants my life to be something very special . . ."

I sensed the Holy Spirit speak through my words. I asked the men to raise their hands if they believed that Jesus Christ could take their pasts, as he had mine, and replace the pain with abundant life. Arms by the hundreds popped up over the heads of the crowd. There was no other sound or movement.

"Pray out loud with me," I instructed. I closed my eyes and, with all my being, led the men in talking honestly to God while his presence was obvious. As soon as I said amen, I worked my way off the platform, and the missionary took my place to continue telling them about Jesus. He offered free Bibles and literature to any who wished to come to the van.

I sat inside with my heart racing furiously. My knees shook. The strength that I had had while speaking vanished. I felt weak and awed that God had really used me in a powerful, unexpected way. I whispered, "Thank you, Lord, thank you," before moving to the door to help distribute Bibles.

After that night, none of the inevitable personal spats or tiresome walks or long days discouraged me. I had felt God's anointing as I never had.

Only as we headed back toward home did my mood change from settled contentment to despondence. I dreaded going back to school for a third year of dumbbell classes. Sharing my faith in such incredible circumstances far outweighed any positive value I could see in finishing college.

Before we drove into Long Beach, R. H. Castillo, one of my teammates, whispered quietly to me in the van. He'd decided to go back to Mexico permanently. On the spur of the moment I asked him if I could catch a ride if I decided to return. "Sure," he said, "I'm leaving in two weeks."

On Sunday I told Louie I'd decided to drop out of school to go back to Mexico. Nothing in Long Beach could compare to my memory of the masses of people with sad eyes that we'd spent weeks with. Besides, the missionaries loved me; they'd begged me to consider coming back after college. Why not now? Louie counseled me to talk to Dr. Hubbard that very day.

"Is this what you really feel you should do, Carolyn?" Pastor Hubbard asked, when we were seated in his book-lined office.

"I can't get Mexico out of my mind. Yes, this is what I want to do," I assured him.

His wisdom showed as he gently took me step-by-step over my reasons for wanting to be a missionary and finding my place of ministry. I assured him that I'd come back and finish college after a year or two. I just wasn't ready for more school yet.

"Would you be willing to share your testimony in the evening service?" Dr. Hubbard asked, after listening to my long explanations.

Hours later, on a long summer's evening, I stood in front of more than a thousand people and related what God had allowed to happen through me in the last weeks. The passion I felt for the people poured through me. For the first time I publicly declared, "I am going to be a missionary."

When I'd finished and taken my seat on the platform, Dr. Hubbard took his place behind the pulpit. "If Carolyn is going to go for a full year to Mexico as a missionary, then we need to support her." He instructed the ushers to get out the offering plates. I sat in disbelief, thinking that I, a nineteen-year-old nobody that no one had cared existed a couple of years ago, was being supported by an entire church! Everyone I had known in my past life would have chosen to punch me in the face and tell me to get lost rather than encourage me in anything I decided to do. I was very moved.

After the service, people surrounded me in the foyer. One by one they hugged me and commended my courage. I could hardly think. It all happened so fast.

As the crowd began to thin out, I saw Jean Fonner, the wonderful woman who had persisted in calling on me less than two years ago, waiting to talk to me. After I found my place in the youth group it was rare for me to see her in the large, active church. I caught her eye and smiled. She just waited patiently.

After the others left, she walked up to me and hugged me tight. She held my hands supportively for a moment before she spoke. "I think it's wonderful that you want to go to the mission field." She paused and just smiled, making me feel like a child she was proud of. She had been such an angel of light for me; I knew she understood what I felt even though I didn't have words to tell her. "I have one question, though, that I must ask you."

"What's that?" I said enthusiastically.

She looked at me with such compassion. "Carolyn, are you running from something?"

"What do you mean?" I answered warily, stepping back half a step. I felt puzzled and vulnerable, as if I were transparent before her.

"You are such a young Christian, Carolyn. Have you ever thought about going to a Christian college? Then when it's time to go to the mission field, you'll be much better prepared. I think this is one of the most important decisions you will ever make."

I must have looked dismayed; my defenses rose.

She repeated her question, "Are you running from something? I just sense there's something you're running away from." She hugged me again then walked away.

A few others came up and gave their support and love, but Jean, one of hundreds who had patted me on the back that night, had spoken the only question my soul seemed to hear.

What was I running from?

The Offer

The next morning as I fixed breakfast, Jean's words reverberated in my head, as clear as they'd been the night before. Why, out of fifteen hundred people, did she question my choice? And why a Christian college? Christian or not, more school wasn't for me.

The phone rang from the next room, interrupting my thoughts. "Hello?"

"Hi, Carolyn, it's Dean Parker from Faith Baptist. How was Mexico? I've been praying for you every day since you left."

I told him about my decision to go back to Mexico in two weeks.

"Well, if you're free until then, why don't you come and spend the weekend with Esther and me? You'll get to meet our boys, and you can go to church with us here in Thousand Oaks."

"I don't have any plans for next weekend. Sounds great!"

Dean and I had worked together in directing youth camps the previous summer at Forest Home Conference Grounds. He and his wife always treated me like a part of their extended family. They'd asked me to come spend the weekend before, but I'd never been able to schedule it.

Early in the week I retrieved my first car, a 1941 Plymouth coupe. I'd purchased it for two hundred dollars during the last year with a loan from my grandfather. I'd paid nearly every cent back. It ran great, had torn patches in the upholstery that I covered with a blanket, and was painted bright red. Having my own transportation for the first time in a while gave me such freedom. I felt exhilarated as I drove east toward the Parkers' on Friday evening.

Danny, Tim, and David ran out the door to look at my car before Dean had a chance to introduce them. They thought my heap had class. Within a few minutes Esther had enticed us into the kitchen with hot chocolate and ice cream. The boys urged me to tell my adventures in Mexico in vivid detail. The conversation was animated and boisterous all round.

After about twenty minutes there was a lull, and I noticed that Dean was studying me. "Carolyn, I have a question for you. Why are you going to Mexico?"

"You just heard my stories. God used me in amazing ways. I can't wait to get back!" His serious tone startled me.

He continued, "I sense something is going on inside of you."

"What's that?" I inquired.

"Are you running from something?"

First Jean, now Dean Parker. I couldn't believe my ears. They used the same words, and neither of them even knew that the other existed.

"You know what you need to do? You should consider going to a Christian college instead of staying at the state university. If you're going into the field of Christian education and are as excited about missions as you appear to be, you need a good, Christian college education."

Amazed that they took such an interest in the direction of my life, I felt as though I were hearing a tape of the same speech Jean had given me a week earlier. Was God trying to tell me something? "I'll think about it, but I'm planning to leave for Mexico in less than a week."

Dean needled me a little: "People have been known to change their minds."

The next morning after breakfast the whole Parker family and I loaded into their station wagon to drive to Big Bear for the dedication of Pine Summit, a new campground. The ceremony was brief, and we tramped all over the wooded lot before heading back down Interstate 10 from San Bernardino. Dean exited at Citrus Avenue in Azusa.

"Where are we going?" I asked. No one had said anything about another stop.

"Oh, we have something to show you," Dean answered, as he and Esther exchanged knowing glances. He pulled the car to a stop in a small parking lot on Citrus and Alosta. "Here it is!" two of the boys chimed in unison.

"What?" I didn't see much.

"Azusa College."

I rolled down the window and peered out at the few buildings scattered around the block. The marquee on the front lawn read Azusa Pacific University Welcomes New Students. Dean put the car in gear and slowly passed an old two-story building that looked like a ranch house. A row of low adobe buildings sat off to the left.

"Those buildings are the dorms," Dean pointed, as we circled through the campus. "There's the gym." As I looked out I saw a small, rounded building at the center of campus. Within minutes we were back at the front entrance.

"That's the whole thing?" I laughed a little.

Dean grinned, "It's a small Bible school. There are about two hundred enrolled now."

"Two hundred? Long Beach State has fifteen thousand!" I'd never heard of a college this small.

I looked out the rear window as we drove onto the main road. There was something quaint and appealing about the school. We drove on down Citrus to Foothill for a mile and parked in front of a small, white stucco house.

"I want you to meet my sister, Pauline, and her husband, Don Grant. He's chairman of the Music Department at Azusa."

Two and two began to make four; this whole trip had obviously been planned in advance to show me the college! I had nothing to lose, so I went along.

A tall, slim man in his early thirties welcomed us when we rang the door bell. One look around the room told me how important music was to the whole family. A piano occupied the central position in the living room, and scores of music, some handwritten, lay on the coffee table. Pauline greeted me before she and Esther started catching up on all the family news. Don and Pauline's three young children bounded in to play with their cousins. This whole clan seemed so happy together!

Don soon motioned for the adults to head toward the kitchen and asked me to watch the six kids at their games. I could hear the sound of voices chatting excitedly in the other room, but I couldn't make out any of it.

Don and Dean soon reappeared and sat down beside me on the sofa. "I hear that you're thinking of going to the mission field," Don began.

"Yeah, that's true," I said, knowing Dean had already filled him in.

"I'd like to show you around the college," he offered.

Dean laughed, "Well, I already gave her a quick run-through. It took us about three minutes."

"I can show you my office and the music studio. I have the keys." He patted his pocket and led us to the car. It was getting dark now.

After parking and heading toward a small building, Don spoke up. "I apologize for the place looking so deserted. Most of the students are out at the L.A. County Fair."

His office was cozy and welcoming. "Like the rest of the campus," I thought. Even though it probably occupied less than five percent of the area Long Beach State did, I found myself liking it.

Dean left us alone, and Don and I sat and talked. His friendliness and personal concern amazed me. I'd never had a teacher just sit down and talk to me. His commitment and enthusiasm for the college was contagious. He talked about the Azusa Chorale that was just starting. He described his small classes and the personal interaction that that fostered. He talked about some of his students as if they were almost friends; he knew a lot about each one of them.

"Have you thought about going to school before going to the mission field?" I could tell by his tone of voice that he was interested in what I really thought.

"Well, to be honest, I've considered it over the last week, but never before. I think if I decide to go to a Christian college it'll be Biola. I know they have a professor named Thelma Bain, who teaches Christian education."

"That's great, Carolyn. It doesn't matter which college you choose. The important thing is knowing that you are exactly where God wants you."

I appreciated Don's openness. I thought for sure he'd try to convince me to enroll at Azusa.

"If you'd like to see a Christian college in full swing, I'd be glad for you to come back and have lunch during the week. Would you be able to come sometime in the next few days?"

"I have some packing to do, but I don't own much."

"Why don't you come back on Tuesday and meet some of the teachers and students. You can even sit in on a Bible class or two; I'll set it up for you. We can have lunch after that."

"Great." His friendliness won me over.

Dean was waiting in the car. As we traveled back over the

few blocks, Don asked out of the blue, "Have you done much in the way of athletics?"

I laughed, remembering my years of street football and my baseball escapades with Mrs. McGee. "I'm athletic, all right."

"For some reason, I thought so. That gives me an idea," Don mumbled.

"What?"

"I'll tell you Tuesday."

Three days later I headed back to the campus. I met Don at his office, and he immediately ushered me into a classroom. Dr. Malcolm Robertson, the dean of instruction, was teaching a class on the Old Testament. Don left, and I became completely absorbed in the wisdom and information this man exuded. I looked around the class. Did these students know how lucky they were? I'd never heard anything in school like this. I didn't want the class to end. That was a first. Maybe Jean Fonner was right.

Don showed me to another class. An energetic, gray-haired man, Mr. Peterman, who was also the librarian, stood near the chalkboard drawing a time line. The class was on the Book of Acts. First, he prayed to start the class, and then he gave a short talk on the early church. The students immediately began to ask questions. Halfway through the class the door opened, and Don Grant motioned for me to leave.

I sneaked out the back and found Malcolm Robertson with Don. After brief introductions, two other men, Glen Adams, the registrar, and Cliff Hamlow, the coach, joined us. For the next half hour the four quizzed me about my life and plans. The class on Acts let out, and we still stood outside, chatting comfortably.

The coach said, "I'd like to borrow Carolyn for coffee." Then he turned to me, "Is that all right with you?"

I didn't know how to answer. I didn't like coffee, but I'd be glad to talk to him. "Sure."

Coach Hamlow grabbed a cup of coffee in the cafeteria for me and a Coke for himself. I should have told him I didn't drink coffee, I thought. But I hadn't, so I sat there and sipped the hot coffee as we talked, trying not to grimace at the taste.

The coach started telling me about the Physical Education Department and recent changes. We discussed my past athletic involvement and skills, and he told me they were looking for someone to take on the women's P.E. classes.

"What are you doing for the rest of the day?" he asked.

"I'm having lunch with Don Grant, then I'm free."

"Good. Check back with me after lunch. I need a few more minutes of your time."

Don and I joined the rest of the faculty in the faculty dining room. I couldn't believe that they all fit in one small room! The conversation around the table was friendly. I felt as though I had known these people for years; they treated me like a member of their group.

After lunch, I met some of the students. A few seemed to recognize my name. Others stood back and looked me over as though they knew something about me. I figured it must be my clothes. My khaki culottes, white blouse, and tennis shoes were the best I had.

Coach Hamlow came to the Music Department office. Standing near the door, he came right out and said, "Carolyn, I want to make you an offer. If you'd consider coming to Azusa, I would like to hire you to teach the women's P.E. classes until we are able to hire a full-time women's coach."

"Wait, wait a minute. Me . . . teach?" I was trying to decide whether I could handle studying for another year. I needed to slow things down; I was starting to feel disoriented—all this was so unexpected. Coach Hamlow assured me his offer was serious and told me not to decide right there on the spot.

"I'll think about it," I told him. "May I call you in a couple of days?"

He patted me on the shoulder. "Take whatever time you need. I'm so glad we met today. I'll look forward to hearing from you."

I drove away knowing that in three days I was to leave for Mexico. The warmth of Azusa had taken me by surprise; nothing in my university experience had prepared me for the atmosphere of a small college.

The next morning I drove to Biola College to meet Thelma Bain, one of the most respected Christian education professors around. If more education was in the offing for me, she was the one teacher I longed to learn from. I didn't have an appointment, but she invited me in anyway when I knocked on the door and introduced myself.

For the next hour, I told her what was going on in my life. She listened and counseled me on what Biola could offer. I knew she had a class scheduled soon and made an attempt to close the conversation. She told me not to worry.

"I think you're on the right track, Carolyn. I agree that you need to pursue Christian education if you want to be a missionary or youth pastor or camp director. But, as you know, both Biola and Azusa have started classes for this year. We don't allow students to enroll this late in the semester. My recommendation for you is to take Azusa's offer if they will give you a teaching position and help pay for your education. You can always transfer here at a semester break if you want to."

As she hurried off to her classroom, I knew what to do. I drove my red Plymouth straight to Azusa and found Cliff Hamlow in the gym. He had me hired and registered before the afternoon was out. When we walked out of the administration building, the stares and whispers, "Is that her?" told me how quickly news could travel across campus.

I went home elated and exhausted, trying to grapple with my new identity as both teacher and student at a Christian college. Two days previously I'd been going to be a missionary, but the Lord opened amazing doors to change my plans. I couldn't wait to call Louie and tell him.

As I dialed his number, it hit me. I had to tell Pastor Hubbard and the church. They had set aside all that money for me to go to Mexico. What would he think of me? The people at church would be so disappointed.

After conferring with Louie, I phoned the pastor at his home, and he agreed to meet me in the morning. In the same book-lined office, I retold the events of the last ten days. He didn't say anything as I talked. But when I finished, he leaned back in his swivel chair and rubbed his chin, a warm grin coming to his face.

"I thank God that he is working in your life and that you are being sensitive to his guidance." He didn't reprimand or shout—he rejoiced with me. We agreed that I'd have to tell the church on Sunday, but he promised to help me by confirming the new path that God had opened for me.

On Saturday, I parked in the students' parking lot at Azusa College and unloaded my one small suitcase. Clutching my purse, which held my last twenty dollars, I thanked God again for Jean Fonner. For the first time, I couldn't wait to get ready for classes. I wasn't running from my education anymore: they could teach me here what my heart hungered to know.

The Prank

Many times in the next months, I headed toward a sunny patch of grass underneath one of the elm trees on campus. There, in my few quiet moments, I took time to be amazed at God's movement in my life. That I was a student, let alone a teaching assistant, was more than I could believe. Just a few years past, if shown a list of what might be ahead for me, I would have scratched off immediately anything that hinted of academics or God. But here I was, immersed in life at a Christian college.

I studied harder than ever, trying to erase the negative tapes in my head. Before tests or while agonizing over papers, I'd hear the words again, the accusations that I was dumb, worthless, a fool for trying so hard. After I adjusted to my new routine, I did well, but the tapes kept playing.

Often my roles of teacher and student went hand in hand. Don Grant convinced me to sing at performances with the Azusa Chorale on weekends while recruiting prospective students at intermission. For one part of each day I served as an official college representative, the other, as a typical, fun-loving prankster.

During my first year on campus, the upper division women students returned from their junior-senior banquet to find their rooms rearranged outside on the dorm's center patio. Bedroom slippers lay next to the bed, clock radios played softly, and millions of bright stars shone overhead. Nestled snugly under the moonlight, none of us slept much during the impromptu slumber party that night.

Word of the all-night fun spread like wildfire across the small campus. Don Grant told his kids, and soon he confessed that his oldest son had convinced him to set up a family slumber party in the backyard.

On the scheduled night, at midnight, two friends and I loaded twenty-six alarm clocks, set to go off at ten-minute intervals, into my Plymouth and pushed it across the gravel parking lot so the dorm mom wouldn't hear us. Revving the engine once the car was safely on Alosta Avenue, we drove the short distance to the Grants' dark house. Three cots were lined up neatly underneath the porch light. Don, Pauline, and seven-year-old Glen slept peacefully. I quietly crawled over the fence and planted the clocks, as if they were Easter eggs, in the branches of the hedge and in the flower beds—and the last one right under Don's cot.

The next morning the Chorale met for rehearsal. He didn't say a thing until one of my cohorts asked, "Have any alarming experiences last night, Professor Grant?" By lunchtime the cafeteria was filled with laughter as the story moved from table to table.

My world kept constantly expanding. Conversations on school policy, higher education, tomorrow's biology exam, and last night's basketball game went on side by side. On weekends when the Chorale wasn't traveling, I loaded up my Plymouth coupe and headed for Thousand Oaks to help as part-time youth director at Dean Parker's church. I loved working in the church, but it was different without Louie and Wes and all my friends at Bethany to guide me. I soon found, however, that they'd trained me well, and the challenge of helping the Parkers start a church in a place where few churches ministered confirmed my desire to go on in the field of Christian education by studying under Thelma Bain at Biola.

My decision didn't sit well with my friends at Azusa. Hardly a week went by that someone didn't bring up the topic of my staying until graduation. But my determination never wavered. I wanted to be the best that I could be, and that meant going to a school that offered a Christian education major.

My first semester at Azusa flew by. As finals approached I realized that I should transfer to Biola after Christmas break, but the opportunity to coach for another term and finish the classes that were full-year courses appealed to me, too. After a visit to Thelma Bain, I determined to complete one full year at Azusa before I moved on to Biola. It would be easier to transfer at the beginning of a year rather than between terms, anyway. For the time being, Azusa offered me everything I could want.

Every Monday, Wednesday, and Friday the student body crowded into the small chapel. Wednesday was missions day, and often Dr. Haggard, Azusa's president, spoke, his passion for reaching people never wavering. He helped us to remember that the world was much bigger than our campus.

I remember one Wednesday service vividly. Perched in my regular seat near the front, I waited through the daily announcements to hear the president preach. Dr. Haggard stood behind the wooden pulpit and spoke with his characteristic fervor. "You've all heard about mission needs and ministries around the globe, but we have foreign mission opportunities here in our own backyard. Thousands of migrant workers live in tents just miles from the university. Mexico is less than four hours from here. You, as students, can do much to help the needs of people nearby. What are you going to do?"

His sermon struck me in a tender spot. I knew exactly what

he was talking about; all the feelings that had gone into my short-lived decision to return to Mexico as a missionary came rushing back. He was so right. We, as students, could do a lot. I knew God hadn't put the desire to minister in my heart to wait until I had a degree behind my name. As soon as he concluded I hurried from chapel to the cafeteria for the job on the serving line I'd taken to help meet expenses. As I poured milk and the students filed by, I asked, "What did you think of chapel?"

"Oh, it was a typical Haggard chapel." "Who knows? I wasn't paying attention."

Finally, Jim Hosclaw, a junior biblical literature major, met my gaze when I asked him. "It got to you, too? I can't get Dr. Haggard's challenge out of my mind. Tell me what you thought, Carolyn," he said as he headed toward the end of the food line.

"Save me a seat. I'll come eat with you."

As soon as I could find a replacement to pour milk, I grabbed a tray and sat down next to Jim. Between the two of us we felt we could conquer the world! Three weeks later we made a trip to scout out mission opportunities within a four-hour radius. Back on campus we had more dreams than hours in the semester. After one chapel service sharing the plans for ministry, training was under way.

Within weeks thirty-five others joined Jim and me in a car caravan headed to the migrant camps near Indio, California, during the first week of Christmas break. We came back knowing Dr. Haggard's prophetic message was right; there were incredible needs just minutes away from the campus. A multimedia presentation we gave on our return to Azusa portrayed the grateful faces of the people we had seen and the extent of their need for love and help. The rest of the campus community was inspired. By second semester we had over fifty readying for Mexico. My life became a whirlwind of exciting ministry.

A committed core group of students emerged who wanted to do something regularly for our neighborhood. We knew local youth-gang violence had been erupting throughout the Azusa, La Puente, and Buena Park communities. Someone suggested a "Teen Pub," and when a Catholic church in a densely populated Hispanic neighborhood only two miles from the campus offered us their parish hall, we jumped at the chance, offering Ping-Pong, pool, table games, refreshments, and a place for the local teens to play "their music" at any volume level they chose.

On opening night we collected knives, razor blades, and drugs at the door. For the first time, members of rival gangs hung out, wary but unarmed, in the same room. Nearly two hundred tough teens, most bearing some gang insignia either tattooed on an arm or sewed onto their jacket, filled the room to capacity.

The guys cued up at the pool table like pros, thriving on the competition; the girls hung back, waiting to be noticed. The ratted hair styles and tight miniskirts were their weapons to entice the guys away from the games. As the kids stood around the room and talked, the sameness of their dress and their nervous glances around showed they were just kids looking for an identity, no matter how tough they seemed.

I often watched the girls, my heart filled with compassion. I wanted to sit each one down alone and say, "You don't have to fight; you don't have to prove anything. I know how you feel, and I know what can change your life." The hardness kept most of them at a distance; only a few ever stayed long enough to trust the friendship that we offered. I could see myself in them. No matter how hard the girls tried to shock me with their drinking or sexual exploits they couldn't tell me anything that I hadn't seen during my high school years in Oregon.

Sometimes the other student volunteers asked me why I was able to relate so well. Begging off with an excuse or changing the subject, I never told them anything about my past or my family, neither of which I considered important to my life at Azusa.

As often as possible, I still headed toward Downey and Al Johnson's church to work on plans for the next YUGO trip. Our new Azusa group was joining the larger program over Easter break. As the time approached I felt excitement at the Mexico trip, but also a strong sadness over the end of the school year that was rapidly approaching. My determination to go to Biola remained unchanged. As the dorms emptied during Easter week, I found myself teary-eyed as my friends raced off for a long break. If it was this hard to say good-bye for a couple of weeks, what was it going to be like at the end of the year?

When it came time for one of the choir buses to leave on tour, I found myself fighting back tears. My attachment had grown even stronger than I imagined. Three of the faculty stood with me in the crowd of well-wishers waving as the loaded bus filled with scores of my excited classmates pulled away down Citrus Avenue.

Don Grant, Glen Adams, and Malcolm Robertson, came up beside me. "Well, Carolyn," Don said, "are you still going to leave us at the end of this semester?"

"I don't know, Malcolm. It's really hard, especially at times like this. I just feel strongly that I am supposed to train under Thelma Bain. I haven't figured all of this out yet."

Don looked at me, "Carolyn, you're going to be in Mexico this week. Why don't you commit the next few days to pray about that one decision. Talk to us when you return."

"And listen," Malcolm assured me, "if God wants you at Biola that's where we want you too."

"I really appreciate that," I said as I looked into the faces of these very special men. "I'll talk to you all when I get back."

That night the endless last-minute details for the Mexico trip sent me to meet with the other leaders at Al's house. I was never happier. My friends at Azusa were behind me no matter what decision I made about Biola, and we were taking a whole bunch of Azusa students to Mexico tomorrow! The excitement in the room was almost tangible. Even after all the others had completed their final plans, I remained, charting out the sleeping arrangements on a ream of scattered sheets.

Al walked over and inspected my work.

"You're an organizational wonder, Carolyn. Don't know what I'd do without you."

Al complimented me a lot, but this time his tone of voice didn't match what he said. I looked up from the table and saw obvious pain written across his face. He was even-tempered and optimistic no matter how complicated things got. Something was up.

He sat down across from me and straightened my papers into a neat pile before he spoke. "You've never told me much about your past."

I sat straight up in my chair and crossed my arms defensively. Expecting to hear about some big problem with the finances of the trip, or some advice about what college to go to, I was taken completely off guard by his question. I felt almost as if someone had just knocked all the air out of me.

He went on. "It just dawned on me that I have never heard you talk about your parents, your mom, anything like that."

"Why? What does that have to do with anything that we're doing?" I retorted.

"Nothing, really. But I need to tell you what happened today."

Wishing I could stop him from telling me, but knowing him well enough to know he'd tell me whatever it was anyway, I sheepishly conceded. "Okay, tell me."

"Your mom called me at the church today. She talked to the pastor before she was transferred to me."

I felt the color drain from my face and gripped my hands tightly together so they wouldn't shake. "How did she know where to find me?"

"I don't know that, Carolyn. She wanted to know if we knew you. And, of course, we said we did. After she identified herself as your mom, she called you all sorts of things I don't want to repeat."

"Tell me what she said, Al," I said, feeling frantic and afraid. The pain, oh, the pain that coursed through my heart as he hesitantly reconstructed her tirade. He scooted his chair close to mine and held me supportively by the shoulders as he spoke.

"She was really out of control and said we shouldn't have anything to do with you—that we should kick you out of the church because you never belonged there and never would. Are you sure you want me to repeat exactly what she said, Carolyn?"

I knew Al was trying to ease the pain, but I nodded, knowing I had to know what to expect if she or Dad had got drunk and planned something crazy.

"She called you a no-good son of a b———; she said that you were no good. In fact, she actually said that you were trash and we had no business letting you into the church! I'm sorry, Carolyn, I wish I didn't have to tell you this."

I held my head in my hands, tightly squeezing my ears, hoping my mother's voice would disappear. I could just hear her—see her—screaming into the phone. Al peeled my hands away. "Listen, Carolyn, I've already talked to the pastor. We know you and can see what God is doing in your life. What your mother said doesn't make any difference to anything. I just felt I had to let you know what she's doing. The pastor heard that she's called other people before this."

"What will she do next?" I groaned, devastated. I thought I'd kept my whereabouts hidden from anyone she might ever happen to talk to. Why did she have to announce to the whole world how much she hated me? Why did she want to hurt me? Hadn't she done that enough already? Why was she so intent on ruining my life? Just because she'd ruined her own? And why now? Everything had been so perfect, why now? Now that she knew where I was, would she tell my dad? What if he got crazy enough to come after me with his gun and finally get rid of me forever?

Al shook me gently, breaking into my anguish. "What are you thinking, Carolyn? Tell me."

I couldn't look at him.

"Carolyn, please."

I turned and said, my voice devoid of emotion but my heart seared with pain, "I'm wondering if my parents will always be an albatross around my neck."

The Outcast

Mexico charmed and invigorated me as ever. Al and I didn't talk anymore about my past, and everybody ministered with every ounce of energy they had. With each move to a new village, the presence of God seemed stronger. On the last night, the high school and college kids all stood to tell what an impact the week had made on their lives. As many testified, I smiled a bit; God had been talking to me too. It was as if he'd been telling me to stay at Azusa. After months of having God work with me about Biola, I now knew loud and clear what I was supposed to do.

Driving back from Mexico to the campus I thought about my changed decision. This choice reminded me of the beginning of the year, when I quickly chose Azusa over Mexico, a decision that was to influence my entire life. It didn't make much sense, but I felt a settled peace at the thought of staying where I was for the time being.

Our bus arrived just after the choir bus returned, and many people were already milling around campus excitedly retelling their experiences of the week. Malcolm, Glen, and Don stood by the baseball diamond watching our team play. One of them spotted me and called out, and I practically ran over to greet them.

"Well, did you pray about it?" Glen asked.

"I sure did."

"So . . . what's your answer?" Don said with eager anticipation. Malcolm just stood back and smiled.

I looked into their faces. "You're not going to believe this.

In fact, I hardly believe it myself, but I spent the whole week praying about next year, and I feel that God wants me to stay here. That doesn't make sense, because I want to learn from Thelma Bain, but I really have a tremendous sense of peace and knowledge that God wants me here."

As Don and Glen whooped with joy, Malcolm, confidently standing there with his arms crossed, said, "Carolyn, I want you to come to my office tomorrow at ten. I'd like to talk with you."

At 10:00 A.M. sharp I stuck my head in the office of the dean of instruction and found Malcolm waiting. "Hello, Carolyn, have a seat. I want you to know that I prayed for you all this week while you were away. I've been thinking about something all year, but I've felt I needed to wait to talk to you about it until you decided what God had ahead for you. It was important to me that your decision to leave or stay at Azusa was made purely through God's guidance."

I sat perched on the edge of my chair, deeply moved by Malcolm's compassion and prayers.

"Now that you've decided to stay, I have an offer to make that I've already talked over with the president. Carolyn, we want you to stay here at Azusa and finish your bachelor's degree. While you are still a student, we want you to keep teaching physical education just as you have been doing, because we feel you're doing an outstanding job. When you graduate we're prepared to send you to the graduate school of your choosing, anywhere in the country, so that you can earn your master's degree; then we want you to join our full-time faculty in Christian education."

I thought I must be dreaming! Here I was finishing up my first year at Azusa, a place I'd never even heard of nine months ago! And now they offered me a professional teaching position. I thanked Malcolm profusely and ran toward Don's office in a daze.

I stood quietly at the door until Don looked up. He smiled widely, "It's 10:30, Malcolm must've talked to you."

"You won't believe this," I started in.

Don interrupted me midsentence. "Let me guess, he offered you a full-time teaching position."

"How did you know? Isn't that great?" I literally bounced up and down with joy.

The puzzle pieces of God's leading began to fall into place. The only thing that didn't fit was my desire to train under Thelma Bain, a highly respected woman educator. Maybe I could still go and take an extra class with her next year. But I was awed that the leaders at Azusa, my friends, believed in me without ever asking where I had come from or what I was like before they met me. They evaluated me for what I was today. Honored and infinitely moved, I simply had to marvel at God's hand in my life.

One month later, I received a personal note from Thelma Bain announcing her resignation. At fifty-eight years of age she had decided to marry for the first time. She wouldn't be teaching in the field of Christian education again.

What a miracle. God knew all along that Thelma wouldn't be teaching again. Even if I had transferred to Biola I wouldn't have had one single class from her. God took care of me and gave me a supportive Azusa family like none I'd ever had before.

I plunged into my classes with increased vigor knowing that I was truly a part of what Azusa Pacific University was now and would be in the future. I thrived on the activity and challenge of the college—it was my life. Rarely did I even think about my own family or my past. I didn't have either the time or the desire.

Once in a while one of my friends would push to learn more about my childhood, but rarely did I have to do more than change the subject. My reluctance to share the pain of my past was heightened by what I termed "the poor-me syndrome." Too many kids fell into the pattern of feeling sorry about what they didn't have growing up. "My family didn't have this" or "My father was never home." Each time I heard the complaints I had to hold my tongue. I so wanted to blurt out, "You don't know what pain is. Have you been betrayed every day of your life by both your parents? Do you know what it's like to never be loved at home? Never!" Not once did I slip, but I buried my past deeper and deeper inside.

Ever since my mother had discovered where I lived, my dad called every few months. All I had to do was say hello, and the insults started: "You worthless, ungrateful b——, who do you think you are?" Each time I heard his angry, drunken, irrational words, a ton of emotional bricks would crash down upon my heart, making me want to run. All I wanted was for them to leave me alone. There was no relationship. There was nothing. I didn't choose them. Every day I worked hard to turn my life around, putting the bad behind and building the good into my life.

Three fun-filled, ministry-oriented years at Azusa culminated in my graduating with a high grade-point average, but it was the one thousand people who had gone with us to Mexico during my senior year that I considered my finest achievement. The young coed who could only read at an eighth-grade level five years ago walked across the platform to receive a diploma and plaque as a member of that year's "Who's Who Among College Students in America."

Azusa asked me to stay on the faculty as director of the Christian Service Department while I pursued my master's degree in religion and theology at Point Loma Nazarene College graduate program.

On the first day, I took Greek with a classroom full of men.

The tapes of insecurity I thought I'd erased played louder than ever in my head. "Carolyn can't read. She can't learn Greek. She will never pass a theology course." Starting all over, but this time sure that I could do it, I gave my classes all I had. It paid off.

Between classes and studies, my new job at Azusa let me do what I loved most—help kids help people in need. During my first year the hippie movement and antiestablishment mentality swept university campuses across America. While the culture at large tried to deny the radical shift, hoping the counterculture would go away, Azusa students rallied to the challenge and weekly headed to the communes springing up throughout Southern California to share our faith, friendship, and some food, when we could provide it. We encountered drug-frenzied satanists and gun-toting Hell's Angels, but we thrived at the front lines of ministry and education at the same time.

I entered the classroom as a Christian education professor at Azusa after completing my master's degree. Moving into the academic classroom after teaching P.E. for a few years sent my tapes reeling once again. "Who are you fooling, Carolyn? P.E. is one thing, but you, teach religion?" I had to thank God daily for bringing me this far, reminding myself that I would be able to do anything he wanted me to do.

After just a few week in the classroom I realized that there was still much I wanted to learn about Christian education, so I enrolled in Talbot Theological Seminary. I announced my decision one day in the faculty lunch room as we sat casually around the table.

"You don't want to go to seminary," one of my male colleagues blurted out.

"Why do you say that? I'm serious about this."

He didn't answer but other voices began to join in. "Don't

go to seminary. You'll regret it later." They all seemed to agree.

Finally someone had the courage to tell me why not. "Who will want to marry a woman with a seminary education?"

I laughed uproariously, "Is that all you can think about? Why would I want to marry anyone who didn't want me to have the best education I can get?" None of their arguments made any sense to me. I felt confident in my need to be as prepared as possible to teach Christian education and equip young people for full-time ministry in the church. And I felt secure about being a woman. I knew the remarks really came from my peers' desire that I have the best, but it wasn't as if my education had kept my man out of my life this far!

Bill, my high school boyfriend, had wanted to marry me, but I wasn't ready. Then I'd dated Dick, a tall, good-looking guy at Azusa, while I worked on my first master's degree. He soon called our dating "going steady," and just as I was getting used to spending time with him, he began talking about marriage.

The faculty room discussion brought back memories of the night that Dick and I broke up, both of us in tears. We really loved each other. After dinner one evening, he told me he'd found in me the one he wanted to spend the rest of his life with. He then went on to describe what he wanted in a wife.

"Carolyn, I want you to be my wife. I want you to quit teaching here at Azusa. It's okay if you teach part-time, or at an elementary school. I really don't want you to work at all. All I want is for you to be my wife and raise our children."

The inner resistance I felt that night taught me that I didn't have the gift to focus my life exclusively around a brood of kids and a husband. There were so many exciting areas of ministry I wanted to explore. The Lord had absolutely transformed my life, and I wanted to spend the rest of my life serving him.

I did desperately want to be loved and cared for, and I felt I had deep devotion and love to give to a future husband, but I saw myself being able to function best within a mutual ministry with my life's partner. I'd wait for God's best in my life. I was unwilling to quell the expanding call to ministry I felt to alleviate the sometimes lonely wait for a mate who understood and shared my calling.

Dick and I agonized long and hard before we parted. I couldn't stop being who God wanted me to be. God had reached into my life for a reason; now I was committed to serve in whatever way he planned so that I could be available to others the way Jean Fonner and Louie had been to me. I could withstand the pain of whatever it cost me to remain steadfast in my plans. So despite protests and advice from my faculty peers concerned about my marital status, I headed toward seminary.

The day classes started, I headed to Talbot early to orient myself to the campus. As I was standing in Meyers Hall, trying to decipher the room directory, a thirty-year-old man with twinkling eyes walked out of his office and headed toward me. "You're Carolyn Koons, aren't you?"

I looked down, trying to remember if they'd given me a name tag at the registration desk.

The man laughed, "I'm Norm Wright. You're going to be in my class. I heard that you were coming. Why don't you make an appointment to talk to me sometime? I'd like to hear about what you're doing at Azusa."

Norm became an energetic model teacher for me. He made us experience every aspect of the theory he lectured on. I found myself on overnight survival camping trips, in family counseling sessions, and in church settings working with local pastors.

Job offers from a number of churches tempted me to leave seminary and the college. Louie Files and Wes Harty had taught me to love church work, but I intuitively believed seminary could teach me what I couldn't learn elsewhere. I just wished I were five people, there was so much I wanted to do.

After two years in the Christian Education Department at Azusa, I received the highest honor in my life. Along with four other faculty members, I was named Outstanding Educator in America. Azusa had taken a real chance on me, an unknown person who had just showed up one day. My world just kept getting bigger and better.

I began to feel as though my parents didn't exist. A full year passed without a phone call from my father. Maybe they were getting over their projected anger at me. Maybe they were getting on with their own lives. I felt at peace.

Then the news came that Grandpa Goodson had died. It had never occurred to me before that he was anything but eternal. His gentle spirit and kindness had served as a watershed for me when there had been nothing in my life but rejection.

I could only imagine the heartbreak that uncomplaining man had felt as he watched two of his sons drink themselves into early graves. I wondered if he knew that his kids had all been waiting for this day so they could get their hands on his money.

Running from the pain my parents caused had not allowed me to stay in close contact with Grandpa, and now that he was gone I felt a tremendous loss. I'd never told him about my faith—that increased my grief. Should I go to the funeral? The decision sent me into a tailspin. My great grief at not knowing him as I had wanted to finally overruled my dread of facing my parents again. I wasn't sure how much any of the other family members had cared about him, so maybe, even though it made no sense, my presence at his funeral would let him know I'd always loved him.

Carefully dressed in a dark suit, I nervously drove to the memorial hall. I hadn't laid eyes on any of my family in nearly five years—maybe even longer since I'd seen Gary. The last time we all were together I'd been a high school kid. Now I was a thirty-two-year-old professor with two graduate degrees nearly behind me. But none of that mattered—to them I'd always be the outcast. Even I didn't know which was really me.

As I walked up the sidewalk to the funeral, I spotted Clifford on the steps. His personable charm showed right away, "I'm glad you came. Come and sit with Madilyn and me." He guided me around to a side door where the relatives were assembling.

Clifford's easy banter made me realize how relieved I was to not have to face the family alone. Outwardly I tried to appear a mature, educated, composed woman, but I felt like a misfit, an insecure little girl who didn't know what to say, where to sit, or how to act. I could organize and inspire thousands in Mexico or lecture for hours at the university, but I couldn't figure out how to act around my family.

We entered a small side area with metal chairs lined up neatly in rows. My mother sat in the front row with Gary one empty chair away. Madilyn was behind them. After fumbling through a strained greeting with my mother I headed toward the second row. Madilyn, always warm and understanding, patted my shoulder and gave me a reassuring hug. "Good to see you again." Her sparkling eyes confirmed her genuine welcome.

The organ music began softly. A few people mingled

around the casket arranging flowers or lighting a candle in Grandpa's behalf. I couldn't relax, even though my father was nowhere to be seen.

The side door flew open. He barged in and made a beeline for my mom, slowing only to turn and sit down beside her. Even from a few feet away I could smell the liquor. He reeked. As he was halfway into his chair, my presence registered in the rage exploding on his face as he flushed bright red. He stood up and towered over his chair, just inches away from me. Every inch of him exuded hatred. "You God-d——b——. What are you doing here? You don't belong here." He ranted uncontrollably at the top of his lungs. My eyes were riveted on his, but I heard the astonished gasps and felt everyone shrink back in fear all around me.

My mother grabbed his arm grimacing, "Sit down, Cliff," and Gary stood and put both hands on his other shoulder, shoving him down. The organist mercifully played louder. Clifford stroked my arm, as tears streamed down my face. I didn't know what to do. Maybe I should walk out. Instead I remained, paralyzed in shock.

"It's okay, Carolyn, just ignore him. Stay here beside me. You'll be okay," Clifford whispered, just as Dad wrestled free from Gary's grasp and turned around in his chair. "You aren't one of us. You don't belong here. Get out." The foul accusations flew again. Gary, too embarrassed to be gentle, roughly jerked him around.

The black-robed minister began the invocation, but I didn't hear any of the service. Tears gushed down my face and I was convulsed in silent sobs. A dark cloud of pain descended on me. It was all I could do to refrain from screaming at him, "I didn't come here to see you. I just wanted to show my grandfather that I loved him. All you ever wanted was his money! All you ever do is hurt me. Will you never stop until you see me dead? Is that what you want?"

The service ended, but my tears had just begun. At thirty-two years of age, I cried all the way home. Would that man ever stop hating me?

The Touch

In the days after my grandfather's funeral, the intense pain I felt forced me to once again sever all connections with my family. My people-filled life at Azusa sometimes felt like a new family where I could grow up all over again in a home where people saw enough potential in me to put up with my immaturities and stubborn attitudes. I flourished on the outpouring of love and affirmation.

Still, each time my parents unexpectedly broke into the present, an emotional club bludgeoned my self-esteem. When I'd picture my father, I'd see myself through his eyes and feel worthless. My memories were like quicksand—with the first horrible thought, the rest would pull me downward.

My father's enraged face haunted my dreams. In recurring nightmares he chased me, brandishing that same black, loaded .38-caliber handgun. He'd come into my classroom and cry out in a frenzy, "This time I'm going to do it. I'm going to kill you." When he had me trapped against the chalkboard, he'd grin delightedly at my students, turn to point the gun at me, and squeeze off one fatal shot point blank into my head.

And now, finally, one spring day my dream was coming true. He called Azusa and left a message with Elsie at the switchboard. "Tell Carolyn that her dad called and that I'm on my way, and this time it's for good."

How well I understood his message! He was on his way to kill me. At first I ran in panic but then I stopped—there was no way I would spend any more of my life fleeing from him. That night, alone, I held a deathwatch in my own home. In my mind, he was just outside, waiting for me to let down my guard—pow, with one shot it'd all be over.

Springing up from the rocking chair, I gasped—startled awake by the ringing telephone. The hands on the clock pointed to 5:30 A.M. Who would call me at this time of the morning? What if it was my father? Should I answer it at all? What if it was someone trying to warn me of danger ahead?

"Hello?"

"Hi, Carolyn, this is Madilyn."

I shrank back against the kitchen wall in relief, sliding down to sit on the tiled floor. "Oh, Madilyn, it's so good to hear your voice."

"I'm sorry to call you at this hour, but it's your dad."

A wail, like the final cry from a wounded animal, escaped my lips, and the receiver shook until I clenched both hands firmly around it.

"Carolyn, are you okay?"

"Yes," *I assured her quietly, my voice quavering.* "What's up, Madilyn?"

"Your dad is in the hospital; he's had a stroke."

"When?"

"Apparently he made a phone call after he finished his shift yesterday at work, got in his car, and peeled away. He suffered a stroke at a stoplight about a mile away. Another driver saw him slump down and pulled over to check on him before calling an ambulance. It looks as though he'll be out of commission for a while."

"Thanks for letting me know, Madilyn."

"You bet, and, oh, there's something else."

"What's that?"

"Clifford and I don't think you should come to the hospital."

"Don't worry about that. I won't come anywhere near the hospital."

"Take care of yourself, Carolyn, okay?"

"You too. Give Clifford a hug for me."

"Sure thing. 'Bye."

"Good-bye."

I hugged the receiver tightly to my chest, the full message sinking in only as I heard the dial tone buzz. I was safe. Tonight I was not going to die. God was truly watching over me.

That was the last I heard from any of my family for a long time. But facing the immediate threat of my father hunting me down had reopened scars I thought had healed completely. Each time someone tried to befriend me at Azusa and make me a part of an extended family, I would balk. No group of people could get too close to me. The depth of anguish, unknown even to me, kept me overtly friendly but emotionally distanced from all but the most persistent—like Lillian, one of my classmates.

Mexican by heritage, Lillian's contagious warmth and hospitality made her mother, sister, and confidant to many, including me, at Azusa. Her flashing dark eyes and Latin exuberance could cajole even the most reluctant into an impromptu family.

Steve Peters was one who became a true brother through her friendship. A pastor's son from a small community in the Mother Lode country, Steve, even as a student, was one of the most dynamic chapel speakers on campus. He and the others from Twain Harte talked constantly about their home in the Sierra foothills as if it were a wilderness Shangri-la. Carloads of students traveled the four hundred miles, only to return enthusiastic converts. Lillian was no exception.

The Twain Harte community church, Chapel in the Pines, sent a group down to participate in one of our Christmas Teen Pub programs, and after that, still somewhat hesitant, I agreed to spend the weekend at the Peterses' home.

Lillian and I packed the car and drove up Highway 5 through the San Joaquin valley and through the beautiful countryside leading to Twain Harte, a town of one short block tucked into a pine-covered mountainside. The men seemed uniformed in blue jeans and flannel shirts. The importance of hard work and fresh air pervaded talk in the community.

Chapel in the Pines, a tall, redwood structure complete with bell tower, was surrounded by towering trees. The parsonage next door served more as a foyer than a private home.

Pastor Russ Peters met us at the door when we arrived. Everything about him reflected his disciplined, mature nature. Tanned and lean, he jogged a couple of miles each day, ate only nutritious foods, and spent a daily hour alone in prayer in addition to any sermon or lesson planning. He padded quietly around the house, but his presence pervaded it. When he did speak, whatever he said was worth listening to.

Alva Peters was the gregarious one. A natural mother-figure to all, she loved her ever-expanding brood. There wasn't a person who walked through the door of Chapel of the Pines who didn't immediately become part of the family.

Together, Russ and Alva pioneered the church's ministry in Twain Harte with years of loving care from the inside out. Russ built much of the chapel, using his carpentry and engineering background. The church family flocked to the sanctuary on Sundays, eager for spiritual nourishment.

Even the family feeling that I had experienced at Azusa didn't prepare me for the Peterses, who had four children of their own, most of them grown and with children when I met them, and innumerable foster children—all of whom made up a large extended family.

I found myself holding back from their openness and vulnerability. My trained instincts warned me that these people could probably ferret out my inmost pain—I wasn't ready for that. Part of me craved being part of a real family, but another part felt convinced that a family would never bring anything but more agony—and that part was stronger.

Around the dinner table that very first night the family held a mock election and laughingly told me that the decision was unanimous; they wanted me to become an official part of their family. I found myself rigidly polite. "I don't need a family. How about just being my friends?"

Steve, Lillian, Alva, Russ—all howled in unison at my terse response. Steve feigned shock, "Are you kidding, Carolyn? Don't you know that there are hundreds of people in line desperately waiting to be accepted into this family?"

Alva took up the joke, though she looked at me thoughtfully, "How about a one-year trial basis?"

I sheepishly grinned, embarrassed but enjoying the attention. Yet I still didn't answer. All the other people in the room could go around calling Russ and Alva, Mom and Dad, but I knew I couldn't do that.

"I can't call you Mom and Dad because those aren't positive words for me," I finally admitted.

Russ spoke up quietly, "That's okay. To be a part of our family means to be just who you are. If you want to call us Russ and Alva, that's just fine."

"We'll see," I said noncommittally, pushing my fork into another bite of roast beef and hoping to change the subject.

The banter went on, but I feared what I had got myself into. I loved these people and felt their genuine concern, but I didn't know how I could be around them without letting down my guard.

Lillian and I took many more trips to Twain Harte. It became a respite for me. What I experienced in that church was amazing. The group of three hundred people really tried to meet each other's needs. There weren't any programs. Russ and Alva dealt with people's lives: troubled marriages, unemployment, poverty, alcoholism, incest, suicide. The church people, many of whom had suffered devastating hardships, turned to each other for love. The people of the church tried to love each other's broken pieces back to wholeness.

Alva and Russ took to calling me their "rebel child," an apt description of what I felt. To consider Russ and Alva as my mom and dad brought back too many painful memories of my real parents. I really did love the Peterses, but I didn't need parents.

They kept talking to me about love and healing. And the more they shared their lives, the more I realized the depth of my pain. Obviously, my negative concept of mother and father affected my relationships with people. How else was my past holding me back? Maybe it was even hurting my attitude toward God. How could I trust God in everything? The Peterses, just by loving me, raised so many questions I'd never thought about before! I learned that I experienced my faith through Jesus as God's son rather than through God as Father. Fathers were distant and untouchable, and they brought pain.

Thanksgiving rolled around nearly six months after my first trip to Twain Harte. Accepting the Peterses' invitation to dinner, I joined nearly thirty people, foster children and extended family, as we all piled into the small parsonage to feast. Seated at the laden oblong table, I truly did feel encompassed by a huge, loving family.

After dinner and the dishes Alva and I were standing in the hallway leaning against opposing doors when Russell came whistling in from the church, where he'd been preparing for the evening's service. He smiled and came to join us in the narrow corridor, pausing just a foot from me to lift his arm above his head ready to rest it against the door jam.

Immediately, as I saw his arm go up, I stopped midsentence, drew my hands into fists, and hunched down, my arms raised protectively in front of my face.

Alva and Russ jumped back. What was I doing? Realizing

that I'd reacted as if Russ were my real father, I giggled nervously and straightened up as the blood rushed to my face in embarrassment. "Sorry, it was a reflex response." I looked at Russ, "I thought you were going to hit me. I'm rather used to my dad cornering me. I don't know what came over me."

Russ studied me soberly, "You need prayer for that."

"What do you mean?"

He continued, "I've sensed your need for prayer to heal your past for some time."

"Oh no, Russ, I'm really fine. But thanks."

Alva shook her head, her rosy cheeks flushed with feeling. "Then why did you put your fists up as though Russ were going to hit you?"

She was right and I knew it.

"Let me give you a book," Russ said as he headed toward his study. He returned to hand me a small paperback: *The Gift of Inner Healing,* by Ruth Carter Stapleton.

I accepted the book and left them without another word to retreat behind the bedroom door, where I threw myself across the bed and tried futilely to clear my head. After a few long minutes I ventured outside to the back porch.

Sitting in an old metal lawn chair, I looked at the beauty of the untouched woods. What I saw with my eyes didn't match the state of my heart. Something was throbbing painfully inside me. For the first time I acknowledged that I'd have to let go of the pain someday; no matter how hard I'd tried, I'd never really buried my past after all. Even at thirty-three my Christian family and my biological family still kept colliding, keeping me from fully belonging to either. My childhood pain and anger resurfaced more often than ever these days.

Opening the slim book, I began to read as Ruth Carter Stapleton described the inner healing of the Holy Spirit's touch that could erase the deepest causes of my pain. The idea that my pain was not necessarily a result of my own sin, but that of my parents, struck home.

That was it. For years I'd been suffering under someone else's sin and anger. My mother had vividly taught me that my father hated me. In some perverse way she loved to shove his anger at me by making me live in constant terror of him and his loaded gun.

I knew I needed to be set free from my mother's sin and my father's anger, but up until now I'd thought I'd have to deal with all the pain in one horrible moment, and that, once I began, a raging torrent of anguish would overtake me. I was afraid I'd be left to drown in pain. But as I read more about the process of inner healing, it became clear that what I faced was a day-by-day journey, not unlike my Christian faith: I'd have to choose each day to leave the past behind.

The starting point was to go to the root of the problem, my very earliest memories, and relive them, allowing the Holy Spirit to replace the pain with positive images as I began to see that even at the worst moments I wasn't alone. Since most of my childhood memories were bad ones—I couldn't conjure up even one that made me smile—I warily read on, not sure if I could make this journey and survive. Hope for healing was as frightening as it was encouraging. I had learned how to live with pain, but if I took this journey, I'd have to let go of all my defenses. Was it worth the risk to be free? I truly didn't want to be bound by someone else's anger anymore, but the unknown process ahead had no guarantees. Maybe the pain would lessen—maybe not. I might just stir up a whirlpool of darkness from the past that would suck me back into the emotional tunnel that I knew led to bitterness.

I kept reading, astonished at how each page seemed to describe me. The author told about the tendency to keep people at a distance because of deep-seated fear of yet another betrayal. What my parents had done to me, I'd never allow anyone to do again. Never!

Each time one of the paragraphs made me shift uncomfortably in my chair, I wondered, How else are my memories causing me to be fearful and guarded? Ruth Carter Stapleton kept writing about the lifelong struggle to discover the unconscious blocks caused by unseen pain.

The sun slipped down into early evening as I devoured her words. In the twilight I strained to continue, until one statement nearly jumped off the page. "Forgiveness lies at the heart of all inner healing."

Why should I forgive? I didn't deserve all this pain! I didn't even know if I felt hatred and anger or just plain pity for my father, a man in bondage to anger and violence. I did know that I wanted to stay as far away as I could from him, because each time he came close he inflicted pain. But forgive him? I wanted to get rid of him and keep him out of my life, not forgive him.

That night I read snuggled in my bed until I finished the book. I knew I needed to begin right then to walk back through my past, but the process terrified me. I lay awake for a long time tracing the pattern of the wallpaper on the ceiling with my eyes as my mind held the fortress walls tight. None of my memories escaped to haunt me as I slept.

On Sunday Alva asked two of her friends to come over and pray for me. As the four of us gathered in the parsonage study I prayed that I'd just be able to make it through the next hour. Unused to this much vulnerability, I tried to just accept the prayers in gratitude, but it was hard. These wonderful women had such faith and such commitment to prayer. Encircled, I listened closely as they asked God to give me the strength to open up and let the Holy Spirit heal me. How I needed their prayers! The depth of the Spirit's presence touched me deeply.

Late that night I drove alone over the many miles from Twain Harte to my home, carefully watching the curving roads for oncoming traffic. Doubt threatened to overtake my earlier hope. Maybe I should wait for a few days and think about this inner healing business to make sure that I wasn't heading into some emotional trap. I didn't want to start something that I couldn't handle. What was the use of delving back through all my memories unless I knew the process was going to work?

That whole week I kept rereading sections of the book when I was home after work, hoping there would be some promise that I'd missed the first time, something proving that it would be worth the trek back to the past. Nothing assuaged my fear; there was a definite risk.

I woke up on Saturday morning to a day of no commitments. Barefoot, I padded into the empty living room of the spacious three-bedroom condominium I'd just purchased. Unable to afford to furnish it completely, I'd carpeted the whole place and filled the kitchen, family room, and master bedroom with comfortable furniture; the rest of the house was practically bare.

Sunshine poured into the picture window in the front room and glistened off the chrome on my well-worn turntable. An old chair, ready for donation to Goodwill, sat in the corner by the window bathed in warm sunshine. Retrieving my Bible and Stapleton's book from the bedside table, I settled into the old chair.

"Lord, I'm ready," I prayed aloud in a whisper. "I don't know where this is going to take me, but I'm ready. We can go back to the beginning now."

I leaned back and let my mind flow freely. The years flashed by in a jumble until I focused in on my earliest memory. I was just four years old and living in Montana with my mom and brothers while Dad was away at war.

One night Gary and I, sent to bed early, were supposed to be sleeping but instead were playing catch with his robe across the room, tossing it from my single bed to his. When we heard Mom's footsteps in the hall, we quickly burrowed under the covers and forced our breathing to be even and deep. She tiptoed to my bed and carefully peered into my face before turning off the bedside lamp and softly closing the door. Shadows darted in through the window in the darkness. I hated the dark; it was so hard to breathe right when I couldn't see.

"Gary!" I whispered, "Gary." He was asleep.

I listened carefully to the voices I heard out in the kitchen until the murmuring stopped and the front door clicked open and then shut. The car engine rumbled and then leveled off as the car was backed away from the curb.

My heart raced in panic as I lay terrified in my bed. They wouldn't just leave us here! Flinging back my blankets, I shuffled into the dark hallway. No one was in the bedroom or the living room. The porch light by the back door cast a dim glow around the kitchen. Empty. We were alone.

I ran back to our room and stretched to my full height to flip on the light switch, but Gary didn't stir. Jumping on his bed, I shook him. "Wake up, Gary. Wake up!"

"What do you want?" He muttered grumpily and rolled over, turning his face away from me.

"Mom and Clifford left. Where'd they go?"

"Maybe the bar? Are we alone?" His eyes began to widen as he rubbed them, reluctant to waken.

"I don't wanna stay here. I'm scared!" I replied, avoiding his question.

"We can't go anyplace. It's dark out," Gary reasoned and snuggled deeper into his warm bed.

I began to cry. "I don't wanna be in this house! I wanna find Mommy."

Gary sat up and looked out the window into the dark night. He hesitated, and I tugged on his arm.

"Okay," he reluctantly agreed and pushed me away, "get dressed."

He scrambled for his jeans, and I tried to follow his lead, but the sash on my robe wouldn't budge. Slumping to the floor, I yanked harder and harder, tears flowing freely as I choked back the big sobs rising in my throat.

"Quit crying, I'll help you," Gary promised. I stood up and together we pulled.

"I'll get a knife," I offered.

"No," he ordered, "we'll get beat again if we cut your clothes. We're just going to have to stay here."

"No, no, no, no!" I wailed.

"Then wear your robe," he concluded disgustedly.

"Then wear yours, too," I pouted defiantly at my brother. Surprisingly, he obeyed. It was then, I knew that he was frightened too. He didn't want to stay home alone any more than I did. He pulled his blue robe over his pyjama top and jeans and grabbed my hand, "c'mon."

At the end of the sidewalk the houses on our block were just silhouettes against the starlit sky. Standing in front of our house, I wiped my tears on the sleeve of my robe while Gary surveyed the distance to the twinkling lights of town that lay to the east.

"We can't walk on the road like this," he motioned at our clothes, "let's take the shortcut."

Without replying I followed him across the street and down a dirt path that led to the top of a grassy knoll. The railroad yard lay quietly before us illuminated by the night sky. The big black trains rested on crisscrossing tracks. Gary again grabbed my hand, and we scurried *down the knoll and stumbled over one track rail, then another. I hoisted my robe with one hand so that my toddler-length legs could lift high enough not to trip. Each time I lurched forward, ready to fall, Gary balanced me with a short tug on my other hand.*

We passed the center tracks where the trains scheduled for early-morning departure waited. Gary pulled me behind the caboose of the closest train. "Follow me, like this," he crouched carefully, and, imitating him, I slowly moved from car to car hesitating in between each long enough to peer across to the other side of the train.

"Gary?" I whispered loudly.

"Shhhh," he pointed through the gap between the cars where several ragged men huddled around a small fire. My eyes grew larger, terrified. I took the next steps gingerly, trying to keep the gravel from crunching under my feet.

Finally Gary whispered, "Run," and I raced around the train station that bordered the edge of downtown. Panting, I glanced back over my shoulder at the railroad yard and shivered, glad to turn back to the neon lights that announced the open bars on Main Street.

"Hold my robe," Gary said as he slipped it off and walked into the first bar. I huddled in the doorway while he checked. We repeated this scene up one side of the street and down the other.

Gary entered the last bar, where a tall wooden counter could be seen from the street. "How old are you, kid?" I heard a deep voice ask Gary after the door swung closed. He didn't answer. "I said, how old are you?" The voice was gruff this time.

"Twelve," Gary lied, then banged through the door and ran down the street. When I caught up I chastised him. "You're not twelve! You're six." He'd just had his birthday.

"I know." He didn't say any more but started scouting the parking lots up and down the street. His head hung down in consternation. He sighed, then stopped walking. "The late show," he breathed excitedly, "we haven't checked there!" We ran one block farther to the theater.

"The car!" I spotted it first. We literally threw ourselves on the hood. Such comfort we found in hugging that old car! Gary slid his hand across the broad side of it and tried the door on the driver's side. "It's open."

I ran to his side, and we both jumped in and curled up on the front seat. After a few long minutes, I dared lift my head to peer out the front window and watch for Mom and Clifford. I heard the town clock chime, but not knowing how to count, I just knew it rang many times. I lay back down and dozed off.

"Jump in the back, hurry!" Gary poked me hard in the back, "the show's over."

Half-asleep, we huddled on the floor in the backseat as we heard voices approach the car. Mom and a strange man slipped into the front seat. The man reached back to unlock the door for Clifford.

"What's this back here?" the man asked as he touched my head.

"Don't," I retorted.

"Carolyn!" my mother gasped. She whirled around and flailed away in the darkness leveling blows on both Gary and me. She wasn't in the least glad to see us.

As I remembered back nearly three decades, I was still terrified as I walked again over those dark railroad tracks. I realized that even my first memory from early childhood taught me that I was unloved and abandoned. I imagined Jesus walking with me holding my hand. I heard him say to me, "I'm going to heal that memory for you." Then he and I walked near the theater and stood at a distance watching my mother swear and pummel Gary and me in the car. Jesus, in my mind, took a jug full of healing water, and poured it over the entire scene. He then swept his healing hand over the entire memory. I felt as if the whole event, my first memory of abandonment and terror, had been wrapped up in a small package that I could actually hand over to Jesus. He lifted the memory up to heaven, and the pain left.

We walked to the next memory and the next. Once again I was cowering on the hard piano bench in the moving van as my father hit me with his powerful fists again and again. As tears rolled down my cheeks Jesus sat down next to me and protected me from the blows. I relived the rejection I felt when all the others could sleep and laugh freely while I remained isolated and fearful, trying not to breathe or move and hoping my dad wouldn't beat me again.

Then I came to a memory that had only been a vague, fuzzy recollection for many years. After years of counting only five members in the family: Mom, Dad, Clifford, Gary, and me, I remembered my baby brother.

My arms ached as I lifted the heavy roller off the neatly pressed handkerchiefs. Most afternoons I helped Mom in our dry cleaning business in downtown Livingston. At first it had been fun to iron sheets, but soon I tired of the drudgery. Today Mom hollered at me to stop early, we were closing the shop so that she'd have time to fix a special dinner—Dad was home from the army.

She wrapped the new baby snugly in a warm blanket and hustled me down the street toward home. Once inside the door she handed me the baby and instructed me to watch him while she cooked and changed clothes. Tottering slightly with the awkward bundle in my five-year-old arms, I carried him to his cradle in the living room.

The wonderful aroma of roast chicken with mashed potatoes wafted through the house, and promptly at 5:30, Clifford, Gary, and I squeezed around our tiny kitchen table hoping Dad would be on time. Fifteen, then twenty, minutes passed, and he didn't come. Mom left us waiting while she went and paced in the living room, swearing and complaining to herself while the baby slept placidly.

Nearly forty minutes after he was expected, Dad staggered in, roaring mad and reeking of whiskey. I quickly resumed my seat in silence. Fuming, Mom piled our plates with cold food and roughly laid

them in front of us. We three kids began devouring the food, oblivious
to the tension in the room.

Before any of us had a chance to shovel more than a few bites of
food into our mouths Mom started in with a sarcastic remark about
Dad's drinking. One remark escalated into a full-fledged fight. Dad's
voice boomed angrily. Before I realized what had happened Mom stood
up and shrieked in fury as Dad picked up his plate and threw it across
the table at her. She ducked just in the nick of time as the plate splatted
against the kitchen counter, spewing food from ceiling to floor. Dad,
in a rage, reached for Gary's plate as Mom headed for the swinging
doors to the living room. I crawled under the table just in time to see
the plate miss Mom by an inch and crash into the doorjamb, breaking
off a piece of the wood and spraying mashed potatoes and gravy with
the broken porcelain. Everyone was screaming and yelling. Clifford
reached from under the table to grab Dad's leg, but with one motion
Dad turned around and smashed him in the face, knocking him across
the room.

Dad scooped up the remaining plates and glasses and rumbled
through the swinging doors pitching them every which way.

"Get the police. Hurry! Call the police!" Mom screamed in panic
as she tried to protect herself behind the overstuffed chair. Clifford
darted out the back door and disappeared into the darkness. Gary and
I ran to the hallway for protection.

We heard glass shattering everywhere. When the crashing stopped
Mom's pleading sobs began as Dad started in with his fists. She kicked
and screamed like a wild animal, but Dad's fierce anger was too much
for her. Finally her screams turned to moans, and Dad barreled
through the swinging doors to the kitchen. I jumped quickly to the far
end of the hallway in fear that he might see me and start in on a second
victim. But instead he stormed out the back door.

Only moments later we heard sirens, and Mom struggled to the
front door as several policemen arrived with Clifford. Two sped out

the back door as soon as Mom pointed in that direction. The other two looked in disbelief at the food-stained walls and furniture.

The two men calmed Mom down and sat her on the couch between them as one opened up his spiral notepad and began writing. As he asked questions, his partner stood up and walked over to the cradle. He looked away in horror before beckoning the other man to come and look too. He too shook his head sadly.

While they took a look around the house, I sneaked unnoticed to the cradle. The baby's eyes were closed, and he was covered with a dark red liquid. I reached down to run my finger along the side of his face, but as soon as I touched him I was horrified. "It's blood! The baby is covered with blood!" Quickly the policeman scooped me up and ran into the kitchen with me under his arm assuring me, "It's not blood; it's jam. It's just red jam!" But before he could shove my hand under the running faucet, I stuck my thumb in my mouth to taste the red stuff. It wasn't jam.

I never saw my baby brother again. The policemen left, and the others brought Dad home the next morning. It took me weeks to work up the courage to ask my mom what had happened to my baby brother. She said he died of a cleft palate. No one ever mentioned the baby again.

Recalling the horror I had felt as a little girl at seeing my baby brother's lifeless face made me queasy even after all these years. But Jesus walked with me into the rage-filled living room, and together we prayed over that pain. He tenderly held my nearly forgotten baby brother and the entire chaotic memory up in his hands. I helped him throw the entire bundle up to heaven.

As my memory kept pouring out the painful past—step by step—Jesus faithfully helped me imagine the scenes anew with his presence pervading the most horrible times. But then we got to the gun. I froze, unable to move in the old chair. I knew the gun was next. I'd been remembering for a couple of hours, and every time the vision of my mom pointing that gun in my face raced across my mind, I quickly went on to another memory. Once again I tried to go back to some other time, but this time I couldn't. The gun had to be next, but there was no way I would face it yet. Maybe another time. I quit praying and left the room.

The book had said that inner healing was a process that would occur over several days, weeks, or even years. The gun was more than I could handle now. I found my shoes and my jacket and left the house.

It took me a full week to be able to go back into the living room and face the gun. Just remembering the cold, black metal gun pointed at my face sent me into convulsive sobs that wouldn't stop. Every pain that I'd felt at eight years of age came back with all the same power. I was curled up, cowering in my old chair, just as I had then against the cedar chest. I was reliving, not just remembering, the past.

I closed my eyes and saw my faithful friend, Jesus, reach over me and wrap his tender, loving arms around me as I crouched in fear in front of my mother as she swung the loaded gun in my face. He promised to protect me and gently took the gun from my mother's hands. Together we threw it up to heaven; the gun was completely gone.

Then Jesus led me without a pause through all the times the gun had haunted me throughout my life. I gave every rejection and fear to Jesus, who gladly took it. Right up to my grandfather's funeral we went. Jesus took them all.

When I stood up from the chair, evening had fallen, but I felt I'd just risen from a long, refreshing nap. For the first time in my entire life I felt free. My heart didn't feel guarded or heavy. I *was* free!

As I looked out the window at the gray night and the stars sprinkled through the heavens, I imagined that each was one of my healed memories. I knew that this inner process had just begun. The pain would come back in spurts, no doubt, but I felt confident that the sky would just become brighter with each memory I flung into God's heavenly realm. I no longer feared that rummaging through my past would lead me nowhere. The bright evening sky comforted me with a deep, settled peace. How well I slept knowing I was truly on the path toward freedom!

The Smile

Healing brought newness to my life. My season of running from my past slowly came to a halt, turning into a time of inner springtime. The newly plowed soil of my heart was prepared for sowing. The seeds of added purpose and challenge seemed to be dropped daily into my life.

Each year the Easter trip to Mexico bloomed bigger than the last. Planning and coordinating what we now called Mexicali Outreach kept me busy from morning to night as literally hundreds grouped to cross the border with us—an invasion of enthusiastic Christians. By the time I'd orchestrated a dozen trips like this, I thought I'd been through it all before. But as the pain of my memories lessened, I felt a new sense of expectation. This year something inside me was different.

On the first night in Mexico, my staff gathered for the last briefing before both morning and the ministry dawned—full of promise. My heart was particularly stirred as I looked around at the group of people in the tiny base camp building. I was so blessed. My fear of family closeness hadn't stopped the Lord from filling my life with people who loved me.

With a glance at my prepared agenda, I started in. "You've done it again—you're really first class! I really appreciate all your work. Everything's covered, and this week is going to be fantastic once again. In fact, I have a feeling this is going to be the best Mexicali Outreach ever!

"I know you've all worked your tails off and we need to turn in early, but I must tell you something, something rather personal. I'm not going to cry, so don't get nervous." They chuckled, but I focused every ounce of energy on keeping my unusually intense emotions under control.

My staff often coaxed me to share my past with them, but I never really allowed myself to expose the deepest pains. Today I felt led to reveal some of the memories I was continually struggling with as God led me through the healing process.

"As a child I did everything I could think of to earn love and acceptance." I swallowed, then said flatly, "I wasn't very successful, so I changed my tactics; the more rejection I felt, the worse I behaved. It was just as though I'd decided that if my world treated me as if I were bad, I'd show them what bad really meant. In time, all I knew was how to get into trouble. Inside, I was really lonely, and my frantic search for comfort constantly got me in trouble." As I spoke I wondered if anyone listening could really imagine how desperately lonely and unhappy my childhood had been.

"But then, when I was a junior in high school, I faced something that utterly contradicted my whole defensive way of life. Someone told me that, in spite of what I did and what others thought of me, God loved me. God's love was so clear to me, so real, that I decided to love him too and live the rest of my life serving him."

I wanted to be really clear to my listening friends, so I continued. "I mean, the first source of real love I knew was God, and I decided to return that love by making him the most important concern of my life. As days and weeks went by, I found his acceptance was so contrary to the rejection and betrayal I'd come to expect that I couldn't deny him. He changed my life. I gave in to him without a single reservation."

Feeling on safer ground, my voice became steadier. "From that day on, my life took on new meaning. The emptiness of rejection was being replaced by committed friendships like ours. You are all very special to me. You're like family.'' Everyone smiled broadly, and a few exchanged knowing glances. I smiled to myself at my frank openness, so unlike how I had been when growing up, or even more recently, and went on.

"And God has helped me to accomplish things beyond my dreams—teaching at the university, organizing Mexicali Outreach—and loving every minute of life. But God, because he loved me, did more than change circumstances in my life—he changed me. I guess I feel as if he's been preparing me for something special; after all, I'd gone to some pretty dark and bitter places in my heart as a child, and he'd totally transformed my life. In a really personal way, I know exactly what we're going to be able to offer the people here in Mexicali when we offer them that same life-changing love. Do you know what I mean?''

I watched them smile and nod. Knowing they were with me, I finished.

"I want this year's Mexicali Outreach to be the greatest one ever, and I think it can be. I want this experience to touch everyone here, of course, but I have a personal goal as well: I'm praying that God will use this week to help me be more receptive to his will. Above and beyond all else, I want God to change me.

"So tonight I'm saying before all of you: I'm ready for whatever God has in store for me; I'm ready for this week.''

Little did I know what I was confessing or committing myself to. I just sensed a strong inner urging that pushed me forward. The Carolyn Koons I knew was being redefined. No longer bound by my ever-healing past, I felt new vistas loom wide before me.

The next morning dawned with the opportunity to visit a

men's prison eighteen dusty, winding miles from our camp. Hand-picked Mexicali veterans and some varsity basketball players piled into a van prepared for a rough-and-ready basketball game with an unruly inmate team. The small musical group came with portable piano to entertain during halftime, hoping to communicate God's love through song and testimony.

Louie Files, my longtime friend and youth pastor, was among the staff. We all anticipated an unfriendly and unkempt place, but the filth and degradation we found at the teeming prison surpassed our most gruesome expectations. The cement walls and dirt floors and the unsanitary eating facilities were nothing compared with the toilets and private areas. The men, understandably, were a near-boiling mass of pain and emotion. Yet, as we'd all learned, if we looked deep enough into their eyes, we could see each man's longing for love.

After numerous delays the two teams were circled around center court ready for the tip-off. Elbowing and furtive moves that redefined the rules kept our basketball team alert and invigorated, yet no matter how many baskets we scored, the prison scorekeeper insisted, with a sly, amused grin, that the home team was one point up. No one minded, and by halftime the person-to-person contact on both court and sidelines subsided into a spirit of friendliness.

The game ended as we expected: the prisoners won by one point. On our way out of the prison, as we toted the equipment to the van, the prison chaplain caught up with me. "Senorita Koons," he said, "if you have time today, will you please visit the boys' prison, too? I can make the arrangements."

"Boys' prison? I've never heard that there was a prison for boys."

He assured me that two hundred fifty boys aged five to

seventeen lived year-round in La Granja, a prison located farther into the heart of the Mexicali farmlands.

I couldn't imagine saying no. After numerous exasperating detours along a rutted road bordering a wide irrigation canal, we spotted a chain-link fence surrounding a long, low U-shaped building. Five acres of hard, uncultivated ground housed the boys—a few of whom we could see from outside, some barefoot and scuffling in the prison yard while others leaned listlessly against the gray concrete walls.

Bored and unmotivated, the boys stared vacantly. My heart beat faster and my fist clutched in despair as we unloaded the van outside the main entrance.

Louie's hand touched my shoulder when we stood outside, "What's wrong, Carolyn? What's bothering you?" He still knew when to prod at my unspoken feelings.

I slowly pried my aching fingers away from the fence I'd been clutching as the pain and anger continued to rise inside me. "I guess I'm really mad, Louie. This is absolutely disgusting, and we haven't even been inside yet."

And once inside, the outside seemed tolerable. Degradation oozed from the one slimy toilet the entire population used; reeked from the fetid barrel of drinking water. Senor Manuel, the prison warden, ruled as master of the pitiful place. With one resounding gong of the prison bell he sent every boy scurrying in panic to fall-in in military formation, an arm's length from the next boy in the center of the basketball court. We watched as Senor Manuel waited, arms crossed, for the last boy to find his place before he singled out the latecomer, grabbing him by the neck and shoulders and shoving him to the ground as he drew his billy club from his belt. I couldn't watch, but I heard the sickening thuds of his club as it struck the boy's head and back.

These boys' lives were controlled by brutality and force

and a travesty of discipline. Their bunk beds in the dreary, overcrowded room were lined up side by side; the windows held no glass, allowing in the early afternoon sun but also, no doubt, the bitter cold of night. My heart ached. The memory of the many months I'd spent in Minnesota daydreaming that someone would rescue me from my horrible emotional prison reminded me of what these boys must feel inside, no matter how hardened they appeared.

Senor Manuel served as father—the embodiment of hatred and violence—to these boys just as my dad had to me. I seethed as he walked by, and Barbara Fraley, one of our team, hissed in anger, "You snake," before her husband, John, quickly hushed her. The evidence of that man's evil showed everywhere I looked. It was more than I thought I could bear.

I turned to Danny, the keyboard player in our music group. "Play, Danny. Play something happy." Emotionally worn out, I slumped down onto a trunk that we used to transport our puppets. Danny immediately began to play the tiny electric piano, and the first note sent the boys clamoring close for the best seats.

Amelia Rattan, a vivacious forty-year-old missionary, stood beside me. In low tones she whispered, "That beating really upset some of the team. That poor boy!"

Quickly I looked for the young victim again but couldn't find him. Instead, my eyes caught sight of one little guy, maybe eight or nine years old, on top of one of the bunks in the back corner of the room. Several older boys sat on the same bunk. As the little tyke attempted to climb down, obviously dying to get close to Danny and the piano, the others pushed him back toward the wall. Undaunted, he came right back and kept struggling to get past. My heart leaped wildly as one of the older boys wickedly jabbed his fist into the little one's stomach. Tears filled his eyes, and he gritted his teeth, doubled his small fist, and started to swing wildly. Still laughing, the older boys threw their arms over their faces to ward off the little tornado's attack. With the help of reinforcements, a whole gang of the older boys shoved the small boy off the top bunk and onto the hard floor.

Without a glance back, the boy clawed and climbed his way over the enraptured crowd until he could squirm his skinny body into the front row, only about four feet from Danny. I couldn't take my eyes off him. I kept shifting to a new position trying to look into his handsome little face. Each time I did I was mesmerized by his eyes—they betrayed the story of his all-too-painful young life. He became enthralled with the music and immediately opened his mouth to sing wholeheartedly as he swayed back and forth in rhythm. His body relaxed, and a huge, radiant smile swept across his face. His dark eyes, so full of depth and feeling, captured my whole attention. How could he just forget his sad life so quickly? His resilience and joy touched something very, very deep within me. I felt a crazy kinship with him, for I, too, knew what it was to fight for every ounce of life when everyone seemed to want to take it from me. The little terror in that prison tapped an unknown stream of compassion and tenderness inside me. Just the night before I'd told the staff that I knew from personal experience what we had to offer the people we would meet. Little did I expect that a fiery young boy could be what God had in mind to change my life.

As I sat enraptured by the boy in the blue denim jacket with the roughly carved cross hung by a dirty string around his neck, the other team members made comments to me—all independently.

"Carolyn, look at the little boy in the front row, the one with the blue jacket and the cross. Look at the expression on his face, and especially in his eyes!" Barbara exclaimed.

Danny was next. When he took a break while the rest of the group sang he hurried over. "Carolyn, look at the cute little guy in the front row with the big smile."

After a bit, I felt a tap on my shoulder and turned to hear Louie say, "Carolyn, have you noticed that little boy in the front row? His eyes are something else."

I couldn't believe it! Was there only one boy in this room, or over two hundred? Who in the world was this captivating little stranger, and what was he doing in this filthy prison? What could he possibly have done? Perhaps he had stolen some candy, or maybe bread for his family? Maybe he'd just been out on the streets, and they'd caught him begging. Whatever it was, I knew with everything in me that this child did not belong here.

"Let's go over and talk to him." I nudged David Johnson, one of this year's student directors and also one of our interpreters. We spotted the blue jacket behind the piano just as we heard one abrupt note sound as he gleefully pressed down one of the keys. Seeing us approach he jerked himself back and covered his face in terror. *"Hola, chico,"* David spoke tenderly and touched the boy's shoulder. He uncovered his thin face when he realized that we weren't going to hit him for touching the piano. David asked him more questions, but the boy remained silent, visibly trembling beneath his tattered shirt.

Finally, the little tyke opened his mouth to speak. Relieved, we both relaxed—until we heard a series of repeated syllables and high-pitched shrieks escape his lips. His eyes filled with tears as he dropped his head, now totally embarrassed.

I was crushed—not because the boy was unable to talk to us but because the joy had fled his eyes. The once-radiant little face now registered terror.

We reassured him before heading for a guard who looked friendly. Somehow we had to find out this kid's story.

Armando, the guard, winked at the boy and had to restrain his affection as we asked who he was. "Yes, that's Antonio. Antonio Hernandez Sanchez. His mother didn't want him, so she just dumped him off here at La Granja. He's been living here since he was about five."

I was furious. This darling little boy had lived half his life in this hellhole just because someone didn't want him? How could someone reject this bright-eyed waif? Not only had his mother rejected him, she'd left him in a place like this: deprived of love, beaten, starved, intellectually stunted, spiritually denied, and probably sexually molested—and probably more besides.

I had to get to the bottom of this. If Antonio's mother had just abandoned him, there must be a way to get him out of here and into a good home. Prison was no place for a kid just because his parents didn't want him!

Amelia suggested a visit to the Office of Juvenile Records, so as the rest of the team pitched in to help the boys on their daily work detail to clean up the place as best they could, Amelia, David, and I sped back to Mexicali over the long, bumpy road.

Once inside the dingy, crowded room, we waited in line, trying not to breathe too deeply of the stagnant, smelly air. At last we walked up to the first of five desks in a line.

"We have just returned from La Granja boys' prison and would like to see the records of a little boy named Antonio Hernandez Sanchez."

"Oh *si,* Antonio! You met Antonio? What a tragedy." The woman behind the desk responded without the slightest hesitation and walked directly to the appropriate file along the long wall of filing cabinets and immediately pulled the dog-eared record of Antonio's life. A picture fell from the folder as she opened it at her desk. For a sober moment I looked into the saddest eyes I had ever seen.

"Yes, this is the boy we found at La Granja. I just can't understand why the authorities let his mother dump him off in the prison."

The secretary looked to David for the translation. "Oh no, senorita! Didn't they tell you? Antonio Hernandez Sanchez is in prison for murder. He's been there since he was five years old!"

My body stiffened as I felt the shock of those terrible words. Surely I'd just misunderstood what she said, but Amelia cross-examined the clerk. "Who could a five-year-old murder?"

"They say that Antonio murdered his baby brother."

I felt sick and numbly lowered myself onto a chair. Visions of my own baby brother covered with blood in his cradle flooded my mind. How could Antonio murder his baby brother? Surely no one who sensed the buoyant spirit of that little kid could believe such a stupid story. How could his mother blame him for such a horrible act?

The secretary sat uneasily behind her desk adjusting her glasses and scrutinizing the documents in Antonio's file. She skimmed the pages and summarized them for us: "At 2:00 A.M., the Tijuana police were notified to investigate the death of a baby boy in one of the shacks on the outskirts of Tijuana near the dump. When they arrived, the mother and a man she was living with led them to the back of the flimsy little shanty. On the floor lay the broken body of a lifeless infant. A bloody wooden bat lay nearby. 'Antonio did it! Antonio did it! He killed his brother! He killed his baby brother!' His mother shrieked the terrible accusation over and over, pointing a finger at the lifeless body.

"The police found Antonio in a state of shock at a neighbor's house. They took him to the men's jail and locked him up after notifying the mother to come down the next morning at 8:00 A.M. when the office opened so that she could formally press murder charges against her son.

"By noon the next day, when his mother hadn't appeared, the police checked the shack, only to find it vacant. Then the police realized that she, or the man, was most likely the real murderer."

I barraged the secretary with questions. "Why did they keep him in the prison if they thought that the mother had done it? Why didn't they put him in an orphanage?"

The secretary looked at me pleadingly. "This is a terrible thing that has happened to Antonio. Somebody needs to get that little boy out of prison."

By the time all the Mexicali teams reconvened at our base that first night, the entire camp was buzzing with the story of Antonio's plight. Before I could even give consent, a P.A. system was erected out on the open area beside the base camp building. It took only one announcement for the mass of people to eagerly assemble, each grabbing a piece of wood from the bin to sit on.

As I listened to the voices of five hundred young people sing out in praise, I found myself uncharacteristically nervous and shifting in my chair. Today had turned out to be one of the most unusual, and emotionally draining, days of my life. I prayed that I'd be able to communicate clearly; I wanted each and every person in front of me to be able to meet Antonio in the special way that I had.

A hush fell over the camp as I retold our amazing story. The young people hung on my every word, and Antonio's plight became indelibly etched in their hearts.

As we opened for prayers for Antonio and one young

person after the other stood up to pray, a calm came over my spirit; I felt God's presence and direction. I'd been praying for years, and I knew God heard my voice, but this experience was different somehow—more specific. "You asked me to change your life, Carolyn. I want to use you to get Antonio out of prison," God told me. "Take one step at a time, and don't take no for an answer."

Immediately after the service my good friend Happy sat down beside me, "Carolyn, if you can get Antonio out of prison, there's a good possibility that Jerry and I could adopt him. We'd certainly like to try."

"And I'd certainly like you to try!" I laughed in amazement and threw my arms around her. Happy had served a number of years in Mexico as a missionary and knew the language and culture well, and Jerry, her husband, worked with troubled youth at juvenile facilities. What a perfect pair for Antonio!

The week sped quickly by, but before we left, David and his girlfriend, Sue, accompanied me back to La Granja bearing a pair of brand new black-and-white tennis shoes and a silver bracelet engraved ANTONIO that I'd purchased on the spur of the moment. When Antonio gingerly untied the curly ribbon, I felt more tenderness than I ever had in my life; my emotions were going wild. That kid did something to me that no one had ever done before.

As David, Sue, and I drove away from the prison compound I wondered if Antonio had really believed us when we told him we'd be back. Could he even survive the month or so it would take us to go through the legal and immigration systems to free him? I prayed he could.

A month later I traveled to Mexico to appear before the judges, who assured me that I could have any boy in the entire

Mexican prison system but Antonio, since he was the only boy in the system being officially held on murder charges. Discouraged, I stopped in once again to see Antonio before driving the five hours back to Azusa, but this time his sparkle had dimmed. After our last visit, the other boys, jealous of his special attention, had beaten him unmercifully and destroyed his new shoes. The poor urchin had scabs from his nose to his knees. His once-sparkling eyes were sunken and dull beneath the black-and-blue bruises. Though he refused to tattle on the other boys, the guards told us what had happened.

Once back at home, I decided to try the second tack—if I couldn't get Antonio from Mexico, I'd try to start the ball rolling with American Immigration. In order to get all the necessary forms, I stood in for Happy and Jerry, consenting to a home study of my house so that the four hundred miles between them and me wouldn't delay the adoption process any longer.

But nothing happened quickly. The lawyer I'd hired turned the case over to his associate; the forms I'd filed in triplicate required page after page of financial and physical history; and the judges in Mexico recessed for time to research all the records on Antonio's case—the process stretched into months. Before I knew it a full year had gone by, and once again Mexicali Outreach was heading toward the border. We'd seen Antonio a few times in the last year, but often when we arrived after the long drive down we were told that he was "out" on a special work project and had to return home, our time wasted.

Determined to make progress on Antonio's adoption, I headed to the lawyer's office to meet the new associate Lupe Puga, assigned to the case. A young, dark-haired, attractive Mexican woman walked directly and briskly to meet me and introduced herself, and I found myself feeling frustrated. Where was Senor Dominguez and the associate he'd told me about over the phone?

All the other lawyers were on vacation. But when Lupe picked up an overstuffed file and confided that she'd studied the case line by line and was the only one in the office sure that there was a way to get Antonio out, I knew she was my kind of lawyer, however young or inexperienced.

She'd sent a doctor out to examine Antonio for the required physical. The doctor estimated Antonio to be around ten although he looked somewhat undernourished and small for his age. Lupe also reported that Antonio was a real fighter, not willing to let anything slide, and that he was continually involved in fights at the prison. She smiled wryly and shook her head, "Whoever gets this boy must be prepared for a battle. He may be small, but every ounce of this kid has struggled to survive at all costs!"

A warm glow spread through me; it was with that same attitude that I met life myself. Maybe that's why I was so drawn to little Antonio. But Happy and Jerry would have their hands full with this one, I thought. "Lupe, that's okay, we'll take him any way we can get him. Let's just get him out!"

"Yes, we'll get him out. Just listen to this juicy discovery. While digging through the records, I was surprised to find not a single mention of a trial. So I researched further and found out there never was a trial. I'm going to court at the earliest opportunity and insist that they try this case! What do we have to lose? Antonio is already destined for a life in prison if we don't try!"

Lupe finagled a trial date only three months away, and with all of us working together via long drives to Mexico and expensive phone calls, we planned a strong case for Antonio's release. Just as the court date approached, my schedule at the university crescendoed, and we finally decided that Amelia, one of the team that had first visited La Granja, would stand in for me.

On the trial date, each time the phone rang, I raced to answer it hoping for some news. At last Lupe called. "We won, Carolyn, we won! In thirty short minutes it was over, and Antonio was found innocent. Listen to this, Carolyn," Lupe's voice sounded triumphant. "Antonio's verdict of innocent will be registered in Mexico City. He was proven innocent of the crime and will not have any kind of prison record ever, anywhere."

"Lupe, that's great, just fantastic! When can we get Antonio out of La Granja?"

"Today sounds perfect to me, but realistically it will be more like a month or so. Papers must be drawn up and signed, then mailed to Mexico City and recorded, then sent back here before we can get him out."

It took several weeks for all the paperwork to be finished, but the minute I received Lupe's call I rounded up David, my faithful interpreter, and sped down the freeway to Mexicali wondering if six years in a boys' prison without the love of a mother or a father had done irreparable damage.

Lupe joined us at La Granja, and in our intense discussion about Antonio's future, we nearly bumped into the prison director. Lupe described the reason for our visit.

The director's beady eyes belied his lame efforts to sound friendly. "Hello, senoritas. I'm sorry, but Antonio isn't here."

He tried to distract us as best he could, but Lupe, David, and I had had our fill of excuses for over a year. Exasperated when all his attempts to dissuade us failed, he scribbled an address on a dirty scrap of paper. All of us smelled a rat, and after futilely searching out the address only to find it did not exist, we returned to La Granja. Not surprisingly the director was gone for the day and the records unavailable without a court order. So the next day we returned, to the dismay of the prison director, a court order in hand.

Silently, Lupe handed him the court order. The despairing man's nerve was finally broken. "I'm sorry. I don't know where he is." He immediately walked into his office and shut and locked the door behind him. Lupe wasn't about to let his rudeness deter her. After twenty minutes of snooping around and interrogating the guards she returned, her face taut with anger. "I'm so sorry, Carolyn, but Antonio has been sold into child slave labor."

"What! What do you mean, slave labor?" I protested, refusing to believe my ears.

"The prison director has been selling the boys and pocketing the money. It's a big racket in Mexico. They sell the children and use them in any way they want to. Most are never seen again."

The drive home to California was full of questions for me. Why now? Antonio was almost free after six long years. Why did you let this happen now, God? I didn't understand, but the commitment to get Antonio out of prison at any cost overrode everything, until that alone restored the peace I had felt all along.

Lupe put all her energies into exposing the reprehensible prison director as well as finding Antonio, only one of many boys that monster had sold for profit in his years at the prison. But months slipped by, and there was no trace of the boy.

It all looked hopeless; just when all the legal and bureaucratic battles ended, Antonio disappeared. Yet instead of giving up, I just kept praying. The sweet, haunting face of that little Mexican orphan caused a searing pain in my heart. I sensed there was still a bond between us, even though he had been missing for nine months.

Two and a half years after I first met Antonio, in July, the phone rang as I cleaned my house on a sultry summer afternoon. A heavily accented male voice demanded, "Are you Carolyn Koons, the lady who's interested in the adoption of Antonio Hernandez Sanchez?"

"Yes, yes, I am!"

"Senorita, are you still interested in the boy?"

"I definitely am! Have you heard from him?"

"Yes, senorita! He has just been placed back into La Granja prison, and you better come for him quickly if you don't want him to disappear again." Click.

A friend from church made good on his offer of a private plane if I ever needed to go to Mexico in a hurry. Antonio was alive! After another phone call, I rushed to the small airport and boarded the twin-engine plane. Amelia awaited me at the other end. She handed me the Mexican release papers, and I gave her the important American documents. I raced back across the runway to return to L.A., desperately wanting to see Antonio, but knowing even a one-day delay in hand-delivering the final papers to American Immigration might keep us from getting Antonio across the border in time. Amelia headed to La Granja for Antonio, confident she could hide him with a friend in a remote village until my return, in case the prison personnel in charge of the slave ring attempted to get him back.

Ignoring every speed limit, I dashed across Los Angeles to the immigration office. Mrs. Myers, the officer in charge of Antonio's case, was delighted to see me after the many months of agonizing delay. She carefully checked the papers from La Granja, the courts, the juvenile judges, and the lawyer's office. Each signature was properly placed.

"Congratulations, Carolyn! Everything is here and signed. We'll mail these to Washington, D.C., today. They'll look them over, put an official stamp on each one, and send them to Mexico. They should arrive in Tijuana at the American Consulate in exactly seven days, and then you can immigrate Antonio into the United States."

Amelia called and assured me that she had Antonio and that he was delighted to be with her and anxious to see me. My heart catapulted wildly; he was really safe!

I hung up and immediately dialed Happy and Jerry. They were ecstatic about the miracle that had brought about Antonio's release, but as we discussed the adoption further, we all began to realize that things had changed in the two and a half years it had taken to get Antonio free. Happy and Jerry had a baby of their own and another on the way. Jerry had taken a live-in job working with fifteen very tough adolescent boys. None of us felt that moving Antonio from one harsh environment to another would do him any good at all. We talked at length—just as we had so many, many times, and began to see that maybe part of the reason it had taken so long to get Antonio out of prison was that it was taking me so long to accept that God wanted to totally change my life by leading me to adopt Antonio myself.

Even though I agreed and could confirm the changes in my heart, the mere mention of the idea sent me into a state of apprehension. As we kept talking, I glanced down at the official papers spread out on the table before me. In all the rush of the day, I had failed to look at them closely. Now my eyes rested on the most shocking words I had ever read. Clearly printed and officially notarized was the name *Antonio Koons.* I actually was going to be Antonio's mother!

The Son

And so on July 18, after having just one week to battle the terror and anticipation of becoming a parent to a boy who had spent seven years in prison for murder, I became Antonio's mother. As my first act of motherhood I declared that day his twelfth birthday, since no one knew the exact date. After a teary reunion and a gleeful shopping spree, we headed, along with Alva Peters, Antonio's designated grandma from Twain Harte, to the lovely Hotel Lucerna to spoil Antonio with a hot shower and dinner. Try as he might to eat every morsel in sight, there was still plenty left over, which he determinedly stuffed into the pockets of his new pants, sure that he'd never again be offered so much delicious food.

Watching my new son's eyes dance with excitement as he began to explore the simple pleasures I just took for granted endeared him to me even more deeply. We could barely communicate—me in English and him in Spanish, both of us relying heavily on gestures and sign language—but how I already loved him!

The next morning we drove to Tijuana early to escape the heat only to be told that Antonio had to have a passport. A passport! How did we get a passport? With a birth certificate. But what if Antonio has no birth certificate and no certificate of abandonment? "I'm sorry, senorita," the official declared, "but you will have to live with Antonio in Mexico for two and a half years before you can legally immigrate!"

This couldn't be happening. It just couldn't. My mind reeled into overdrive. There had to be a way. After making the four-hour trip on a winding mountain road from Mexicali to Tijuana and back over and over again trying to obtain a birth certificate for four full days, not knowing what else to do, I dialed Lupe's number, knowing full well that she'd left for vacation as soon as we'd picked up Antonio.

With the first ring I hoped she would answer; with the second ring, I chided myself for trying; on the third ring, mocking doubts stung my pride; I sat in despair through the fourth ring; by the fifth, I moved to hang up. Just in time, I heard a cheery hello and jerked the receiver back to my ear.

"Lupe—hello Lupe, is that you?"

"Yes, this is Lupe. Is that you, Carolyn?"

Lupe had just stopped by her office for five minutes to check her mail. Antonio and I rushed over after she promised to cancel her plane reservation and stay to help us one more time. She listened with sober attention to a blow-by-blow account of our four-day journey. After thinking it through she agreed that I'd have to stay in Mexico if I wanted Antonio.

Discouraged, yet determined not to quit, I exclaimed, "There's got to be a weak link in this law somewhere, Lupe. Think!"

"Sure, just get a signature from the governor of the state. Unfortunately, he doesn't do things like that," she sighed.

Lupe paced around the stifling office tapping her finger against her chin in deep thought as temperatures soared upwards of 115 degrees. "Carolyn, I have one crazy idea. About three months ago," she began, "I attended a conference in Mexico City for officials from all the various states. One day I was invited out to lunch by, would you believe, the governor's personal executive secretary. During the meal she asked me to tell her about anything exciting I was working on. As we parted she asked me to keep her informed on my progress with Antonio's case."

"Let's not disappoint her, Lupe! Keep her informed right now!" I gestured toward the telephone, and after a long, animated conversation in Spanish, Lupe made an okay sign with her fingers.

Clinging to our last thread of hope, we raced over to the executive offices and were ushered into an oak-lined room with fine leather furniture, polished marble floors, and walls lined with rich oil paintings. Antonio stared wide-eyed at the luxurious surroundings.

Fifteen minutes passed before Senora Romero emerged from the governor's office, and I held my breath as she handed me a document and pointed to the bottom of the page. There it was—the governor's signature! Lupe and I squealed with amazement, and Antonio jumped up and down.

Senora Romero bustled us down two flights of stairs and personally handed the document to the director of the passport office. "It will only take a few moments, senorita, to prepare this passport," the director said respectfully.

Ceremoniously, only moments later, he opened the last passport, looked at Antonio's huge smile, and announced, "Antonio Koons!" Antonio knew exactly what to do. He had to stand on his tiptoes to see over the counter and reach up for his treasured passport. The director's hand reached down to meet Antonio's, and he asked, "Antonio Koons?"

"*Si!*" His proud voice rang out clearly, and my heart leaped in joy. The director leaned over and spoke directly into Antonio's beaming face, "You are a very lucky boy. In the seventeen years I've worked in this office, I have never known the governor to personally sign anyone's passport." With my little son hugging his passport tightly to his chest, Carolyn and Antonio Koons could now go home.

We spent the first week in Glendora at my condominium experiencing what it must be like to have been joined in an arranged marriage. Neither Antonio nor I knew anything about the other's lifestyle, likes, or dislikes. And to top it all off, we still couldn't speak the same language.

One afternoon when David was visiting to help translate, I asked Antonio to decide whether I should learn Spanish or he should be the one to become bilingual.

"English! I think I better learn English!" he said to David —in Spanish.

"And maybe you'd like an American name," I suggested. "Shall we call you Antonio Koons, or would you prefer Anthony or Tony?"

He didn't understand at once, but when he did, he was delighted. "Tony," he said. *"Me llamo Tony."*

Tony and I spent the remaining weeks of summer, mostly alone, learning together. I soon found that after years in an institutional environment, Tony needed lots of structure and a regular daily routine. As for me, the freer and more unrestricted my life was, the better, but for Tony I compromised, determined to commit this first year to my new son—no speaking, no traveling, unless he went with me. He was my number one priority.

I learned to make tacos the way he liked them, and he learned to keep his room neat and his bed made. But I also soon discovered Tony, like me, had a will of steel. Nothing could make him do what he didn't want to do. Years of mere survival had honed his defenses to protect him at any cost. I, someone who hated conflict after years and years of my own pain, was now family to Tony, a boy whose emotional scars were just as deep.

Enrolling him in the right school was a task I only hoped I'd done well. No school in the area was properly equipped to handle a non-English-speaking twelve-year-old who had never sat through a structured day of school in his life. Believing that keeping Tony in the same neighborhood as our home would speed up his socialization and help him to make friends influenced my decision.

Toward the second week of school my secretary buzzed me in my office with a call from Tony's principal. "Carolyn, just a little while ago, Tony ran out of Mr. Bradley's class and off the school grounds. We thought you should check at home and see if he's there."

I couldn't get out of the office fast enough. Why would he leave school? Was he sick? On the way home I swung by the park on the off chance that he'd gone there. He hadn't. Frantically I pulled the car into the garage and ran up the walk. Immediately I sensed something was wrong. All the draperies were tightly drawn, and the dead bolt on the front door was pulled.

There was an eerie feeling about the darkened house. "Tony, are you here?" I called and went in.

A look of terror on Tony's face brought me quickly to the sofa, where he was curled into a fetal position, clinging to a pile of pillows.

"Tony, what happened?"

Mingled sweat and tears rolled down his face, and in a fit of uncontrollable trembling, he began to shout, "Make him stop yelling! Make him stop yelling! I can't stand it! It's just like prison!" he sobbed.

All this came with difficulty through stuttering and hysteria. "What are you talking about, Tony?" I wrapped him in my arms—giving him a little protection in a world that seemed so terrifying.

He repeated himself over and over until I shook him lightly. "Look at me. Tell me what's wrong, Tony!"

"Mr. Bradley," he managed. "He yells at us. He yells at us just like in prison. Mom, Mom, make him stop."

Tony was too far gone for reason. I just rocked him in my arms until he began to relax. "Son," I spoke gently, "your school is not a prison, and no one is going to hit you." I knew that in Tony's mind, Mr. Bradley had become Senor Manuel at La Granja, where hitting had always followed yelling. The hurt and pain of his past had left him little reserve for dealing with conflict.

Little by little I learned the roots of Tony's inner conflicts. His strong disrespect for male authority, especially angry male authority, I rightly assumed related back to Senor Manuel at the prison, but then I discovered his scars were far deeper than that.

One day Tony came home from school angry; it seemed like good therapy for him to vent his feelings, and it gave me an opportunity to direct his interpretations, so I encouraged him to talk.

"You know, Mom, one time when my dad was really mad at me," he recalled, "he chained my arm to the bed and started hitting me with another chain that had a lock on the end." He pulled up his shirt and exposed his scarred back. "That's where he hit me, and on my legs, too. He hated me bad." Tony's face contorted as the tears rushed down his cheeks; the pain of his memories was still very real.

"Did he hurt your hand too?" I asked, touching his badly scarred fingers.

"No, that was my mom. If I didn't do something, she got real mad, and one day she put my hand in the fire."

I cringed. The horror was more than I could bear. Tony's dad beat him and his mom burned him. And my own dad brutally beat me and my mom held a loaded gun pointed at my face with her finger on the trigger. I knew my own pain and could only begin to suspect the depth of torture in my own son's life.

I had a feeling that teaching Tony new things about life would be a lot easier that helping him deal effectively with the pain of his past. First me, then Tony. Oh, how I wished Tony could forget the past, but I knew—how well I knew, that someday he would have to face it head on to be healed.

Over the next months, Tony woke screaming from nightmares, "Don't hit me, Don't hit me." Then, when his teacher yelled he retaliated with a powerful karate chop, and he left a schoolmate with a concussion after defending one of his friends from a gang of other kids on the way home from school. Tony knew one way to survive, and that was to fight like a mad animal to the death.

With a school change midyear, Tony managed to last a full year in school, although he found himself suspended every few weeks. It seemed to him that all Americans liked to do was make up rules, and to one who had lived in a prison where "Only the strong survive" was the only one—they all seemed strident to Tony.

My work suffered, and I found my ability to concentrate, always one of my strengths, had waned to a feeble sense of just trying to keep one step ahead of the next disaster. Two out of three days with Tony were pure hell, but I knew underneath all his aggression was a great kid, a truly great kid. Everybody who knew him at all agreed, but his pain was taking a real toll on me.

Able now to converse almost fluently in English, Tony reluctantly moved on to the seventh grade with his special, beloved reading tutor, Mrs. Spurling, consenting to work with him individually for another year. She was the only reason at all he could imagine for enduring the torture of going to school.

Throughout the semester I kept close tabs on Tony through Mrs. Spurling, who became the tender grandmotherly figure that he desperately needed in his life. He was reading at a third-grade level, which was just fine, considering that he was in only his second year of school. He was seeing a speech therapist for his stuttering, but it was still too soon to expect results. (I wasn't terribly concerned; I believed that when Tony finally worked through his other problems, the stuttering would take care of itself.)

One day well into the semester, she said, "Tony seems to have lost his spark lately."

I agreed. "He's been very quiet at home these last few weeks. That's usually an indication that something is building up somewhere else in his life—at school, for instance."

"He just doesn't seem as happy as usual. He's special, Carolyn, and I love him very much." She winked and gave me a little nudge. "Tony and I understand each other, you know! Tony's problem lately might be that he and Mr. Lantz, his classroom teacher, aren't getting along. Mr. Lantz seems to be developing a reputation as a yeller, and you know how Tony reacts to that. Why don't you go talk with the principal?"

The principal, Mr. Cook, had good things to say about Tony's development both socially and academically. I brought up the tension between Tony and Mr. Lantz. "Have you ever confronted the coach about the way he yells?"

"Well, I've mentioned it," he confessed. "He's new to teaching and has a lot to learn; I'll speak to him again."

Days later, I was sitting out in my secretary's office expounding on Tony's improvement in school. (You'd have thought I'd know better by then.) Just then the phone rang. My secretary answered it, responded briefly, and hung up. "Mr. Cook would like to see you. Tony's been suspended from school!" My barely inflated heart sank—right to the bottom.

I walked past Tony and the school secretary directly into Mr. Cook's office. It was hard to tell whether Tony looked hurt or confused, but typically he was both. I forced myself to ask the dreaded question: "What happened?"

"Mr. Lantz's class got a little out of control today, so after several warnings he told them to 'shut-up' and take out a piece of paper and write fifty times, 'I will not talk in Mr. Lantz's class.' Everyone took out a piece of paper, Carolyn, except Tony."

"What did he do?" I hardly dared to ask.

"According to Lantz, and Tony agrees, he flew out of his chair and said, with that defiant tone he uses, 'You make me!' He ordered Tony to sit down. He refused. Lantz tried to grab him, but Tony was too quick for him and jumped out of the way. When Tony started laughing at him, Lantz became even more angry and grabbed at Tony again. This time Tony jumped on top of a desk and started leaping from one desktop to another all over the room.

"Mr. Lantz made one foolish attempt after another to catch Tony, until the whole class was laughing at him. Finally, he yelled at Tony to get out of his room and down to my office, and told him he was suspended. And I heard every word of it clear down here," Cook sighed.

"I'm sorry, Carolyn, but Tony will be suspended for the remainder of this week and all of next!"

"I'm sorry, too, Mr. Cook! Couldn't this have been avoided? Haven't you talked to Mr. Lantz about his yelling?"

"Yes, but apparently it hasn't done any good. Both you and Mrs. Spurling warned me that this would happen. Really, I do hate to do this, Carolyn, but Mr. Lantz is totally unglued at this point."

"That makes several of us, doesn't it?"

Tony and I drove home in silence, then automatically

gravitated to the couch. "All right Tony, tell me what happened."

To my surprise, he repeated Mr. Cook's rendition almost verbatim.

"You mean that you actually did jump from desk to desk?"

"Yes," he answered emphatically, but without a trace of arrogance.

"Tony, were you right or wrong?"

"I was wrong," he admitted, slightly embarrassed but not hesitating.

"I don't get it, Tony; if you knew it was wrong, why did you do it?"

He looked me straight in the eyes, "Mom, Mr. Lantz told us to write something fifty times, and he didn't even write it on the board for us to copy. I don't know how to write that stuff. I don't want the kids in that school to know I can't write, because they'll think that I'm stupid." Tony was determined as he leaned forward on the couch toward me, "And I'm not stupid! I'd rather get kicked out of school than have the kids think I'm stupid." He folded his arms and put on the triumphant look he must have used on Mr. Lantz. "So, I won!"

It was impossible to argue with his logic, but for future reference, we certainly discussed the benefit of some constructive alternative solutions to such a dilemma.

The next day I stopped in to see Mr. Lantz, not to defend Tony, but to clear up a few things. When I explained why Tony had reacted the way he did, Mr. Lantz was shocked.

"Didn't you know that writing was difficult for Tony?"

"No." He looked mortified at my question.

It was beyond me how he could have had Tony in his history class for months and not know he couldn't write. I took a deep breath and continued, "Mr. Lantz, are you aware that you yell at your students?"

He looked at the floor. "Yes, Miss Koons. I'm trying hard to stop; I'm very sorry. Mr. Cook talked with me yesterday. I'm sorry about Tony. We'll get him back in class right away, okay?"

"No, we've worked out his lessons with Mrs. Spurling, and he'll manage fine at home. This punishment is justified because Tony knew exactly what he was doing. But he does need to learn that yelling doesn't solve anything."

Mr. Lantz looked embarrassed.

Tony returned to school, but the cease-fire didn't last. By the third day they had declared war against each other. Koons versus Lantz, or Lantz versus Koons—regardless of who had fired the first shot, it was now mutual.

A couple of weeks later, Tony came home seething about something. He threw his books on the floor and crashed into the chair. "Mr. Lantz thinks I'm bad!"

"What?"

"Mr. Lantz said I'm no good. He said that I'm bad, that there's nothing good in me!" Tony was furious, and he said it again, "He thinks that I'm bad, so I'll show him! I'll be bad, real bad! He doesn't know what bad is!"

"Oh, Tony. Oh no." I groaned. His words echoed in my head—haunting reminders of the nearly identical words I'd screamed out in my own sixth-grade year. Mr. Lantz was to Tony what Mr. Stokes was to me. I knew how deeply Tony's teacher's words must slice into his already faltering self-image.

Within days, Tony exploded. A simple game of keep-away at lunchtime with another boy's cupcake uncorked the already pressurized pain in my son. Mr. Lantz, hearing the noisy ruckus, entered the lunchroom just as the cupcake was passed to Tony.

The principal recounted the rest to me as I beat a now-familiar path to his office, "Mr. Lantz was infuriated and started screaming at Tony, accusing him of stealing the cupcake and starting the whole incident. Tony denied it, and the other boys came to his defense. That made Lantz madder still. Mr. Lantz lost control, grabbed him by the neck, and wrenched him backward off the bench. Tony went crazy; he jumped up, reached into his pocket and pulled out a knife, and pointed it at Lantz."

My son, with a knife? I felt the last of my strength crumble into desperation. All I wanted to do was run and scream myself. How could I handle a problem like this?

Mr. Lantz was called before the school board to determine his fate as a teacher, and the welts stayed on Tony's neck for well over a week. He felt blamed for starting the cupcake fight and saw pulling the knife as pure self-defense. Exasperated and weary, he looked at me and said, "If everyone thinks I'm so bad, I guess I am!"

And so he was. Tony's typical attitude was now defiance. He balked at any kind of authority. He hated school and proved it by continual fights both inside the classroom and out. He was sinking fast, and we both knew it. I soon became the object of nearly all his pent-up anger. "You can't make me do anything. I don't have to obey you," he'd retort to the most simple request. In his mind adults, whether prison guards, teachers, or moms, were the enemy. I exhausted myself trying to keep him from exploding; I was failing fast.

One day, a meeting at the university kept me late. I always tried to be home when Tony arrived from school. He was home already sitting at the table when I walked in. He seemed to wear a permanent frown these days, and his eyes were dull and lifeless. Trying to be pleasant, I greeted him, "Hi, Tony, how was school?"

"I hate school!" he retorted with his face displaying all the feeling boiling inside.

Okay, I thought to myself, I won't rise to the bait. I'll just fix dinner. Tony likes hamburgers. I'll make something that will make him happy. I had to coax myself into each move. Now, get the meat out, Carolyn. Now get out a plate. Better start the barbecue. It took everything I had to concentrate and not lose my composure.

Pretty soon Tony said, "What's for dinner?"

"Barbecued hamburgers."

"I don't want hamburgers."

The meal was nearly ready. "I'm sorry, Tony, if you wanted something else you should have asked me before I started fixing hamburgers."

"I don't want hamburgers," he repeated sullenly.

"We're having hamburgers. If you don't want them, you don't have to eat." You can starve, I wanted to say, but held my tongue, knowing from experience that this simple confrontation could easily escalate into a major war. I ate a thick, juicy hamburger in boring silence while Tony just picked at the hamburger bun. We might as well have been eating cardboard.

"Tony, how's Mrs. Spurling?" I interjected, trying to lighten the mood by talking about one of his favorite people. He shrugged his shoulders—so much for conversation.

After dinner, I moved from the table toward the sink. This was Tony's cue to clean up the dishes, one of his regular chores. He didn't budge; he just sat at the table looking angry and defiant. He probably felt the strain as much as I did.

"Mom," Tony spoke harshly, "do I have to go to school? I hate it!"

I'd been hanging up a hand towel when Tony spoke, and it fell to the floor and stayed there. I couldn't bring myself to respond to his question. We had been over the issue dozens of times. What more was there to say?

All of a sudden, my mind started racing, and the things that I wanted to say were awful. I was rapidly losing control of my emotions. The months upon months of tension and exhaustion had taken their toll. Faster and faster, my thoughts went wild! My body began to tremble, and I held on to the towel rod for support while Tony's voice droned on about school in the background. A strange sensation of darkness seemed to be closing in around me, and I imagined that the ceiling was slowly moving down to crush me. It was so heavy and so dark —I had to escape. Leaning on the refrigerator for support, then the doorway, then the wall, I managed to get into the bathroom and lock the door.

I finally found the switch, the light came on, and the fan began whirring. Shaking even more now, I leaned up against the sink. Slowly I looked up at my reflection in the mirror. Emotions welled up in my body, and I could hold in the flood no longer.

"God," I bellowed, "what have you done to me? I asked you to change my life, not ruin it. You're destroying me." The pain and anger spewed out, making me feel old and ugly. "You gave me a son, and I can't even stand to be in the same room with him. It's not fair!"

Tears began to stream down my face. So very angry and so very tired, I cried without restraint for what seemed an eternity. If God doesn't care, why should I? I can't take it anymore! I quit! I've had it and I want out! I hate it, God. I hate it. Nothing about my life is right anymore. I'll quit my job and disappear. No one will ever find me. I'll sell the house and leave—go to Washington or Oregon—anywhere!

What about Tony? a voice within me asked. You can't just dump him.

I was so tired, so confused. I'd take Tony with me—maybe I could find someone who'd want him. I cried all over again as I remembered the prediction of my failure one cruel woman had flung at me soon after Tony came: "You'll dump him in a year!"

The escape became a detailed plan in my mind. I had to start packing, but the sobs continued to well up from deep inside me and overflow again and again. "God, you've always helped me," I cried, "and I've been faithful to you. Why are you destroying me now? I'm a failure and it's your fault! I give up! I quit!"

As I finally quieted, my will collapsed. It had always been strong; this was the first time in my life I had given up. As my will came crashing down, a little, limp, pathetic me, totally vulnerable, remained—and God's mighty arms were there to catch me. What a shock to find God at the end of my broken will.

His comforting Spirit was so tangible, so real, that I hardly dared to breathe. I felt myself a disciplined child gathered gently into the restorative arms of a loving parent. I was ready to listen, and he was ready to talk.

Looking in the mirror again, I saw past my reflection into my own childhood. Memories—so vivid I could smell, feel, taste them—stabbed at my heart. Why was this happening? I rarely looked back at my childhood. I had walked away from all that ugliness; it was not relevant to my life today. But there it was, my own past, flashing before my eyes in the mirror, as if I were drowning. It was eerie!

My dad constantly reeking of alcohol—his violent anger constantly raging—my baby brother lying in a pool of blood —my mother standing over me with a loaded gun—my sixth-grade teacher telling me that I was no good—shooting up vacant cabins with my friends just to prove we really didn't care and that maybe, just maybe, we were bad just like everyone seemed to think.

I was snapped back to the present. Suddenly it was Tony's face I saw in the mirror, not mine. He was a survivor, just like me.

I stood there, still staring into the mirror. "Carolyn, you are just where I want you," the Spirit of God seemed to be saying, and those were the words I didn't want to hear. "Tony is just like you." Just like me! And that was exactly the problem. Every time I tried to deal with Tony on just about anything it cut so deeply because it so vividly reminded me of how I had been myself. "Tony has forced you to look, once again, at your past and remember how I took you through it and gave you a new life. Now you can show him how he can make it, too. I'm going to do the same thing for Tony that I have done for you. Be patient, Carolyn, Tony is just like you. Remember how long it took you to trust my healing? Only you, Carolyn, can show him the way."

The Mirror

Standing there, looking at my reflection, I saw, for the first time, that Tony was as like me as if he were my own flesh and blood. His life held the essence of my own struggles. No longer could I view him as a little kid that I'd discovered in a Mexicali prison—someone I could rescue and give hope. No, Tony was that same imprisoned, angry, terrified, lonely child that I had been—a prisoner of the painful past.

Tony reminded me of the tough, independent young girl who craved somebody—anybody—who would reach out in love, yet when they did pushed them away, afraid of the vulnerability of love, though wanting it more than life itself. The grace and mercy of God alone was both gentle enough and persistent enough to release me from my bondage. Only that same power could change Tony.

From that day on, our life together began to inch away from the despair of struggling to forget the past—be it Tony's or mine. The bonding we felt helped both of us see that it was Tony and me together heading toward healing as God worked in both of us. Both of us had a lot to learn. Both of us had to be dedicated, with all the determination we had, to making this mother-son relationship work. Failing, then succeeding, then failing again and forgiving each other—by God's grace we began building toward the future together.

The confidence that came from accepting that in the truest sense of the word I was Tony's mom—and he was my son— made us sure that nothing could tear us apart. Tony's countenance visibly softened, he stuttered less and less, and his gait was lively. Oh sure, there were those days when he shuffled through the door, hating school and not believing that even I would be on his side, but the tantrums and anger didn't last nearly so long. Tony was growing.

But so was I. The miracle in me that had begun when I first started to take a long look back at my past now settled into a lasting peace and ability to trust both God and Tony. What had been mere words or fleeting feelings began to take hold. My prayers were deep and rich. God communed with me in a way that made his presence felt as I walked through each day and choice in the present—not just saving me from my past— and that was good.

Tony started to tell me more and more about his past. Prison, his biological mother, a special friend named Victor, and those monstrous guards at La Granja—snippets and longer tales started to help me understand what shaped Tony's fears. No longer did his past horrify me or make me fear that his heart was irreparably scarred. Just talking together about his life helped us both begin to deal with it. Each night after Tony reluctantly went to his room—he always resisted bed-time—I prayed for the day when he would be spiritually ma-ture enough to ask for inner healing and embark on the jour-ney of lifting the past up to God and letting God show Tony how he had been near him, loving him and suffering with him, all the time.

I clung to the hope that Tony would someday understand the depth of something I'd said to him during a traumatic and awful moment in the first months of our life together. He'd been suspended from school, and early bedtime was part of his restriction. I tried to ease him from the television at the agreed hour. Right before my eyes he changed, in a split second, from the cuddly little friend next to me on the couch to a fierce, defiant enemy.

He flung angry words like machine gun fire. "You won't let me do anything. The only reason I'm in the United States is because you made me come. This place is just like prison."

The comparison of our home to a prison cut through me like a dagger. Devastated, barely able to hold myself together long enough to respond, I gestured angrily. "Tony, look around our house. Do you see any bars on our windows? In a prison," I went on, "the locks are on the outside so that you can't leave. Where are the locks in our house?"

He looked, "On the inside."

Tony had to come to realize, as I had, that the inner prison, painful memories, only had locks on the inside. God's love alone could offer him the courage to put his hand on the door and face the avalanche of unwanted memories, but the first move would be up to Tony. Once he was ready, I knew God would come to heal him.

Summers became my favorite time of year. The first day of spring Tony began to talk incessantly about going to camp in just a few months. Weeks before it was time, he began piling his gear in his room. Every time he bubbled over with excitement, I had to smile inside, remembering his terror the first time he'd gone to camp. "Please don't make me go," Tony had begged, his pathetic voice following me as I drove down the dirt road toward the camp, "Don't leave me, don't leave me!" I had longed for camp so that for the first time in months I wouldn't have to coerce Tony into doing his chores or coax him away from the television, yet once he left, all I wanted was to hear his voice on the phone. I wanted so badly to know how he was getting along. It took all the restraint I could muster to keep myself from the phone.

When Tony raced off, now, with barely a wave good-bye, it was because he knew without even thinking about it that I'd be there when camp was over. While he enjoyed three weeks of adventure and laughter, I headed to Twain Harte for a relaxed week or two with the Peterses. The mountain community provided the perfect vacation for me, plenty of open space and lots of ministry as people came over to talk and pray.

Each year I took all the books on the subject of inner healing I'd gathered during the past few months. Reading voraciously, for my sake and Tony's, I devoured *Healing* and other books by Francis MacNutt, a prolific Catholic writer on inner healing, and Dennis and Matthew Linn's *Healing Life's Hurts,* which deals with healing through the five stages of forgiveness. Alva and Russ supplemented these and other books with their willingness to talk long and honestly about inner healing. They introduced me to several people in their church who had incredible scars from their backgrounds. God had literally turned their lives around as they faced their pasts.

One morning, over a late cup of coffee, I told Alva, "I can hardly wait for the day when Tony will be ready to pray for the healing of his past. He's come so far in the last couple of years, but when I imagine just how free he could be, I long for him to be able to let go of the past and allow the Holy Spirit to heal him."

Alva let a comfortable silence fall between us. I could tell she was thinking, and with typical wisdom she smiled at me, "Why don't we try something to help Tony on his way. Do you remember those two women who prayed for your inner healing? Why don't we ask them to come over, and let's all pray for Tony."

"You mean now—even when he's not here?"

"Why not? We will pray for the day when Tony is ready for God to heal his memories."

"But Tony is over a hundred miles from here!" I reminded her, a little skeptical of the whole idea.

"But God isn't. Intercession is for us to talk to God about

Tony, it doesn't matter if Tony is here to listen."

Before I could ask any more questions Alva was thumbing through the church phone book. Both women agreed to come over right after lunch. Alva never wastes any time!

Within hours four of us sat in the small prayer room off to the side of the sanctuary in the Chapel in the Pines. Still not convinced, I squirmed a bit, trying to reconcile myself to praying about Tony's memories when he wasn't even nearby. Trying to relieve my hesitancy, I asked Bobbie, one of Alva's friend, "Have you ever prayed before for the healing of someone's memories when they weren't in the room?" She looked across the room, shrugging her shoulders at Sharon, her prayer partner, as she told me no. "Well," I pushed, "do you think it's just a waste of time, or will this really help Tony?"

Bobbie answered with a positive nod of her head and exclaimed, "Sure, there's no reason why our prayers won't be heard. I can't think of any reason why someone has to be here unless he killed somebody or spent half his life in prison or something terrible like that!"

My mouth fell open in disbelief, and with one glance at Alva, we both doubled over laughing uncontrollably. Poor Bobbie blushed and blinked her eyes nervously, looking to Sharon for help. "What's so funny? Did I say something wrong?"

It took me a moment to stop laughing long enough to answer. "No, Bobbie. You said something very right. The person we want you to pray for was accused of murder and has spent more than half of his life in prison."

Her eyes widened as she stammered, "I didn't mean it that way."

"Don't worry, Bobbie," Alva consoled. "God must be speaking to you since he let you hit the right target. It just proves to me that you're already tuned in."

Bobbie and Sharon asked questions about Tony for a few minutes, then we all bowed our heads in prayer as we journeyed, as Tony would someday, through all the pains that I knew of in his past. His mother's sin—the brutality of the man she lived with—the death of his baby brother—the prison— we walked through each phase of his life, each of us bearing part of the pain for Tony. We all sensed that God was healing Tony and touching him even as we prayed.

Tears flowed for hours as we lifted up Tony. By the time we chorused our final amen, I felt exhausted from seeing anew just how much my wonderful son had to bear in his heart. But I also sensed new promise that, little by little, God would restore him to inner freedom.

Back at home I watched Tony, busy at school and oblivious to the minute, but obvious, changes in his attitudes. Weeks passed without a major incident. Progress could be measured by how far we'd both come and also by how far we had yet to go, but we were moving forward. My heart rejoiced. Life was good to us.

In January, just before the new semester at the university began, my brother Clifford called with the news that my mother had been hospitalized with a stroke the night before. He asked, "Will you come?"

The calm I had been feeling changed immediately to panic. My father would be there, and she'd promised that he'd kill me if she died before he did. What if she didn't make it? All the fears that I thought had been put to rest roared back. I physically shook and fought the urge to run even though I stood in my own kitchen with no reason to fear.

I knew I needed to go. As estranged as we had been, if she died without my seeing her I knew I'd regret it. Clifford and Madilyn agreed to meet me at the airport in Tucson, Arizona, where Mom and Dad had been visiting Gary, and drive me to the hospital.

The brief one-hour flight from Southern California carried me only a few hundred miles from home, but emotionally a great distance—far beyond the security of friends or familiarity. When I realized that my whole family hadn't been together in the years since my grandfather's funeral, the sad truth sank in: all we ever shared was death and pain. Never had any of us given each other hope.

Clifford stood at the jetway when I disembarked, and within minutes we were outside my mother's room. Gary, his wife, and Madilyn stood on one side as Clifford and I entered the room. Mom's gaunt face registered a flashing glimpse of relief—as if she had wanted to see us all together again. No one said anything, and the awkwardness brought back that little-girl feeling of not belonging all over again. "Hi, Mom," I offered, struggling to know how to act. Our family never hugged, and kissing, even a slight peck on the cheek, was an absolute (though unspoken) taboo, so no one extended as much as an outstretched hand in greeting.

We tried clumsily to chat. "What are you doing these days?" "How is everybody?" "Our daughter is ready for college in the fall." Any outsider would have thought we were strangers meeting for the first time. We knew so little about the very basics of each other's lives. Mom barely spoke, her voice sometimes drifting off incoherently when she tried.

After a few strained moments, Dad walked in. Every one of us visibly tensed. A heavy silence filled the room, and every eye was on me.

"So you decided to come, huh?" was all he said.

"Sure, she's my mother."

Nothing else was said beyond a few feeble words of good-bye before we all divided into carloads and headed toward Gary's house near the army base, forty-five minutes away. Gary was now a career man. He's stayed in the military from the day he was inducted at seventeen.

Once inside the small house, we all found it hard to know what to do. The time just crawled by. Dad had started drinking early that morning and obviously had no intention of stopping. His voice and snide comments resounded throughout the house. I spent the day moving from room to room trying to avoid him. Gary and his wife made constant references to his drinking. Neither of them wanted him around. Whenever he came by he pushed their kids around—he'd even beaten them while they were gone. Apparently Mom's stroke brought out even more of his belligerence. I guess he thought that cussing out the doctors would help her to get well.

Night finally fell, a blessing to end a day full of anxiety. Everyone simply found a place to lie down. I spent an unrestful night on the living room couch before flying back in time for my afternoon class at the university.

Ten days later Mom was dead. She survived surgery but never came out of a three-day coma. When Clifford called me at home he promised, "I'll let you know when the funeral is."

I put the phone down and repeated over and over to myself, "She's dead. She's dead." For a moment I didn't know what I felt. This person, nearly a stranger to me, someone I went years without even seeing, no longer breathed or spoke. My mother was dead, but even her death didn't reconcile us. Still numb, rationally aware that my mother was gone but emotionally empty, I gathered my books and my briefcase and drove the three and a half miles down to the university. It would do me no good to just sit home alone.

I walked through my outer office without greeting anybody, but within thirty seconds Don Grant peeked in and entered without asking, shutting the door firmly behind him.

"Your brother, Clifford, just called me."

I looked at him in disbelief. "You're kidding!"

"No, he was concerned and wanted to make sure that you were okay and that someone here knew what had happened."

My brothers hadn't ever thought about me before, as far as I knew. I was shocked.

"Let's go for a drive," Don said and motioned toward the door.

Without hesitating I followed Don's lead. I was very quiet as we drove down the freeway and turned off on the country roads in the hills around Chino and Brea. Don knew the true meaning of friendship. He knew when to talk and when to just be nearby.

"What are you feeling?"

"I don't know. In all the years I hardly really discussed anything with my mom. Still, it's hard to believe that she's dead."

The first words, however unfocused, brought my deeper feeling to the surface. Now that I'd started, I blurted out, "Do you know what this means, Don?" Tears welled up in my eyes. "Remember what I told you when my dad started to come after me a few years ago? She always said that she was the only thing that would keep him from killing me. Do you know what it means to have my mother die? She told me as an eight-year-old girl to pray that Dad died before she did. And Don, I have to admit that I prayed earnestly that would happen."

By now I spoke through streaming tears. The words poured out. "Don, my dad is so angry that he really might try to kill me. Everything I've dreamed for my whole future is now up in the air."

Speechless, Don didn't know how to comfort me other than just to listen as I spilled out all the frantic fears spinning around in my mind. I could still hear my mother's voice, "You'd better pray that he dies before I do, because I'm the only thing that's keeping him from killing you."

"Why, Don?" I finally asked, spent with tears, "why do I have to keep facing this?"

The rest of the week was a blur. Within a few hours the funeral was set, allowing enough time for everyone to return to Long Beach. Don and Pauline offered to take me. "I won't let you out of my sight. I don't want your dad to try anything." Clifford promised to watch out for me too. He vowed that there was no way Dad would get near me as long as he was around. Other friends of the family promised to make sure there wouldn't be another dreadful scene like the one at my grandfather's funeral.

My relief at knowing I had protectors between me and my father throughout the room made it easier for me to walk into the little church and see the casket that held my mother. The protective emotional barrier she had erected between me and my dad had fallen.

Arriving early enough to meet the relatives in the pastor's study, I left Don and Pauline seated in the front of the sanctuary. Clifford and Gary had already arrived with their families. I stood quietly, just inside the door, looking for Dad. He was behind the desk talking to the pastor.

He turned only a moment after I spotted him. His eyes flashed with fury. "You son of a b——! You sit down here," he ranted and lunged the few feet to grab me by the neck of my blouse. He shoved me backward, and I lost my balance, tumbling onto the couch. Clifford and his son started to make a move toward him but hesitated. His perpetual smell of liquor filled the room.

In my embarrassment and fear, I felt a short twinge of pity. My father had spent his whole adult life living a stormy life with Mom. I'd never seen another relationship like theirs— they practically killed each other with their hatred on a regular basis, but they couldn't live for very long without each other. Now Mom was gone. What was life going to be like for him? What would he do? Now that he didn't have her as the target for his anger, maybe he'd turn on me.

Gary sat down next to me, leaning protectively close. "Don't pay any attention to him."

The terrified pastor haltingly said a few words about the the order in which we'd file into the church. Nothing had changed in the years since my grandfather's funeral. We were all uncomfortable and frightened. It became poignantly clear that any time my family rallied together there would be more pain.

Only moments before the pastor prepared to open the study door, my father filed past me appearing to be engrossed in conversation, but when only inches away he spun toward me, grabbed my arm, and jerked me up from the couch. Pain seared through my shoulder as he roughly pulled my arm at an unnatural angle. "You sit next to Clifford; get in line."

I wrestled away from him and quickly stepped out the door, feeling again like a little girl being shoved around by an alcoholic, angry father. Everyone else fell in line and filed past: Gary, Dad, then Clifford. I was to be next, but I let everyone pass. Madilyn brought up the rear and I fell in after her, leaving ten people between me and my father. I didn't want to be anywhere near that man! I felt like more of an outcast than ever.

A few dozen other mourners sat sprinkled through the front pews. The funeral was a total blur. Some words were said by the stiff minister, a man who had never spoken more than a formal greeting to anyone in our family. I leaned forward and looked down the line of people; there he was at the end of the pew near the aisle—the man who might kill me someday. If not physically, he'd surely do me in emotionally. He could do it now; there was nobody that could stop him.

I shuddered just looking at his angry face and nervously clenched my fists. "God," I prayed, "what is going to happen to me? Is my life almost over? Did you bring me this far and work so many miracles in both my life and Tony's to let this happen?"

Then Tony filled my mind. My son—now I had Tony to consider. Whenever my dad threatened me before I only had to worry about myself. Tony had been deprived of a mother most of his life, was he going to have to watch me be ripped violently away from him?

Am I going to have to spend the rest of my life hiding from this insane alcoholic? The police aren't going to stop him. They can't even act unless a threat is proven. Who'd believe my dad has been wanting to kill me for over twenty-five years!

The half-hour memorial service was lost on me as I tried to predict the future. But hard as I tried, I couldn't plan for the next year or even the next month. All I could do was worry whether my mother's prediction was true. Would my father really kill me now? How much of a real barrier had she been between that vengeful man and me? "God," I silently screamed, anguished beyond any words, "What's going to happen to me?"

The Release

"What's wrong, Mom?" Tony asked when I walked in from my mother's funeral.

"Tony, do you have a few minutes to talk? I need to tell you about my father." In our years together, I'd been reluctant to worry Tony with the constant threat that hung over my head. He knew that I'd grown up much as he did, unloved and betrayed, but I tried to spare him the details. His graphic young mind didn't need any more horrible fears. But now he needed to know—perhaps his life was at stake too.

We sat on the couch, both nestled against one of the arms, as I told him why my mother's death brought me such pain. It's funny, looking back, most people would have chastised me for not feeling more bereaved about never seeing her again, but not Tony. He was the only one who really could understand. When he nodded his head, I realized he, another survivor, could empathize with me. Having a mother who bore him and another who loved him gave Tony a realistic perspective on what true parenthood meant. He and I shared the emotional wound of knowing that the ones who had given birth to us had never really cared.

Tony patted my hand as I talked. His brown eyes flashed with anger when I told him what my father had said in the pastor's study, but when I honestly described how deeply I feared what might be next, he looked puzzled. He stopped me before I could finish.

"Didn't you ask God to heal your fear of that gun?" Tony

remembered that I'd prayed for God to heal all my painful memories.

"Yes, Tony, I did."

"Then why don't you trust God to take care of you? After all, you gave him the gun, didn't you?"

"Yes, I guess I did."

"Well, then?" my pragmatic teenage son leaned forward with a victorious grin on his face.

"Well, then, I need to give the gun to God once more."

"Right." Tony had heard me tell him many times to keep giving the past back to God every time it threatened to overtake him; he wasn't about to let me get away with not practicing what I preached.

So we bowed our heads and joined hands. "God, take the gun; it's yours. And take my dad, too. I want to thank you for every moment that you have given me, because you used the pain in my life to prepare me for Tony. Once again, my past is yours to heal. I bind the pain in Jesus' name."

And together Tony and I chorused a resounding, "Amen!"

The first week passed, and the peace I knew inside quickly returned—a sure sign of how much God really had healed me. Earlier, it had taken months for me to recover from a bout with my dad. Months flew by, and before I knew it Tony was ready for his first date and we were frantically shopping for just the right shirt only an hour before I was to drive him over to pick up the lucky girl. Then a swift year later he came of driving age, just about when we decided it was time to finally commit ourselves to writing a book about my finding Tony and the struggle we'd had in learning to be a family. *Tony: Our Journey Together* was published right after Tony's graduation from high school.

The editor kept encouraging me to follow it up with a

sequel about my own experiences, but I just didn't feel free
to write anything more as long as my dad might get hold of
a copy. If I knew anything about my father, reading about
himself would surely be enough to provoke him to finish me
off. Besides, why would anyone want to hear the gory details
of my past? How could that be constructive for anybody? I
surely didn't want to keep going back over the old memories.
The pure necessity of facing the pain in order to go forward
was the only reason to do it. The last thing I needed was for
anyone to feel sorry for me.

But then the pastor of a local church with a large single's
group asked me to share my testimony one night in church.
He assured me that there were many he knew in our congregation that would benefit from hearing that the healing of past
hurts was really possible.

I spoke often around the country to singles groups and
huge Christian education conferences, but standing before
people I knew and telling them about the pain I'd lived with
was harder than I could have imagined. But God gave me the
words to use. After the service, I couldn't get off the platform
for nearly an hour. People streamed forward to tell me of what
they'd been through and how deeply they longed for freedom
from their past. One woman, stylishly dressed and quietly
refined in manner waited until the others had gone. "Carolyn," she confessed softly, "I've never told this to anyone
before." After a long pause she told me of her childhood—
years tyrannized by her incestuous father. Together we talked
about inner healing. "I need that," she agreed through her
tears. "By sharing your story I've found the courage to face
my past."

Someone in the church sent a tape of my testimony to a
radio program, which aired it and offered the tape to regular
listeners. Thousands of orders poured in. I was astounded, but

God was telling me that he offered healing to all who hurt from childhood anguish. If my experiences could help me love Tony so much, maybe someone else could find hope and release from the deep scars of betrayal. I no longer was the cold, tough kid who felt she didn't need anybody. I knew I desperately needed people—their love, their encouragement, their laughter, and their tears. If I could help someone else to understand that all the pains and sorrows in the past can serve as preparation for a very special journey with God, I most certainly would. So I agreed to let go of the fear of writing, knowing full well that a single word from my father would make me reconsider in a flash.

Early one morning I sat in my cozy nook with a ream of paper strewn across the table as I reworked the first draft of the manuscript. The phone jangled. Friends often called soon after dawn, the only time they knew to consistently catch me at home.

"How's my favorite sister?" Clifford's now customary greeting brought a smile to my face. In the years since Mom's funeral, Clifford and I were learning, very late in life, to know and love each other. We took frequent jaunts on his power-boat just talking for hours. His affirmation did wonders for me, even if I did know it was pretty easy to call me his favorite sister!

"Oh, I'm fine. How's my favorite brother?" I teased in response.

"Well, I've got news for you." His voice changed, and I sensed him groping for words so I waited.

"Dad died last night."

"What!"

His words shot right through me. Somehow without really thinking through it, I had always imagined my dad would outlive me.

"The hospital called me last night. He died of alcoholic poisoning."

There was silence over the phone lines as the pronouncement sank in. I didn't feel anything at all. He'd been there—violent and mean—every single day of my life. How could he and his threat just disappear, vanish like that? Finally the silence seemed too long, and I wanted to clear the confusion in my spirit. "Clifford, what do you feel?" I asked softly.

With a sigh he gathered his thoughts, "Nothing."

"Neither do I," I admitted. A whole life lived, millions of words and emotions communicated, pain and destruction strewn all along the way, and at the end all we who knew him could feel was nothing?

"I'll call you after I talk to Gary to let you know what we plan to do. I don't think that we'll have a funeral or anything." Clifford signed off with a gentle good-bye.

I heard the click on the other end of the phone. Stunned and trying still to delve my emotions to find if I felt anything, I thought about all the relatives—aunts and nephews and grandchildren. He'd parceled out pain to all of us. But now it was over.

"Lord," I looked up toward heaven, "does this mean it's really over? Does this finally release me from the gun that has been pointing at my core for all these years? You mean I don't have to spend the rest of my life looking over my shoulder and wondering if my dad is just a few paces behind me? It really is over, God?" I remembered the pages scattered all around me. "You mean I can finish the book without fear, God?"

The huge mortuary in north Long Beach had the air of a gothic cathedral with vaulted ceilings and ornate stained glass windows. Taped organ music softly played a dirge that echoed among empty wooden pews that could hold at least five hundred people. In the front, near the altar, lay one lone wreath of flowers. Seven of us, Clifford's family and Tony and me, marched to the front, the total group that had gathered to note this man's passing. The frailty of life rang poignantly in the emptiness. This really was an end, not only for Dad, but to an agonized era experienced to differing degrees by these few assembled.

The minister, whom Clifford had hired sight unseen over the telephone, properly greeted each of us personally. He handled himself well in such an awkward position, yet officiating for such a tiny group in the cavernous room made him visibly uncomfortable. We all felt odd, but somehow we needed closure for this passage in our lives. The minister looked sadly at the sole floral arrangement and walked behind the pulpit to direct his remarks toward the seven waiting.

He cleared his throat and opened his Bible, "I am sure that many of you today come to this memorial service for Clifford Arthur Koons with mixed emotions. Some of you may feel tremendous anger and bitterness, others sheer relief in knowing that Cliff Koons, who so dominated your life over these years, is no longer among us. To perhaps one or two of you, today may bring confusion and an onrush of painful memories. Just maybe in some of you there might be just a little sorrow for this tragic man and his life—now fully past.

"Cliff Koons was a lonely man and an angry one, who made some choices in his life that trapped him—leaving him with years of repeated sins and pain. He basically came to the end of his life empty-handed, but you, ah, the seven of you still have your lives ahead of you. You still have choices to make.

"The Son of God descended to earth and died to forgive our sins—our horrible choices and actions—in order that there might be a way to change our lives. He alone brings hope and purpose. He alone can heal the scars and the wretched memories. He can turn lives around, but the choice is always ours. What do you want your life to be? Are you trapped in the pain and beaten down by the scars as Cliff was? Do you want to live that way, or do you want to be set free?

"You see, our past can be our biggest crutch or it can be used as a rod of transforming power for the future. Jesus offers to change all our scars—all those debilitating weaknesses— and give us, in return, a compassionate strength to help others as they journey along life's way. The pain may threaten to break us, but because of Jesus Christ our paths can open wide in ways we can't imagine.

"Jesus is the healer of healers. He gives life so that it can be shared to encourage life in others. The choice is yours. He wants to heal your life and use you. Today you can be set free."

As Tony and I unlocked the doors to our car in the bright sunshine after the service I said to my son, "The minister somehow knew us, didn't he?"

"Yeah, and you and I know the truth when we hear it, don't we, Mom?"

"We sure do, Tony. We sure do."